Speaking of Faith

To: Majorie,
With warm greetings,

Speaking of Faith

The Winchester Dialogues

Edited by

John Miller

[signatures]

CANTERBURY
PRESS
Norwich

© The contributors, 2016

First published in 2016 by the Canterbury Press Norwich

Editorial office
3rd Floor, Invicta House
108–114 Golden Lane
London EC1Y OTG, UK

Hymns Ancient & Modern® is a registered trademark
of Hymns Ancient and Modern Ltd

Canterbury Press is an imprint of Hymns Ancient & Modern Ltd
(a registered charity)
13A Hellesdon Park Road, Norwich,
Norfolk NR6 5DR, UK

www.canterburypress.co.uk

British Library Cataloguing in Publication data

A catalogue record for this book is available
from the British Library

978 1 84825 920 1

Typeset by Regent Typesetting
Printed and bound in Great Britain by
CPI Group (UK) Ltd

Contents

Preface by Dean James Atwell   vii

Introduction by John Miller   ix

1   Lord Douglas Hurd: Making politics exciting again   1

2   Frank Field: The dangers of forgetting   20

3   Maria Miller: A Ministry of Fun?   40

4   Bishop of Winchester Tim Dakin: Out of Africa   64

5   Lord John Wakeham: Fixing things behind the scenes   85

6   P. D. James: The importance of language   105

7   Jon Snow: How to interview a tyrant   123

8   Dean of Winchester James Atwell: Pilgrimage in the blood   147

9   Mark Tully: Where all the great religions began   169

10   John Simpson: Liking difficult places   189

11   Archbishop Rowan Williams: Things to say to psychotic dictators   209

Preface

Winchester Cathedral carries the evidence of well over a millennium of creative interaction between Church and State. The Mortuary Chests, containing the mortal remains of the royal house that united England, reminds us that the Christian faith was a midwife present at the birth of our nation. In chantry chapels, heraldic roof bosses and memorials, including the episcopal son of one of the great voices that ended the slave trade, it is impossible to escape faith informing political and cultural life.

The Winchester Dialogues were the inspiration of John Miller, who so ably conducted the interviews. I jumped at the suggestion that we might use the stark reality of a £20.5m appeal as a good reason to host a series which celebrated 'faith in the marketplace' in our own generation. The series would make a modest contribution to the appeal, raise awareness of it, and at the same time celebrate that identity of the Church in England – exemplified in the very stones of Winchester Cathedral – that continues to be there for the good of the whole. It is no less true now than it ever was that 'Without a vision the people perish' (Proverbs 29.18). For that reason we decided the dialogues would be held in the Guildhall at the centre of the city near the statue of King Alfred. The one exception, which held its own significance, was a generous hosting in the Stripe Theatre of the University of Winchester.

The series was able to gather distinguished contributors speaking of faith from a whole range of backgrounds: senior church leaders, politicians who have engaged with issues of Church and State, well-known correspondents and broadcasters, and a substantial literary figure. People were drawn from across the community eager to hear the perspective of someone often familiar from the media, but not encountered as an individual. The interviewees were without fail gracious, stimulating, candid and encouraging. Our huge thanks to all of them for making this series possible and allowing the publication of their scripts.

It is a delight that Canterbury Press has taken up the opportunity of publishing this series as a book. In particular, we offer our warm appreciation to its publishing director, Christine Smith. The series was captured for posterity by Whitwam, and has been painstakingly typed up by Judi Osman, for which many thanks. John Miller has given freely many hours in editing the scripts. To all involved in this endeavour warm thanks and appreciation. To the reader, enjoy the encounter with a remarkable assembly of interesting individuals speaking of faith.

The Very Revd James Atwell
Dean of Winchester

Introduction to the
Winchester Dialogues

The idea of the dialogues was conceived in response to a front-page report in the *Hampshire Chronicle* of Winchester Cathedral's new and urgent appeal to restore the fabric of the building in September 2012. This stirred me to write to the Dean offering to help publicize it by hosting a series of Winchester Dialogues with leading figures in the Church, politics, the arts and the media. One of the most important things I had learnt in 14 years of running the Winchester Festival was that audiences much preferred dialogues to monologues; and in most cases so did the speakers, as our discussion is much more spontaneous when they don't know what questions I am going to ask. I don't always know myself, as I respond to the thrust of their answers, which keeps us both on our toes.

I remembered how religious discussions were always very popular at the Salisbury Festival, where in the 1980s and 90s I had interviewed Donald Soper, Trevor Huddleston, Bishop Montefiore, Rabbi Lionel Blue, and the then Dean of Salisbury, Hugh Dickinson. So I believed that something along those lines would similarly appeal in Winchester, with the addition of some significant figures from the secular world as well.

The Dean immediately responded with enthusiasm, and we met soon after to discuss the list of our first choices. To our delight most of them agreed in principle as soon as the Dean invited them to participate. Finding possible dates took rather longer; interestingly the politicians seemed to find it easier to offer an early window in their busy schedules than the church leaders. Our first quartet was completed by the Bishop of Winchester, who had recently made his maiden speech in the House of Lords. Other early acceptances came from P. D. James, Jon Snow, John Simpson and Mark Tully, so the series as a whole embraced a wide spectrum of views and experiences.

Individually each dialogue stands alone, and all were very stimulating, but I believe that taken together the sum of the series was greater than the parts. It was most fitting that we opened with Douglas Hurd, whose overview drew on his historical studies of how the political leaders of the nineteenth century handled the frequently vexed issues of Church and State relations, as well as on his own experiences in office in the Thatcher and Major governments. We ended with Rowan Williams, who was delightfully candid about the problems he had faced as Archbishop of Canterbury; he also transfixed a capacity audience with his traumatic near-death experience of being just one block away when the Twin Towers in New York were brought down on 9/11. We gained many such insights from our distinguished guests in these dialogues, which is why we wanted to preserve them in printed form in this book.

John Miller

I

Making politics exciting again

LORD DOUGLAS HURD

Welcome to the first of the Winchester Dialogues. I am delighted to be welcoming back Lord Hurd to Winchester, who has been to the Guildhall several times for these conversations, and of course we think of him as one of our own. Your first boarding school was just down the road at Twyford. Did you have religious education as part of the curriculum at Twyford?

We did. The headmaster was a young clergyman and he took over a school which had really gone downhill quite a long way. It was very old fashioned; they had just got as far as electric light. But the headmaster's wife explained to my mother, 'Of course, we don't have any in our own part because it is so dangerous when it goes round corners.' I think the scientific teaching needed something. Anyway, Bob Wickham was the headmaster, he was in orders, and he was a first-class headmaster, young and go-ahead.

Then you went on to Eton and you wrote in your diary, I think at the age of 14, 'Dined with the Archbishop of Canterbury'.

Yes, I'm ashamed of that actually because the full entry is: 'Dined with the Archbishop of Canterbury – a good man.' He was a good man, but it wasn't quite for me to say.

And you've met several archbishops since. In 1988, you addressed the General Synod with a question and answer, which you describe in one of your books as 'rather fun'.

It was rather fun. It was a time when the Church of England and the Tory Party were not really on speaking terms and I thought that was silly. I was Home Secretary so I broke that down, and I was delighted when Bob Runcie invited me to speak to the Synod, and we got on quite well.

As Home Secretary you had to read the oath that all new bishops had to swear to the Queen.

Yes, the problem was that some bishops vary a good deal in size: some of them are reasonably bulky, the Queen's footstool which they have to kneel on in the ceremony is quite small, so there was a slight sense of unease about the bishop and the footstool. And then I had to read out as Home Secretary the full oath which they had to take, which was to the effect that 'We declare that no foreign Pope or Potentate had any jurisdiction in this our realm of England.' This was a crucial point in Elizabeth I's time. Someone suggested I should change the wording, but that seemed to me very dangerous to do. So I went on reading the old language.

When you were Secretary of State for Northern Ireland, which was your first cabinet post, did you find the sectarian hostility there difficult to cope with?

I found it quite incomprehensible to begin with; you had to get used to it. There were both sides in Northern Ireland always longing for the incoming Secretary of State to make mistakes to show your ignorance, because by definition all the Englishmen were very ignorant about Ireland, and so you had to be very, very careful. A lot of it was quite good fun, which was quite in jest – the jokes they made about each other. But there was an underlying aggravation, and that did take a bit of getting used to.

Did you feel in danger when you were there?

No, I didn't feel at all in danger. I was quite heavily protected by the Royal Ulster Constabulary, as it was then. But I never felt any fear; I felt much more frightened in London than I ever did in the Province. So I didn't feel frightened. The RUC were very frank; they said, 'Well, Secretary of State, it's not that we'll be able to save you from being killed, but we are likely to get the chap who'd done it.' That was a great comfort.

You were at the Brighton Conference when the IRA bomb went off, but you weren't actually in the hotel, were you?

No, I was staying with relatives about ten miles away, and the police woke me up in the middle of the night about 4 a.m. to say that there had been a bomb. They didn't know details then. I was opening the debate – I was answering the first debate – and I didn't know whether there was going to be a debate or not. Eventually it was decided that the conference would go on. If you know Brighton, there are a lot of roundabouts and you go whizzing through and I just got to the conference in time.

But that was a fairly shattering day, wasn't it?

It was an awful day because for a long time we didn't know what had happened, we didn't know how many people had been killed, and all sorts of rumours went round the eating places in Brighton. Sometimes much worse than the reality, and sometimes the same as the reality. It really took all day just to sort out what had happened. The Prime Minister was in charge, she was brilliant. She was very calm, she spoke, and everybody applauded – more for what she was than for what she had been saying. We got away and we drove back to London to my little house in Hammersmith. The police stopped us going into the street saying, 'You can't spend the night here Secretary of State, because there are too many Irish in this part of London.' So we went back first to Oxfordshire, and then the Metropolitan Police said they've bought at some expense a nice little house in Belgravia, into which we were shunted.

In your dealings with the politicians and political leaders, the Nationalists and the Ulster Unionists, did you feel that their hostility to each other was political, religious or both?

Both. The province of Northern Ireland just had too much history for its own good, and the result is when you are driving past a particular crossroads, if your driver is a Catholic that is the place in which the wicked Black and Tans did terrible things in the 1920s; if your driver is Protestant that is the place where his grandmother had been slaughtered by the IRA. Exactly the same crossroads, but the history behind that crossroads varied hugely according to who you talked to.

Did you ever feel then that it was soluble and there would be an agreement?

I thought it was gradually getting better, just very gradually getting better. I had a sort of test. There was a Catholic farmer in the Mountains of Mourne, and I was invited to go and see his farm. He had benefited a lot from the Common Agricultural Policy. The test was when I returned the invitation. I said, come and have a drink in Hillsborough, and he came. His father would never have come; as a good Catholic he would never have set foot in Hillsborough Castle, where the Secretary of State lives. The fact that over the generations that young man had moved and was willing to come and have a drink in a perfectly ordinary way with me was a sign, a small sign, that these times are up.

One of the things I wanted to explore with you was the historical changes between the Church and State. In 1988 you made a speech at Tamworth on the bicentenary of Robert Peel's birth. You made a point in your biography on Peel that he opposed Catholic emancipation for some years quite strongly, and then changed his mind and swung it. Why was that, do you think?

Because Peel was a very practical man and he held strong views, and he changed them when he thought it was necessary. He changed a rule we were talking about, that the Roman Catholics could not sit in the House of Commons, it was illegal. That was his view when he started out, and then he saw over the years that you couldn't run Northern Ireland from London under that rule, you had to allow Catholics to come in; so he changed sides without argument. And of course that infuriated the people who continued to be against it.

It wasn't just Catholics was it, because he made arrangements for Dissenters to sit in the House of Commons.

That's right. I've just been writing about Disraeli, and Jews came later – they didn't get the right to sit in the House of Commons until 1858. So there was just gradual progress, and, of course, women didn't get it till a good deal later than that. Perhaps we'd better not get into that – it's still a little bit sensitive. It took time, and this is a slow process all through the nineteenth century, of gradually moving the posts.

It's hard to believe that Parliament had to change the law to allow Dissenters to marry?

Yes. There was originally a rather strict law that said there was an oath to be taken. The declaration they had to take was quite a stiff one, which caused difficulty, and so Peel managed to turn that down.

And one of the most important things he did, which I don't think many people now remember, was setting up the Ecclesiastical Commission, which was again a real hot potato.

It certainly was. Peel's whole philosophy was 'We don't want change for change's sake, but there are things going on in this United Kingdom which need changing'. Catholics in Parliament was one, and the Church of England was another. The Church of England is now rather short of money, as I understand it, but then it overflowed with money, and it was all going in the wrong places. So you had curates, and from reading Trollope you can see that curates were desperately short of cash and only able to hold maybe one service on a Sunday. On the other hand, you had big colleges, where money flowed in and it was misused on huge feasts and so on. Peel set about it by setting up a commission to deal with that, and he got into trouble over it, as he did over many things, because he was cutting away at privileges that he thought had outlived their usefulness.

At that time the Church of England was really quite unpopular in the country?

In the middle of Queen Victoria's reign, the Church of England had a rather big dip, it lost a lot of ground. Almost all the bishops voted against the Great Reform Bill in 1832, and that was noticed. This business of rich deans (I am sure deans are not rich nowadays) – the contrast between the poor clergymen and the rich clergymen was just too great.

What did the Commission actually do to change that?

The Commission had quite a lot of power. The Commission was able to change the make-up of a diocese. For example, until the other day, I was High Steward of Westminster Abbey, and in Westminster Abbey it was decided by Peel's Commission that there were too many canons, with not enough work for them to do. So he reorganized it so that they took in a part of London, a part of working-class London, and had to look after that; it became part of their job. And so in that sort of way he changed the system, slowly improving it without, he hoped, creating too much of a row.

He had a lot of difficulty with his own party, didn't he, in what you call the sour right of the party, which has not quite gone away?

Well, it's not quite gone away. Old-fashioned Conservatives, I have a respect for, my father's generation, my grandfather's generation and so on. They don't really believe in change but they accept that change has to happen. But there is always in the Tory party a residue, a minority, who are stubborn and against anything that even a Conservative government proposes, and a Conservative leader has to assert himself. He can't just sit back and let them roll over him. He has to be prepared to stand up and stake out his ground, and that's been true now with Cameron; in Harold Macmillan's time, going back through the centuries, that's always been true. Disraeli had to assert himself from time to time against what I call the sour right, who are simply against things because they are against things.

Disraeli and Peel were at daggers drawn, weren't they?

Yes. Disraeli, who was only interested really in his own glory, thought after a time in the House of Commons that he could get the greatest glory by dishing the Prime Minister, who was Robert Peel, Conservative Prime Minister, and Disraeli eventually, after havering about, decided to sit as a Conservative, but he dished Peel. Night after night he got up, and there are amazing speeches; they are witty, they are wicked, and Peel was a really genuine man who repealed the Corn Laws because that needed to be done in order to lower the price of bread. Disraeli took him to bits; he attacked him again and again, and Peel – in those days you wore your top hat in the House of Commons – Peel had a habit of pulling down his hat quite often, so that no one could see what his expression was. He got the Corn Laws reformed, he got it through all right, but Disraeli had his own back later because he beat the government on a completely different issue. Those were exciting days in Parliament. Part of our theme in this latest book is that we needed to get a bit of excitement, genuine excitement not bogus excitement, back into the political process.

It is clear from your biography of Peel, and the new one of Disraeli, that you think Peel was the greater man, the greater statesman, though Disraeli was the greater speaker.

Yes, Disraeli was a great orator. Those speeches must have been great fun to listen to. Disraeli never moved a muscle in his face, he never laughed at his own jokes (something Boris could study, I think), and he kept his features absolutely rigid, and these amazing attacks, very witty, very funny, were successful partly because they came from this deadpan figure, a young Jew saying these amazing things about the Prime Minister. He had great success simply by his sheer technique: he had a white handkerchief there, and after a time, his supporters knew, when he took his hanky out and began to manipulate it a bit, that there was a good joke coming. So they geared themselves up for a good joke and it came.

You make the point in the book that one of the few things that Disraeli really stuck his neck out on was Jewish emancipation.

Yes. I think the one thing we found – Edward Young and I wrote a book together – was that Disraeli really stuck to it; the one conviction that he really held to was about the Jews. He was of course born Jewish. He was christened, he was baptized, a Christian, because his father fell out with the local synagogue and in revenge, as it were, he had all his children baptized in St Andrew's. So it wasn't greatly a matter of conviction that that happened. Disraeli was always proud of being Jewish, and he argued not just the ordinary liberal case that we must let Catholics in, we must let Jews in, to the House of Commons. No, he said, we must let Jews in for quite a different reason: they are superior and we acknowledge that superiority. If there had not been the crucifixion there would have been no Christianity. God never spoke to a European. He produced these remarks out of the blue, and they made an impression, and people began to realize, and he won the case. On the evening when they won the case, and Jews were allowed into Parliament, Lord Rothschild, ancestor to the present Rothschilds, went up and shook Disraeli by the hand, because he realized that without Disraeli's support they would not have got that far.

He also said that without Judaism there would be no Christianity.

Yes, without Judaism, there would be no Christianity. Judaism came first and there would have been no Christianity if it hadn't been for the Jews. Therefore the Jews deserve respect. Instead of which, when Disraeli stood, he was hissed for being a Jew. Jews were people who sold old clothes. 'They work on the old clothes line' – that was the election cry against him, so he suffered to a small extent; it was water off a duck's back. Disraeli didn't care a damn really about what people wrote about him. But they did write bitter things because he was Jewish.

One of the things that cropped up in the nineteenth century was the question of the disestablishment of the Church, which a lot of people thought without Peel's Ecclesiastical Commission could have happened.

Well, anything could have happened. The Church of England wobbled on the edge discussing this. I personally would be against disestablishment. Disestablishment would mean that the Church of England was no longer the national church. I think that would be a pity. I think the fact that the Archbishop of Canterbury is on a different footing from the heads of other churches, the Jews and the Muslims and so on, is a help. We see it in the House of Lords, where there are archbishops who sit there as of right. I think that is a good idea: there aren't very many of them. They have not got enough to swing a vote, but they have got just enough to put an emphasis on the moral side of the question, and it is a good idea that somebody should be there to do it. The fact that he is dressed up in funny clothes is irrelevant really. It is a good idea that we should be reminded occasionally by people in authority that there is a moral dimension to most of the things that we talk about.

Why do you think that so many of the bishops voted against the Great Reform Bill?

They saw the writing on the wall. They saw that their lush living habits were in danger. They saw that what was happening in the Reform Bill to the franchise, letting lots of people have the vote, that it would only be a matter of time before they said, as they are saying now, 'Why does a bishop have to live in a palace? Why can't I live in a palace?' That kind of envious attitude was gathering speed, as the bishops themselves clearly imagined, so they went into the lobbies to try and sort it out.

You have, of course, been on the commission to examine the role of the Archbishop of Canterbury more recently. What conclusion did you come to?

I was asked by George Carey when he was Archbishop if I would chair a small group to look at the role of the Archbishop, how it worked, or failed to work. When we looked into it we discovered some very strange things. We discovered, for example, that archbishops still have no proper handover. One Archbishop of Canterbury told me that when he was elected the existing Archbishop said, 'You must come over; very well done, I am delighted. You must come and have tea.' He turned up for tea on the day appointed and was met by the Archbishop's chaplain, saying, 'Oh, I'm very sorry, but the Archbishop had to go out; something very important has come up, so he can't have tea.' All he got was what I call in my book an 'Anglican wave', which was nothing but a greeting – no serious discussion of the problems which one man was handing over to the other.

So what did you recommend?

We recommended that things like archbishops' voyages abroad should be properly prepared in the way that the Queen's are; that was agreed on, completely modernizing. We felt that there should be a layman who would take over from the clergy the business of organizing the Archbishop's diary. It was a sort of chaotic business we discovered, where the Archbishop was more or less open to everybody to come and see him. An ambitious bishop used to scurry in and scurry out, and say to the clerk at the desk, 'The Archbishop's particularly keen to come to my confirmation class on such and such a day.' And that wasn't in fact so, but nevertheless they got away with it because there was no system of organizing things in a sensible way. So that has changed, it's changed for the better. The current Archbishop is very much a man of affairs, and very much believes in getting things organized right. That is a good thing.

Do you think now the battle for women bishops has been accepted in Wales it is bound to happen in England?

Yes, I do think that. I know it is a sore point; I know it is a very diffi-cult subject for some people, but having accepted as we certainly have, women priests, the logic is exactly the same. To keep out women bishops, which is what the lay members of the synod voted a year ago, is absurd; it doesn't carry any conviction at all. So I am sure what the Welsh did yesterday we will do the day after tomorrow.

It is interesting that the vote was lost on the lay vote, not the clerical.

Is that very surprising? I think if you study the General Synod and the people who are on it you wouldn't be surprised.

What, in your view, having been in office close to the Church in various positions, what do you think should be the relationship between Church and State?

I think it is right that people, whatever they believe or whatever they don't believe, should feel that in the Church of England they have some-where they can go, somewhere they can pour out their complaints, or their views. Lots of people, especially in the countryside, feel this. We live in Oxfordshire, in a cluster of villages; each has a beautiful church; it's very hard to maintain them all. If you started closing them and doing away with them, there would be a terrific rumpus, led by people who never go to church except occasionally at Easter and Christmas. There's a feeling that the Church of England does stand for something other than simply the number of people who go to church in Anglican churches.

You have written, I think when you were Home Secretary, that you were required to be on parade at the Cenotaph in November, and you found that a deeply moving experience.

I did. Sometimes you find a sort of prickle at the back of the throat. I don't know if you do, but I do occasionally. You can never quite tell when you are going to prickle or when your eyes are going to fill with tears. The Cenotaph was such an occasion for me in the days when I used to lay the wreath on behalf of the colonies, as Foreign Secretary. I think on the whole it would be a great pity if that ceremony disappeared. Actually it has increased – the number of people that go to watch the Cenotaph, the number of people who come to Winchester, or their own parish church to remember the dead of both wars, has increased. After a time when we thought it was going to go down it has actually increased, quite substantially. That I think is a good thing; it means that, because memory is an important part of life, what you remember and what you forget is a very important part of deciding what you are.

The Cenotaph service is interdenominational. Do you think there should be more of that?

It works quite well in the Abbey at Westminster, where whenever the Queen comes, or whenever there's a Commonwealth Games, you have the Chief Rabbi, you have representatives of the different faiths. That, I think, will gradually increase; more and more services will be organized on that sort of basis. Westminster Abbey is a Christian, an Anglican, foundation; it has a Royal Charter from the Queen. So no one is actually tackling that. Within that great church there is room for all kinds of different formulae, different ways of organizing services, and the present Dean of Westminster is very good at that.

Given the current international situation, do you think it is difficult to have a relationship between Christian denominations and the Muslim?

Of course it is difficult. It is difficult especially when you reach the point as with Syria, where they learn to kill each other. I went to Syria as a tourist, probably people here did too, three years ago, and thoroughly enjoyed it. Part of the point was that in these towns and villages in Damascus and Aleppo there were people who were Christians, Jews, Muslims, Sunni and Shia, and there were all sorts of combinations and they co-existed peacefully; they lived together and they took some pride in that: 'We are not like those others, not like the Israelis and Palestinians, we live peacefully with each other.' They have thrown that out of the window, they have allowed it to be taken away from them. That is the real disaster, that is why the Syrian war will drag on a bit. Whether the existing negotiations provide a ceasefire, I don't know; the bitterness has been unleashed, just as it was in Ireland. It took a long, long time for that situation in Ireland gradually to come out of the shadows, gradually you forgot all the nonsense. When I was there, people used to drive an extra

30 miles to buy some Protestant vegetables. It was completely absurd the lengths to which they used to go to underline the differences.

The violence from the Troubles in Northern Ireland spilt over into various atrocities on the mainland. Do you think what is happening in the Middle East could do the same thing here?

I don't think so. I think the reaction of Muslim leaders in this country has been restrained. Of course there have been people who have been educated out of reason into unreason, and those people do terrible things, as we have seen, but they are not characteristic, they are not typical, and with luck I hope that we have got out of the habit of either getting over-excited by these people or of neglecting them.

Do you think the Church should take a stronger line about political issues, or is that dangerous?

I think the present Archbishop of Canterbury will take a stronger line on bread-and-butter issues. I think we've had in Rowan Williams an archbishop who was a saintly man and a highly intelligent theologian. We've now got a man also highly intelligent, but who is interested in practical things, bread-and-butter problems, and I think he will make mistakes as all archbishops do, but I think his heart is in the right place, and that will gradually transfer itself into people being fond of him.

Do you think that gay marriage in church is a real issue or a sideshow that is going to make life difficult?

It is not an essential, an urgent, thing, but it is quite an interesting example. We've got a Prime Minister who believes in change not for its own sake, but he believes in changing things that need to be changed, which means changing things that are out of date. It seemed to him, and to a lot of people, a lot of young people, to be an example of something that could be and should be changed, so he set about changing it, and he managed it. Like Peel, he paid a price; it wasn't an enjoyable process, but I think you do need in leadership to be able to show what you feel, if what you feel can be shown to be factually reasonable and indeed obvious.

Is there any constitutional limit on what an Archbishop can do in that field?

Oh yes. An Archbishop is not a great power; he has very little power. He has power over the Church and over the See of Canterbury. He does not have any constitutional power and the fact that he has a voice in the House of Lords is a secondary issue. I think the Archbishop builds up a body of respect if he is good. I think Bob Runcie, for example, who was the first Archbishop I knew, built up that respect. He won a Military Cross, he wasn't anybody's fool, and therefore he developed that hill or mountain of respect which he could draw on at difficult times, and difficult times he had with the Prime Minister, for example when he preached a sermon after the Falklands War saying we should pray for the Argentines, for their dead, as well as for the British dead. That seemed to me to be entirely right, but it didn't go down well in some places. That I think is an example where that kind of leadership, Christian leadership, is important.

Do you think the appointment of the Archbishop should be approved by the Prime Minister?

That's a difficult one, but I think the answer is yes. There is a system by which names emerge, in a very English kind of way, and the Prime Minister probably has two names which he has to choose from, and they go to the Queen and she approves one of them. I think that is about right. There should be someone keeping an eye on this process, so that it doesn't go completely haywire and you find some fanatic edging his way into Canterbury. I think the present system is about right.

Do you think the Prince of Wales saying the title should be 'Defender of Faith', not 'the Faith' is helpful?

I don't know. The Prince of Wales is his own man and he is entitled to his own opinion. How far he will press this particular one, which may have been just something he said when he was pressed on a particular point, without having really thought it through, I don't know. But we will see. The Queen has strong views and a great knowledge of the Church of which she is the head. I am sure that knowledge and that concern will be transmitted to her successor.

You have accompanied the Queen on a number of visits around the world when you were in government. Do you think she takes her responsibilities very seriously as Head of the Church?

Very seriously. She knows the bishops, she knows many of the clergy, and she listens to all the criticism she gets. She is a staunch supporter of the Church, and she goes to church regularly herself. That is just an important part of her life. Thank heaven that is so.

Where do you think the Church and the relationship with the State will go later on this century?

Who can tell? I think people turn to churches when there is trouble; it's part of human nature. In a blitz or after an outrage of some kind people think about God and they remember to say their prayers when otherwise they may not, and who knows what lies in store for us as far as that is concerned? About war and peace or about hunger as opposed to plenty? All kinds of uncertainties lie ahead in the next century and they could go either way. Nations couldn't work things out at the United Nations, so we didn't go through the manoeuvres that we are going through now over Syria. You can't tell; the answer is I don't know, and you don't know, what the future has in store for us.

But are there changes you would like to see?

Of course. I was Foreign Secretary and I developed strong views then. If we could get a situation in which the great majority of nation states accept that there are rules about what you do and don't do, which they have to accept; if that could be really established as working practice, so that you don't just have someone with a veto, vetoing something and others voting in favour; if you could really get an acceptance across the world that there are certain rules, and that human society depends on having those rules respected – that would be a big step.

You spent some time in Beijing, an atheistic country. What was your impression? Was that a difficult society to live in?

It's a difficult society to live in, if you are Chinese; it's an awkward situation, the Chinese situation. In the background there is a lot of religion, but it doesn't really surface, it's not really approved of. There are a lot of Christians and they have increased in numbers. But the doctrine that the Party is supreme, the Leader of the Party is more or less infallible, that is a very dangerous doctrine. I think I am the only remaining British politician that actually talked to Chairman Mao. It was quite an event, quite something. He was a slightly frightening character, frightening to have that sort of person dictating what you thought was a bad idea. If the world could simply progress, if we said that we don't have that kind of subjection to those people who happen to have come to the top of the heap, that would be a big advantage.

Was he more difficult than Saddam Hussein, whom you also met?

Saddam Hussein was a really nasty man. Mao was bigger than that. We know now that Mao was responsible for the deaths of very, very large numbers of Chinese, millions of Chinese, by his different experiments and so on, and they almost all came to grief. They were concealed at the time, and when I lived in Beijing little children ran up and down the street saying, 'Long live Chairman Mao. May he live for ten thousand years,' and that's how they were brought up. Now you wouldn't have that, not quite to that extent. China has grown up but not yet found the right way to govern itself.

We had religious wars in the seventeenth century. Do you think we are in danger of religious wars now?

I think the divisions in the Middle East – the Shia think they have to kill Sunnis, the Sunnis think they have to kill Shia – is nightmarish. You find it in other places – in tribal places in Kenya and Rwanda, and so on. So there is always a danger, there are always people who like their children to inherit the same prejudices as they do, and bring them up accordingly. The sooner humankind can shed that kind of approach the better.

Does your religion make you optimistic or pessimistic?

It tells me you ought to be optimistic and that's difficult sometimes. I remain on the whole optimistic. At the back of most of us, even most of us who have been in power, there is a basic feeling of sympathy and a basic feeling that we need to live together and that if we haven't learnt how to do it we should hurry up and learn. I think that is a basic feeling, and one that the Prime Minister appealed to the other day, which wasn't successful, that when people use wicked weapons they should be in some way held to account. He didn't win that particular argument, that particular vote, but it hasn't gone away.

Questions from the audience

The Queen is the Head of the Church in England and on her coronation she took an oath, I am not quite sure what the wording is but something like 'to uphold of the teaching of the Church of England'. With the recent passage of the Gay Marriage Bill the Church of England was against that, the Queen signed that. Does that mean that the Queen has broken her coronation oath?

No it doesn't. It simply means that on one issue the Queen constitutionally has to accept that whatever her own view is, the Gay Marriage Bill should go through. That's just the constitution and that is her position, and it is one she understands very well. What her own personal view may be could be a different matter, but she has the constitutional duty when the Parliament of both houses have passed a measure to agree to it.

You have spoken about Syria at some length, how would you rate the diplomatic skills of the Russians in this process?

High, high but unscrupulous, both those things – skilful, clever and unscrupulous. And I think they have proved that over and over again. I certainly think President Putin took up, captured, a stray remark made by Senator Kerry, who is the American Secretary of State. He made a stray remark, off the cuff, as one does when one is finishing a press conference and one is slightly tired. The Russians snapped it up and turned it into a proposal. We still don't know whether that proposal makes sense or not, whether it is practical or not. I hope it is, because if it works it would solve that particular problem for a long time and get all of us out of a sticky mess.

We hear today that the satirists and cartoonists have a bit of a hard job through the lack of characters and material in politics. Do you share that view?

I do think that we need a little bit more amusement and excitement in politics. By which I don't mean one side bashing the other more brutally. I mean that people who write for the newspapers, cartoonists and so on, allow a little bit more subtlety, treat us a little bit more seriously so the issues as they arise, the Syria one we have just been talking about, come to people not as a surprise but as something which was foreseeable. I think there are still very good cartoonists. I think Matt in the *Telegraph* is a great cartoonist, as good as any we have had in the past; it is a breed that should be encouraged provided they are good.

What I'd love to know, as a Ted Heath enthusiast, if you'd persuaded him not to have that election in 1974, do you think he'd have solved the problems with the trade unionists and we'd now have a very different country?

Like many of these questions, you can't be sure. I thought there was a strong case for having that election not at the end of February but at the beginning of February 1974. I thought it was more likely that we would win (I was working for Ted Heath at the time) in an earlier election than a later one. Later on we got most of the vote, the majority of votes, we just didn't get the majority of seats, and that's what counts. I don't know. I tried to persuade the Prime Minister to go early, but on the whole the weight of opinion, heavy opinion, experienced opinion (I was very inexperienced at the time), the weight of opinion was against that. He only went for an election when he had to, when there was no other option. I think that was a mistake, but political history is full of such mistakes, as you know. Callaghan made the same mistake; he should have gone earlier.

We have read in the press in recent times that so many of our parliamentarians are fiddling their expenses, and not really living up to the high standards we all claim we live to. In reality, would you think that politicians today are probably less corrupt than the ones of yesteryear?

I think probably they are, yes. I know of one or two cases of people who were pilloried, whose reputations were thrown down the drain on a misunderstanding of what the position was. Their efforts to straighten it out came up against that wall of prejudice which you often find in the press. The press makes up its mind that someone is guilty, no amount of evidence will alter their opinion. I think there have been one or two cases, there may be more, where this happened with this particular row. I am all in favour of having strict rules about what you spend, and I think we should tighten the rules about political spending, I think they could be tighter than they are, and a cap of the maximum that you should spend on an election is desirable. But on the whole if you look back through history, through the nineteenth century or through the eighteenth century, you find a lot of intolerable things going on, and people getting away with it.

My question is along the same lines. I was going to ask you what you thought about the moral breakdown of so many institutions in this country: MPs' expenses, but also the phone-hacking scandals which involved the newspapers and the police, and this latest scandal at the BBC. Would you give the same answer you gave to the previous question?

I find these moral questions very hard to answer. I believe, as I have already said, that we have, in the House of Commons and indeed to some extent in the House of Lords, a set of people whose main motive is the good of the country. Alongside them, you have, as you've always had, a handful of people who are out for their own advantage, their own cash, their own dividends, their own well-being. These two, the selfish and the unselfish, do their job side by side and I think it is impossible to say from the extraordinary examples you have given; these two things co-exist, they happen side by side. You can do your best to root out the bad ones, but to create a complete system wholly free of blemish is beyond human capacity.

Lord Hurd, you made some comments earlier on about Disraeli being a good speech-maker. Would you draw any parallels with what is happening in Parliament now? Are there any good speech-makers? Would you give some examples?

No. I think that is one of the difficulties; there aren't. When I went into the House of Commons in 1974, there was still a residue of really good speakers. By good speakers I mean that when you see their name go up on the board you go into the House in order to listen to them. And there were people, Iain MacLeod, Michael Foot, and several others, who just in terms of not what they stood for but the way they put it were really good. They have almost entirely gone now, and that's a pity because oratory – good oratory – is something precious, it is something to be encouraged and cultivated. I think it is all connected with the kind of people who get selected now as candidates. I have got my views about that – I am in favour of a greater degree of MPs being older. That is not because I am ancient myself, but because I just think to have a House of Commons which is populated by people who have never done anything except politics in their lives, to keep out the people who have run a university, who have taught in a comprehensive school, who have run a trade union, excluding that kind of experience and shunting it in the House of Lords which has much less power, is a mistake. It's your mistake; you are entirely responsible for choosing these people, and if you don't like them you can change them. No one else can do that. So next time there is an issue about a candidate and you have a strong view which is well backed by facts, you should go and act on it.

Do you believe that the European nation state, which is largely a creation of the nineteenth century, has much further to go?

I do think so, yes. I have worked with them quite closely in my time and I think that what I have been saying generally about Britain is also true about the world as a whole. I think we are lucky to have Mrs Merkel as the Chancellor of Germany. When you think who held that position in the past, you count your blessings, and so across the board. Of course there are silly people around, and silly people sometimes get to the top, but I don't think the world on the whole is governed by silly people.

Developing the point about members of Parliament, the working life of a member of Parliament, and the working hours actually in the Chamber, seems to have changed quite a bit. I recall listening to and seeing excellent set-piece debates on foreign affairs, or defence or whatever, that con- cluded at 10 p.m. with tremendous wind-up speeches on both sides. We don't seem to get so much of that, and I am just wondering whether the change of hours and the changing role of an MP, because there seems to be an awful lot more casework that they do, and emails flooding in and out every day, whether you think the change has been for the better or not?

No, I think on the whole not. I think efforts to reform the House of Commons have often produced perverse results, The situation by which now the House of Commons takes a look, takes a fleeting look, at legislation which is quite complicated and is going to affect the lives of thousands of people, and then passes it to the House of Lords, is a mistake. The House of Commons used to take seriously this business of looking at legislation and it doesn't any more. We get a lot of stuff in the House of Lords that is only half-baked. Not because the policies are wrong but because they have not been put into good effect. And it is linked with another point. When I was Home Secretary and we had a controversial bill, we quite expected to have to stay up all night, not every night but every now and then, an all-night session, an all-night sitting. That was a way of allowing the opposition to really let off steam, really to have their say and feel that they had had their say, and that's gone now. Everybody's off to put the kiddies to bed at 7 p.m. The hours have changed, the hours have become much shorter, and you are quite right, the casework is much bigger. I remember when my grandfather was MP for Devizes one of my jobs. a little earlier in the day than this, was to take his letters up to the post and post them. I rather enjoyed doing this. My grandfather's mail, the stuff that came in to him, was four or five letters a day, now it is 50 or 60. A lot of them are written not by the person who signs them, but simply by the person who has organized the cause; that's quite a different business if you get that kind of letter. You could really almost ignore it, because it was written by somebody else. So I think you are on to a good point, that the efforts quite genuinely made by Labour governments to reform the House of Lords, to improve the Commons, to sort it out, have on the whole tended to have perverse results, the opposite results.

The Dean

Lord Hurd, it is my pleasure to say thank you very much for your 'Yes' to the request to come and open the batting for the Winchester Dialogues. Thank you for the huge vision you bring as a politician, and now well-earned, accolade of statesman. Also as a churchman, you are an acute observer of world affairs, and you bring the distinction of an historian. It is so useful sometimes. We all think the world has never been as bad as this, never been as complicated, never been as difficult. What you were telling us about Peel and Disraeli and all the hot potatoes around, Church and State, bishops and the Reform Bill, all those years ago, I can't believe it – they'd never do that now, they're all much more enlightened! The Church of England is still established, despite all the various efforts to the contrary. So thank you very much for the breadth that you have brought and for your huge vision as statesman and historian – we couldn't have done better.

2

The dangers of forgetting

FRANK FIELD MP

Welcome to the second of the Winchester Dialogues. It gives me very great pleasure to welcome Frank Field to the Guildhall for the first time. We hope this will be a memorable occasion for him as well as for us. Frank, I would like to begin with a bit of biographical detail – I think as a committed Christian, but also as a Young Conservative.

I don't know whether I connected the two, but yes, I was. My parents were working-class Tories; that's always given me a very good feel for where the Labour vote really is. We would run you close in Winchester if we had a candidate like that. I am sure we will get one. It is very interesting how my views were changing anyway, but it seemed to me that the race issue is a key one. Not particularly because one is a Christian and our Lord was not white, but because it just seemed to me horrendous that people could be judged by their outward appearances rather than their characters. I was in the sixth form – upper sixth, doing my A levels – and the great campaign of South Africa was coming to a climax. I say I was pushed out of the Tory Party because I helped organize the boycott of South African goods. The truth is we handed out a few leaflets. The Tory Party is really rather clever how they get rid of you. There's a closing of ranks and one was pushed out. It was soon after that Macmillan did that great speech – 'The Winds of Change in Africa' – and one saw people who were appalled by one's views a few weeks before quite happily mouthing the Macmillan line after he had given it. That was a key political lesson I should have learnt, and I never learnt it, in that leadership in political parties is quite important, and political parties, like churches, survive because large numbers of people are prepared not to keep questioning everything.

The House of Commons would be impossible if everybody decided to do what they wanted to do. The government is having enough difficulty now because there has been a real change in members of Parliament, which I think is wonderful, but quite challenging. But I didn't really learn the lesson that first of all nobody thanks you for getting there first in a political change, and that if one is going to be successful in politics then it is quite important to wait until the crowd moves. I have always thought it was exciting to try and suggest to the crowd that they should move.

You were involved in the 'Faith in the City' movement. How significant was that?

I think for quite a long time the two most important organizations I belonged to – the Labour Party and the Church – were dying. The jury is out on both of them at the moment, isn't it? Both organizations. To belong to one is pretty careless, to belong to two organizations is more than carelessness, as the phrase goes. It is very interesting how malleable our constitution is, and we were enfeebled as a party in that earlier period of Mrs Thatcher's government. It was very interesting how other organizations came to the fore to make the opposition. I think I was one, if not the first, to make the case that the opposition had moved out of Parliament and was actually in the Church and the churches, and 'Faith in the City' was a very important part of that.

Eric James, whom I knew, also quite rightly claimed some credit for this. He thought, given his experience of working in south London, that here was a crisis that was brewing and that the Church had a real role to play. I looked at the first postcards he sent to Robert Runcie and Robert Runcie's reply. Runcie, with real skill, did use the position he had as Archbishop, not only in public debates and the Lords, and so on, but as institutions called Archbishops' Commissions, and he established one. I do think it raised the debate, it widened the debate, in that before there was some sort of appreciation of poverty in the inner city, but afterwards it was clear that, beyond the city, the post-war council estates was where a lot of the issues had moved, particularly when the new development was not accompanied with work moving out there. Then of course there was a huge meltdown of jobs, and the beginnings of an underclass in this country. I think the Commission was terrific, and they went round the country and were good in raising questions and listening to people. I think politicians had got out of that particular habit. To be honest, there has not been a Prime Minister like Mrs Thatcher – she was brilliant to deal with. She knew how to behave as a Prime Minister and how to use that office. Given that she was a mediocre Education Secretary, it is extraordinarily surprising that she was such an effective PM. There is obviously a huge downside to everybody, and one of the downsides was that if you are trying to change the debate it is easy in your anxiety to push the pendulum too far, and I think certainly she did that with a few things.

You went to see her two days before she resigned, and had to be smuggled out of the back door of 10 Downing Street. Is that right?

No. She was insistent I went out of another door and I said, 'No, Prime Minister, I have come in through the front door and there is an unmanned BBC camera there. It is a far better story that I don't go out and therefore stay all night than they see me going out.' She said, 'No, you are going out a different way.' The men in grey suits, the attendants at No. 10, took me out through part of the Tudor Palace, over the Tudor tennis court. It was the most extraordinary evening. Shall I say a little bit more about that?

Please do.

There was a huge feeling that kept welling up, particularly on the Tory side, about this woman. Clearly she had lost her bearings in that until about three years before her exit she had people around her who loved her but would firmly tell her things. She was adrift after she had lost that support and was clearly open to hearing voices and so on about what her role should be. I remember one person – a Tory grandee – said how shocking it was, the behaviour to Margaret. It was when Leon Brittan was pushed out, there was a huge, horrible feeling in the atmosphere about his being Jewish. Again things were erupting about this woman and what she had done. After saying this to me, I was talking to someone else round the corner, and he had his arm around Heseltine. I thought, God, what a treacherous set-up this is, you wouldn't have a seat if it wasn't for her. Then that evening Chris Patten and I were being interviewed to be one of the governors of the Pilgrim Society. I didn't realize the interviews involved having you to dinner to see how interesting you were. Half-past seven came and eight o'clock came, then eight forty-five – no Chris Patten. Finally Chris came in, pushed the door open and went, 'The worst day of my life.' I thought, 'Your life, what about *her* life?' I mean come on, let's get real over this. He then regaled us with what had gone on. Going back in the car I said, 'Chris, did you actually say that to Mrs T?' and he said, 'No.' I thought this whole business of not telling people to their faces what is going on was awful, and I ludicrously said, 'I will go and see her.' He said, 'I think that would be a good idea. I will drop you at the House, where I saw her.'

I went to her rooms. Behind the Speaker's chair there is a room for the Chancellor of the Exchequer and a little group of rooms for the Prime Minister. Her door was locked, she had left. So I moved quickly back towards the Speaker's chair and phoned No. 10. The voice I had always spoken to was on that night. I asked, 'Is Peter Morrison there?' Peter Morrison was her PPS, her link with her parliamentary party. The voice said, 'No, he's gone home.' I said, 'Gone home? Tonight?' and she said, 'Yes, that's what I think.' So I said, 'I think I will come over and see her.' The voice said, 'I think that would be a really good idea if you did.' So I took some work, because I didn't expect to see her easily, and walked up Downing Street and knocked on the door.

As you go into No. 10 there is a rather lovely hall, and behind the door to the right is a little cubby hole, which is now occupied by the attendants who let people in and out of the door. It was the place where Violet Bonham Carter used to lie in wait for Churchill leaving Cabinet meetings. She was clearly in love with him and would step out so she could speak to the man, when he was in that great Liberal government, the 1906 government.

The guy came out and opened the door and said, 'Who have you come to see, sir?' I said, 'The Prime Minister.' He said, 'Oh, the Prime Minister.' It was as though his feet were nailed to the floor, his head just hit the wall. He pulled his head back, went in and made some phone calls. A very officious clerk came out and said there was no way I could see the Prime Minister tonight, perhaps I would like to write a letter. I said, 'I cannot write a letter with what I have to say. I'll wait.' I went to the waiting-room and one of the men in grey suits came and asked if I would like a coffee. I said, 'I think it is going to be a long night and I would love a coffee, thank you.'

There was a bluebottle in the room, and I hate flies. I thought, 'If it's the last thing I do I will get you tonight.' Before I could, Tebbit came in and said, 'What do you want to tell the Prime Minister, Frank?' I said, 'I have come to tell her she's finished and that she can't go out on a top note, but if she doesn't go out tonight your side will tear her apart tomorrow. But she can go out on a high note, she's got a big debate tomorrow, and that she should take that option.' He said, 'If you promise to tell her that, Frank, you will see her shortly.' I asked him why he was doing this: 'Because you are her campaign manager, her gatekeeper.' The penny hadn't dropped at that stage. Anyway I got back with my work and in came Mrs T. Up to all the times I had seen her, I'd always played a particular role – she was Big Mama, I really didn't understand the world; I'd explain what my problem was and Big Mama would deal with it for me. This time she came in looking frail; she seemed to be diminished in height. She looked at me; I brought two chairs close together. She said, 'Why have you come, Frank?' It was like I imagine one would be if the surgeon was telling you that you have inoperable cancer. 'Why have you come, Frank?'

'I have come to tell you, Prime Minister – you are finished.' She said, 'It's not fair.' I said, 'I am not discussing fairness, Prime Minister, I am discussing options. You cannot now go out on a top note. I'm not discussing fairness, I am discussing your options.' This went on for a few times and I noticed the door was open, and still the penny hadn't dropped, that Tebbit wanted someone from outside to tell her what he couldn't get across, or others couldn't get across to her. After a few more times, she then said, 'Well – who will replace me?' I said, 'It is obvious who is going to replace you.' 'Who?' she asked. I answered 'John Major.' She said, 'Why John Major?' I said, 'You have promoted him to all these top positions, you've been training him.' 'He's very young,' she said. 'He will age,' I replied.

Tebbit then came in. He again said, 'What have you told the PM?' Then the penny did begin to drop. He wanted to be able to say, 'Look, Frank told you, you are finished; they will tear you apart. You now have to get out, and your great choice is, the one thing you can do, is to go out on a high rather than a top note. You can actually help choose your successor.'

She then went into a cabinet room to make that speech, which was a marvellous speech that she gave. She was choking back the tears in the first half of the speech, and then Dave Nellist, who was a Trot on our side, got up. She walloped him. He was saying, 'If it's all so good why are they getting rid of you?' The temptation was to say, 'Ask the gentlemen behind me.' She said, 'I'm enjoying this,' and the whole thing was raised up. But that was the night before she went. I'd previously dropped in to talk to her.

Did you feel history was repeating itself when the next Prime Minister, who won three elections, was also forced out against his will?

He was, and I didn't know how near he was. He wasn't the most easy to see, compared with Mrs T. It was always easy to talk with Mrs T because she wasn't my boss. It's so much easier when it is not your boss. But I did see him, and I didn't know how near it was, and I pleaded with him. I said, 'Tony, you can't go yet, we've not got a candidate – you cannot let Mrs Rochester out of the attic; you hear her every night clawing away at the floorboards, trying to get out. You cannot let that out on the country; we have got to have time to get a candidate.' It was the first time he laughed and was relaxed. I hadn't realized how near he was to undoing the door and letting Gordon Brown out.

It was all over the Guardian *today, all coming out, with emails and everything.*

Yes. I suppose it is naivety that I was shocked by. I understand that people want to get top jobs, hopefully because they want to do things. But the idea that you destroy colleagues in this way I thought frightful, shocking, deeply shocking. Blair was very brave sending out troops all over the world to do this, that and the other, but he hadn't got the courage to stand up to the bully next door. A terrible indictment.

You have argued lots of times that religion is an important driving force in politics in your case, and should be. You have also said it is very dangerous for any Church to be tied up with an individual political organization or party.

Now you have put me on the spot. There are people who say they are Christians, who say they know the presence of Jesus. I think it is wonderful that they do, but I have never had that experience. Now you have thrown me into great doubt because I have to talk about it. It just seems to me to be a more reasonable position to hold. The position is a better explanation of why we are here, what the purpose of life is. People who I know say 'Jesus walks with me.' Well I have never had that experience, and that's what I have caught from this part of the country, what I have always found so attractive with John Keble. Because Keble said, 'Blessed are the pure of heart because they may see God.' The idea that you get a pure heart because you have seen God. I am not claiming that I have a pure heart, by the way. Just think of the whole business of that sectarian movement, that discipline, that by sheer effort you may get some greater glimpse of what the Great Story is about – that is the position that I am in. Whether I do enough work on it is another matter, but I have never had that personal experience. As for Churches taking sides, I think it is crazy. It mistakes the role of Christians, and of the great institutions. We may be facing a situation in which knowledge of the Great Story dies out in our country. My view is that you get these people, don't you, who say it is perfectly all right, it is in the hands of the Holy Spirit. I would always feel the Holy Spirit would have found it a bit easier if we had done some work beforehand. I think it is very, very important for us, if we are trying to protect our position and to influence our position, and to influence the nature of the society that we have, that we put a lot of energies into schools. As the Great Story dies out in homes, and Sunday schools have collapsed, the only possibility of getting this knowledge over to people is through schools, and again we have to make a distinction that faith is a gift. Again I think the Holy Spirit might find it easier if we did a bit of work beforehand. That gift may be imparted more easily if people know about the story, and also perhaps knowing that some people don't find it easy and find that that is the very nature of the mystery itself.

You have written that knowledge of Christianity is no longer part of our common verbal currency, as it was, say, for the Victorians.

I think that has had a huge effect, these two great revolutions in ideas that occurred in the early stages of the nineteenth century. Then there was the great biblical scholarship work, which started in Germany and spread out, which people tried to contain first, and then tried to limit to the Old Testament, but it spread to the New Testament. There was a huge change in the nineteenth century. Maybe there were always some people who were relieved that they didn't believe 'the story'. Certainly for most people up to 1850, for doubt to visit you was the most horrendous experience; it would divide families and have the most horrendous consequences. The big tripwire for us was whether people took their Easter Communion or not – that was the big division in families. Did you feel you could no longer go in all honesty and make your Easter Communion? What does appear to be happening, after the 1850s as the economy began to revive, was that people found it much easier to take on doubt. It was less threatening, but nevertheless the most thoughtful people were worried about this, in that they wondered whether one could maintain Christian morality without Christian dogma. We largely did in this country maintain that right to the beginning of our lifetimes, and we did so partly because of this extraordinary philosopher at Oxford, T. H. Green. In one sense his primary aim was to give Christianity a form which intelligent people could defend. For that he got rid of miracles, and much more besides. He did take, as some people said, the Christian honey and put it in a vehicle which was much more secular. For well over 100 years we had the best of Christian morality linked up with what was called idealism, which is in all three political parties. I think if we could go back in time tonight and visit people in the 1850s, we would be surprised how long the Christian capital was safeguarded in this new form. It didn't all come over, and there are these latest statements by the Pope, which are wonderful, about how serious it all is now, how it could collapse like a pack of cards. I think that shows that we are now so clearly into this new era, and I have seen it in my constituency at Birkenhead – this collapsed behaviour, this thuggishness, this yobbishness, which was not there when I went there 35 years ago. It is one of the great things about our parliamentary seats. If you are lucky enough, you have something like Winchester or Birkenhead, which is a proper place and doesn't get 'knocked around' by the Boundary Commission. If you are a member for Manchester, if you are lucky, you keep moving around Manchester, the wards and boundaries change. I have had this wonderful tutorial for 35 years, and the great thing it teaches me – I clearly probably won't do this – let me put on record. On Thursday evening when I go to Birkenhead, if I am having a weekend off, I don't find a buzz when I get out at Lime Street. I always find a buzz when I go up Thursday night to do something. I start about 8.30 on Friday morning. I do eight to ten things, ending at 10 p.m., and I do two or three things on Saturday morning. I am copiously learning and listening all the time. If I cease to not come back with a headful of things I should be doing and ideas to take on – that will be time to give up. But the notebooks keep filling up.

You wrote a rather passionate little book called Neighbours from Hell, *which you said your constituents experienced. Why do you think that is, and what do you think can be done about it?*

I think this is all breakdown of behaviour, and particularly the idea of the cult and culture of respectability. If you are well off and you read the *Guardian* and you live in a nice area, you have these high-falutin' daft views about working-class culture. The great mobilizing change before our lifetime was not relying on political parties, certainly not relying on governments; indeed you were deeply suspicious of governments. One of the reasons why Gladstone was such a hit was that people thought he wasn't putting taxes on them, and because he was 'the people's William'. I pause here. There is a really lovely story about the pull of Mr Gladstone. There's a wonderful book on 1910. Before there was the age of eBay, I was looking everywhere for it and I finally found it in New Zealand. When I saw the author, who'd been an academic, obviously, a diplomat and a politician, chatting to him, he said he was at LSE doing this great book *1910* – about all those massive changes in the House of Lords and so on. The Tory grandees would take students off to the country, and it was during the period of the 1958 Torrington by-election, when Mark Bonham Carter was the Liberal candidate. He said he was giving out Tory leaflets on Polling Day itself and somebody, an agricultural labourer, pushed himself through the hedge and said, 'Tell me, lad, who is the Gladstone candidate?' He said, 'Mark Bonham Carter.' The labourer then thanked him and went in to vote. In our lifetime, the only person who would probably pull out votes like that would be Mrs T.

When I went to Birkenhead it was a Catholic seat; it is nothing now – it's extraordinary how these things die out. It was a trade union seat; it is nothing now. So all these great structures of people's lives have been lost and with it this cultural respectability. There is a brilliant book by Geoffrey Gorer on the English character, in which he explains what my position is. What I do think has happened is we are the beneficiaries of an extraordinary period in English history, when this ethic of respectability took hold and that the people themselves wanted to prove their own worth by adopting that culture. Of course, it was family based and was crucial to the survival within a family. Original sin, William Temple said, was about when we are born and finally quite quickly look out, we think we are the centre of the world, and if we are with people that love us they teach us that of course we are the centre of the world, but there are three or four other people in the household who are also centres of the world. We have to negotiate how each centre of the world lives with the other centres of the world. That gives us a social training beyond the front door as we progress in life to school and beyond. That has progressively broken down. You see it in schools; you'll see it here, not thank goodness in such an extreme form, but talk to any reception teacher and they will tell you two things. One is how more wild the children are. In Birkenhead schools increasingly they grunt rather than speak; some mouths are misformed because they've never had the dummy out of them. Some will only know their name if it is shouted at them; others use pencils to stab next door, won't know what a book is – all of these things, and it has got worse. There is something terrible happening in our society. It is affecting most families, but it is affecting the poorest most because they've got least resources. The book *Neighbours from Hell* was about that.

What do we do about it? If you look at Edwardian times, when the great results of this respectability were among all of us, there was clearly trouble and so on, but in working-class communities, if you had difficulties you went down to the magistrates' courts. They sat after hours, and they would sort things out, and they would do it immediately. I was trying to get Blair and Co. to do something similar, with the idea that we would mirror the criminal justice system with anti-social behaviour orders. What was wanted was to stop the trouble, then and now, and to give power largely to 'the grandmas' in the street, to say, 'Look, we've had enough of this. Any more trouble and we'll be down in the magis-trates' court tomorrow.' They can do that now, but when you go to the magistrates' court, the magistrate can issue a summons, but, because it is being brought by private individuals, the police won't enforce it. The little change I was after was that they should give the magistrates or the county court the power to say, 'The whole street is here, this is clearly not a private action, this is a public action and I want them in court at the end of the day. The police must bring them in and we will sort it out now.'

I also noticed from my constituency that once you start misbehaving, to get the same sort of pleasure from misbehaviour you have to keep increasing the intensity of it and the nastiness of it. Then goodness knows what happens to the chemical composition of the brain, which then for the extreme people takes on a life of its own. So *Neighbours from Hell* was a plea for us to move back to a much more contract-based society, so that we all know what our duties are; and it's duties that beget rights, not rights beget duties. What is it we have to do as decent citizens? It would strengthen lots of people to know they are not being weird in doing these things, and I think that by teaching through contracts one hopes that these rules would again become affairs of the heart, so that people would automatically do them – because they had started to do them, and because they are doing them, other people are doing them. We are reaching the stage now where people say, 'Why should I do it? Other people don't do it', and you get a withdrawal from good behaviour.

Who is to blame for that situation? The parents? The education system? Society itself?

I think a number of forces have changed. We have an underclass in this country, and I saw it happen in Birkenhead. I wasn't aware at first, but when I first went to Birkenhead there were 16,000 semi-skilled male jobs in the docks. There was a huge number of similar jobs in Cammell Laird. Even if you didn't do well at school, or did very badly, there would be a job for you and you could bring a wage packet home. Marriage has been the great civilizing force for men in this country. I don't know about elsewhere, I don't know enough about elsewhere. What we had was a disenfranchisement of young males. There were no jobs for them if they were unskilled. At the same time, we were daft enough to have a lot of social security rules which paid you more money if you were a single mother than if you were part of a partnership. I saw this change, a cul-tural change, which was economically driven to begin with. It wasn't from the air – it wasn't a virus. One saw this disenfranchisement of young men who were not worth marrying. They could not fulfil that side of the bargain, and there was no pressure from the mothers' side for them to do so, because they could pick up more money in welfare. That was in my lifetime; it means an economically driven underclass is now a culturally driven one, in that it is thought a proper option for some young women to start their family without a partner. Yet if you look at the figures in the Merseyside region, 80 per cent of poor children are in single-parent families. I have huge resistance from the system. I think we should teach this in schools. If you don't want your children to be poor, you need two wage earners. They may be of the same sex, they may be of different sex, but if you are on your own it is a hell of a life. Usually, despite how brilliant you are, it is a terrible start for your children.

You have also written about ethical leadership in your rather more upbeat book Saints and Heroes, *and the first two you mention are the father and son who were both Archbishop of Canterbury: Frederick Temple and William Temple. William, I think, is better known to most people, but you reckon that Frederick was more influential.*

More influential because he was the one they tried to censor. He was brave and wonderful throughout the whole of his life, unlike William who wasn't. William had it easy because of his dad being Primate. Frederick's mother was a widow, and because of the Exeter connection he won a scholarship to Balliol, but his mother was determined that he should get there. She was uneducated herself, but she taught herself some very important disciplines, like arithmetic, from books that had the answers, so she knew whether she got the right answer. She gave Frederick this wonderful start in life. He was so poor at Balliol that he had to work on the stairs at night because he couldn't afford lighting. He got a most distinguished First. He could have gone to Rugby to teach but he decided to go to college in Twickenham for Poor Law teachers. From the very beginning this man showed that he was exceptional. In one great dispute, Tate, who had been his protector, was less than good to him. He never forgave Tate for not siding with him in this great debate.

When he was appointed to Exeter, there was a real chance that the chapter would vote him out, which they would have, then lost their livings, but they felt so strongly about it. He was just this wonderful uncompromising man. There is a great tale, a lovely tale, at the coronation of Edward VII. Because he was almost blind at this stage, at Lambeth these huge scrolls were held up by the Bishop for him to read the oaths to the King. He put on Edward's crown a piece of cotton so he would know which was the front and which was the back, but somebody saw this and pulled it off, wondering why that was there. The Coronation was hugely long for this 80-year-old and his legs were giving out. Davidson, who was a creep, who had followed him from Winchester, an absolute creep, said to him, 'Your Grace, would you like a lozenge?' To which he replied, 'You fool, it's my legs not my throat that's giving out.'

He was the most senior person before all the royal family. He gave homage and he couldn't get up. The King lifted him up, and he touched the King's crown and said, 'God bless you'; the King snatched his hand and kissed it. We don't quite have a royal family that matches that. He also was determined at Lambeth to give the people of Lambeth a park. Freehold meant freehold, so he could give it, but the bishops, particularly Davidson at Winchester, who wanted to succeed him, was really anxious that he did not give half his great garden away as a people's park. Temple found out that Davidson was up to his oily business behind the scenes, so he then let Davidson know that he knew. So Davidson in typical grovelling fashion wrote and said he so treasured his relationship with Temple and was so, so grateful that he was consulted on all the big affairs – would this continue? There is a lovely letter back, with Temple saying it would continue but the people will have their park. And they did get their park, though the Church Commissioners tried to take it back.

You also say in that book that William Temple made the Church 'crucial' to the centre of political debate.

Yes he did. He did take his role seriously, although I think he misunderstood his role. His father was an outsider who knew how to behave as an insider, and was brilliant when you look at his decisions. William was born an insider and always behaved as if he was an outsider. He was always setting up societies which he could dominate, through which he could run campaigns to influence the Church. I don't know why he didn't get on and just do it within the Church. He set up these bodies, like great missionary societies, so he could attack the bodies, but he was by then Archbishop of York, then finally to become Primate. He was nevertheless a marvellous character, and the great debate is of course whether Fisher should have followed him or someone different, whether it should have been George Bell – but that's another debate.

Talking of bishops, you ruffled a few feathers not so long ago when you questioned whether bishops should sit as of right in the House of Lords.

Yes. It's the whole business of how you do politics. Here we have got an indefensible House of Lords, but it works, and it works better than the House of Commons. The idea that we should follow the daftness of Clegg by having an elected chamber, so all the creeps who couldn't get into the

House of Commons would get in, and you wouldn't know who they were because they didn't have a role and the whips would decide the order of pecking – it would be a most corrupt system, of strengthening the dying party system in this country. What I wanted to see, and any prime minister wanted, like poor old Cameron who understood what he was saying when he talked about the Big Society, was the second chamber to be the Big Society. So he would say, 'What is the Big Society?' 'Which are the Learned Professions?' 'Which are the other professions? Which are the great cultural institutions in our country?' 'Which sides of industry should be represented? What about education? What about science?'

That would be our Second House. All these bodies are far older, and were electing their senior people long before we all had the vote to elect the House of Commons. I wanted, therefore, the second chamber to be the representation of the Big Society, our great interests who would largely elect themselves, and if they did have any elections there would be an electoral college/commission to do that. I thought the bishops should start it off. The bishops should introduce a bill to say, 'We can't reform the whole House of Lords, but the position of religion has changed in our society; we would like the 26 places plus three to be shared out among Roman Catholics, among Methodists, and then if the other faiths like the Muslims can get together and have representatives, places should go to them as well. What we are doing now is starting the House of Lords reform, which the country would be able to understand and might even support, might even vote for.' And you would see the bishops being really, really influential in politics, because they'd be using their position. Most of them don't turn up; I don't know why they keep their positions. Davidson for all his faults, this oily Winchester man, when the House of Lords was sitting, he had one of the bishops' robing rooms as his office. And Tate – as Bishop of London, then as Archbishop – said, 'You know you cannot sit in the House of Lords for 25 years and not be able to contribute something important to the debates.' They took that role seriously. We've got now bishops who have lost confidence in using their position in the House of Lords to do church business and other business – ethical business for the nation. Of course, if you are uncertain, what do you do? You go back to the womb, go back to your diocese. We don't want all bishops to be doing this because there is a need for them in their dioceses, although there are many more bishop Chiefs than ordinary Indians, so that could be looked at. But with all the modern iPhones and so on it is crazy to think that you can't be a serious parliamentarian and have a really good hold on your diocese. You need to delegate. We need to be serious about women in the Church as well if we are delegating.

You have never hesitated to take an independent line and criticize your own party as much as opposing parties. How did you feel when The Economist *wrote that article headed 'St Frank'?*

I had two feelings. One, it was great that a backbencher had got this page – because that doesn't happen. I don't like that side of it; I don't like this idea that you are pushed up on to a pedestal, because I'm not on a pedestal. I might have just had life easier than others. I haven't got children, so I have no pressure on me to fiddle, I don't have school fees to pay, I haven't got school shoe bills to pay. It is all very different and tough trying to do well by your family, given where lots of MPs come from. I know it is a huge wage compared to lots of people in Birkenhead, but it is not compared with other people on the same social strata as you. I have never had those pressures, and I was lucky enough to buy when it was silly money, before it became funny money. So I've never had to worry about that. That's a huge change, to have these incredibly talented young people working with me. When I left university I expected to get a job; indeed you interviewed people for the jobs that you actually wanted. I expected to have a pension, I expected to have a home and I expected to have savings. Now I have these incredibly clever people working with me and it is difficult enough for them to get a job. The world has changed. You who have got children know this, that your responsibilities to them do not stop when they get a job, if they are lucky enough to get a job. The whole socio-economic ecology has changed. Not for the better, but that is the world that we live in.

Before I throw this open, one last question. What would be your ideal situation of the relationship you would like to see in the twenty-first century between Church and State?

I'd like both to be more confident. When we talk about the State, we are in this extraordinary period now where if you look from the post-war period – 60-odd years – in 52 of them governments have run a deficit. We are not in a new game here, we are in an old game. We have developed a habit where politicians will dog-whistle that 'You can elect us, and you won't get all the bills; we'll just shove it on to our children's children to pay.' Therefore, we are in a serious business now about trying to rein back the role of what we have historically thought of as the State. Yet look at this room – we are living longer, we will draw our pensions longer, we will need more care towards the end of our lives, and we will make greater demands on the NHS. So the bills are going to go up, but none of us, except the lunatic fringe, are prepared to pay significantly more taxes. So one of the things we have to do as a state is to redefine the things that we will do in common, but we won't do through the State. I have tried to get our side first off the tracks on this: how do we do a deal if we pay more towards our pensions and towards our unemployment insurance, and our care, and the NHS, that politicians don't get their sticky fingers on it. For that we are going to have to have a new relationship between having organizations which take on some of the powers of the State, clearly separate from politicians doing that.

We also have to face this huge challenge that maybe we are the last generation which really understands the 'Great Story'. What is our responsibility to ensure that knowledge of that 'Great Story' continues? I talked about schools earlier on. I wanted to talk to people afterwards about whether we can have some cathedral academies here, of getting a real further hold into the community. We know that generally speaking cathedrals are growth points. So we should have the courage to support them in that role. People find it easier if they are in my position to make entry into a cathedral, than to go to an ordinary church service and be landed on the parish council after your third appearance, or something like that. Thinking about the role, why was it that Queen Elizabeth I was so taken by church music? In other countries that tradition of choral music did not survive. It did under her, largely because of our cathedrals. Given that music was largely driven out of the state sector of education, here is a huge opportunity to use our cathedrals as great centres of spiritual, and also of musical, excellence. With cathedral academies we could get music back in a serious way into our schools. But how do we use this extraordinary position we have been given in English society, places in the House of Lords, a wonderful network of cathedrals, 12,000 clergy, paid foot soldiers? How do we use them more effectively to try and prevent this message from dying out? At the same time, how do we rethink the role of the State, when most people are fed up with our politicians?

Which is a good moment to throw this open. Who would like to ask the first question?

Questions from the audience

Talking about being fed up with politicians, now that we no longer have mass membership of political parties or indeed particularly large membership at all, how do you think they should be financed, if they should be financed?

I do not support financing by taxpayers. I think we should limit the size of donations. Political parties should cut their coat according to their cloth. I am making the comparison now between the Leader of the Opposition or Clegg's office or the Prime Minister's office. When Gaitskell was Leader of the Opposition he probably had two people in his office. We have now got offices stacked with people. You have to have other people to control them, and what the message is and all of that. I am in favour of politicians getting real over this and the idea that you are not somehow a serious politician because your party can't fly you around in a helicopter. You get the train like everybody else to do these meetings and it would be much more exciting for people because you could go up and talk to them, which could be very useful. It is an immensely serious point about our constitution over political parties. I have a huge advantage, for a lot of the time I largely do what I want to do, but you couldn't run the House of Commons like that. Because we do elect parties on programmes, and this is the real change again. It is called the theory of the mandate. A lovely person who taught me at university said one of the great things about British constitution is that it is impervious to the ludicrous foreign notions like the mandate. Anyway, Mrs T introduced the mandate and that was: 'I've got a programme, I've got the authority, I am going to drive this programme through and at the end of the Parliament I am accountable, I go back to the electorate and say this was the mandate, this is what I've done, this is what I failed to do.' We had half a day with the Tote – the Betting Board, or whatever it is called. Normally that is a mega-debate, people staggering in making contributions, and I remarked when I spoke how extraordinary that we'd got most people in for our debate. One of the Tories very cruelly pointed out and said, 'Yes, they are mainly on our side, aren't they? Not on your side on this particular issue.' Sixty people were there for that debate, and as they spoke they became members of Parliament; they'd done things or they wanted to do things, they'd built charities up. Wow, this is going to be ungovernable, this group; they are here to do things, and not just climb the greasy pole. That has actually been proved, hasn't it? So how do we get the sort of freedom that we want our members of Parliament to have, but in a way in which governments can drive through a pro-gramme? So that at the end of the day, at the end of the Parliament, they can say, 'We have done what you asked us to do', and don't say, 'Well, of course we couldn't do that, these lunatics you sent in wouldn't let us do anything. They just kept changing everything that was actually going through.' So there is a real tension there, but I do not think the tension is solved by either rich people being able to influence parties or rich organizations being able to, or us thinking that somehow we can put our hand into the taxpayers' pockets. I think we would die even more quickly if that took place. Douglas Carswell has a community centre where they have a fish supper and people come along. It is £5, and at a certain stage when they are having a discussion about their community, he will say, 'I am your MP and I'm a Tory. I must see how many of you want to stay on and discuss Tory politics with me.' But he is also making members. Clearly we need to reinvent political parties in this age and make it cheap to join and fun to join.

What is your proudest parliamentary moment?

I hope my proudest is to come. The Centre for Social Justice, which Iain Duncan Smith formed, asked me to go along to the launch of their report on modern slavery. I have two lovely people in the office, who are both pushing me to do new things. One is what can we do to save the Commonwealth dying; we've done a huge amount of work on that this year. The other thing is about slavery. I know something about it and I went to the launch. As with lots of these launches, they had far too many people speaking; it was getting more and more boring. I thought, I am the fifth speaker, their bones will be aching. Anyway, I got up and said, 'This fantastic report – we cannot let it go back on to the shelves and collect dust. We are going to have to have a new act, like Wilberforce, and that should now be our campaign.' I believe in providential luck. That evening, as I was coming out of voting, Iain Duncan Smith was looking for someone. I said, 'Iain, this wonderful report you published today, it knocked me sideways; it's such a credit to you.' He immediately said, 'It is not me, my adviser Philippa Stroud, when she was running CSJ [Centre for Social Justice], it was her baby. You must come and give evidence before our social justice committee – cabinet committee.' I then met Philippa, and said, 'Look, Philippa, we could make this an Act.' She then spoke to her equivalent, Fiona Cunningham, Mrs May's political adviser. I then went and did the cabinet committee – it normally takes so much time, it's junior ministers. Mrs May came for the modern slavery item. She said what she was doing in the Home Office now, what she would continue to do, that she would probably seek new legislation. We are at the stage now where she promised legislation. It will be on the statute book I hope before the next general election. That's been exciting. It's terrible – you think, 'Why can't one get one's ideas over to one's own side a bit more?' I think there are some lovely examples, what they call chocolate soldiers, two political advisers. One knew her minister Iain Duncan Smith had an interesting list, she'd actually given birth to it, making sure this two years' work was done.

You mentioned T. H. Green. Would you say that sort of thinking is still influential today in the Church?

The English were very good at sorting out what they needed, and it was an approach which they had, and it was an ethic which they had. You can see it in Mr Attlee. I would like to think that Blair was probably the last person who would understand that language. It is the great ethical underpinning of our society, and there's nothing to replace it. It's all part of the heritage which we are just using up. So I very much want to go back. The Chief Rabbi generously said, 'No, Frank, we don't want contracts, we want covenants.' And I said, 'Yes, of course we do, but how are we going to get to covenants unless we have contracts which start teaching us a way of thinking?' The Prayer Book is very interesting, it has this phrase which always used to puzzle me: 'in whose service is perfect freedom'. How can that be? As you get older you begin to see the tramlines are a means of freedom, rather than a limitation of your freedom. What the idealist did for us was to give us a way of thinking about the world which promoted both our own freedom and the freedom of other people as well.

In view of the need for retrenchment of the welfare state, could there be an argument for the disestablishment of the Church from the State? If so, what would that argument be?

You'll never get it because it would be so complicated. And you might get disendowment with it, so you would lose all your money as well. I wouldn't go there if I were you. Again it's choosing it, isn't it? For the best reasons in the world Clegg has got free school dinners for young people in primary school. The idea that we are in a state where we have got that sort of money to throw about is appalling. It means that richer parents in his constituency will not have to pay for school dinners when we are cutting special education needs budgets. It is ludicrous politics, it is grandstanding, and if one has got £800 million to throw around like this, we know that people's life chances are decided very early in life, in the womb and in the first crucial stages afterwards. There are obviously so many people doing this. One of their jobs is to not be so busy, to stand back and think a bit more. If you had £800 million it would be to get over the knowledge about how crucial that stage of pregnancy is, and the first stages of life, and that you have power, particularly as a mother but also as a father; you may not be able to set yourself free to achieve your best self, because the race has already been determined before you get to school, but you can do it for your children. The incredible revolution we have had in neuroscience, whereby we now understand a huge amount more about the formation of the brain, indicates the role of parents helping to form that brain. I had recently a young woman who came in after she had got over the grieving of a friend of hers who had witnessed his best friend stab him to death, and that friend didn't know that it was wrong – and we have got more of these cases coming. You have the part of the brain that gives you human empathy, at the very front of your brain; it is grown particularly during the first year, and after two years the part of the brain that feeds that growth doesn't function. We are getting a whole stream of people coming on who are so damaged that we will have more of this violence than we have ever had before. The great news would be if the government was thinking about what it could do to eliminate this huge bottom 40 per cent of our population who will find it increasingly difficult to get jobs, increasingly difficult to make relationships, increasingly difficult therefore to earn their living and contribute. We have got to become very serious about these foundation years. It's not to spend more money, but whatever money we spend – £640 million for free school dinners – we spend it where we know that we are totally focused on outcomes, when we are spending other people's money, and we are not nearly at that stage now. We have got a manifesto trying to get all the parties to adopt this on the foundation years, on the idea that we should be committed as political parties to let no child fall behind. Not because we should be in business so they achieve their best selves, but we won't have the money any more to continue the way we have been behaving, propping people up in dependency. So that huge issue we actually have to deal with.

How would you say Mrs Thatcher's faith influenced her relationship with other members of Parliament during her years in power?

I don't know if it did at all, directly. She once gave me Graham Leonard, the Bishop of London's, Lent book. It was amazing. She had read through it and she had underlined all the points I thought you shouldn't underline. I don't think people influence other members of Parliament by their faith, they do it largely by who they are and the way they live their lives. I don't think she ever therefore thought in those terms. But can I just end on one rather nice note. After she was kicked out, I said to her, 'What is your greatest failure as Prime Minister?' She said, 'Oh easy, I cut taxes because I thought I would get a giving society, and we haven't got it.' I wrote a paper on that, that we should have anti-social behaviour orders for the rich. If you don't know your responsibilities because you've got wealth, we have clearly got to teach you. I thought we should have a tax system which says that above a certain level we are going to tax you each year. If you give that away, if you form your own foundation, great, but if not we will take it from you, and we will give it to the charitable sector, to other foundations, until you learn what the responsibilities of wealth are. I wrote that up and when Cameron had just got the leadership of the Tory Party he was doing the restaurant in the House of Commons. When he came out, he said, 'I've read your paper Frank, interesting.' I said, 'Are you going to do it?' 'Ah,' he said, 'another matter.' All sections of society desperately need to be taught what their duties are. We have perverted the whole of our society, where everybody knows about their rights. But rights cannot exist without duties; they are based on that, and it's the duties that beget rights. It is the most fundamental change. All the welfare reforms that I have been trying to do have been to get over that very simple point. I could never get Blair; he started talking about duties, but he still talked about rights and duties. Never duties and then rights. Takes a long time.

The Dean

This is the moment to say, Frank, thank you very much for taking the train from London to Winchester and finding time to be with us, with all the pressure you were under. We are enormously grateful. It is lovely to have had this relaxed space with you, which has been something very precious to all of us.

3

A Ministry of Fun?

MARIA MILLER MP

It is a very great pleasure to welcome the Secretary of State for Culture, Media and Sport, and also Minister for Women and Equality. I think what I would like to do, Maria, if I may, is to begin by asking you something that comes under the latter responsibility. You have been very strong in your support of women bishops. Was that a difficult row to hoe?

My position has been that the Church needs to make the decision on women bishops, but I think when I go round I see how much women do in the Church, not just here in Winchester in the cathedral, but also in my own constituency in Basingstoke. I see people like Jo Stoker doing a fantastic job. I really ask the question why we wouldn't want women to be involved in every part of the Church's life. So ultimately that is a decision for the Church. I have been really pleased to see that the Church has brought forward further recommendations, which I think are going to go to Synod later this month. So maybe this will be a speedier process than anybody thought, and I think really a good decision.

It was interesting that the Bishops and Clergy were all in favour of women bishops, and it was the laity who threw it out in Synod.

Well, I am told by Tony Baldry who is the Second Church Commissioner that I should never try and understand the voting process around Synod, and I will take his sage advice on that, although I should also declare an interest that I too am a Church Commissioner – something I actually found out by accident in the members' tea room. I am an ex-officio

Church Commissioner, which means that I am the Church Commissioner talking about how you get hold of money to mend churches, so that is something I think is very important and I am very proud of that job. I do think that it is a very complicated voting process, and I do think it is important for everybody to feel it is the right thing to do. That's why, although I have very strongly supported women bishops, I do think the Church needs to feel comfortable with that as an evolution in the way it works.

An even trickier issue is the one you have had to speak on in the House of Commons, which is same-sex marriage.

Yes, well, I don't feel it's difficult to talk about marriage. I didn't make myself very popular when I first got elected at the Conservative Party Conference by giving a rather long speech about marriage. The *Daily Mail* liked it – I got a very big double page spread from them – but I think everybody else thought I was a bit out of touch. Why was I talking about marriage? I've been married since 1990 to the same person, and he's brilliant and wonderful and I can't imagine my life without him, and we have got three wonderful children; some of you know them quite well. I think that it is something that everybody should want to be involved in. I think that marriage is a great institution; it keeps us all centred, but also as we get older we can look after each other. So it wasn't very difficult for me to talk about marriage that might be between two people of the same sex, when it came to the State's involvement in that. What I again wouldn't ever want to do is to try and tell the Church what to do. So I was most fortunate that the Bishop of Leicester, who is a very good man indeed, is the Church's spokesman on these issues, and he and I have built a very good relationship, and I think he feels happy now that what we have done as a state, in introducing same-sex marriage, is that we have really protected particularly the Church of England and the Church in Wales, but also protected other Churches as well who wanted to be able to marry people of the same sex. So I could probably turn it slightly on its head and say that this Bill, this Act, is about religious free-dom because the Quakers, the Unitarians and the Liberal Jews do want to be able to marry people of the same sex, and I respect that as much as I respect the fact that the Church of England may not want to marry people of the same sex. So I think we have come to a good position and I hope that at the end of the day I just want more people to be able to get married and be happy in their lives.

But it has been a very divisive issue within the parties, within your own party, the Labour Party and the Liberal Democrats. There are strong divisions right down the middle of those parties about whether it is a good thing or not.

Yes, but interestingly when you look at society in general there are those divisions, and discords are less pronounced. I looked at some polling recently, and you should never ever do politics through polling because it is difficult. I looked at the attitudes towards women and same-sex marriage, and a lot of women are very supportive; in fact, the majority of women are very supportive of same-sex marriage. I wondered whether that is perhaps because women are more used to some of the discriminations we face as women – our gender makes us more understanding of other people who get discriminated against as well. I'll put it very simply. I was sitting next to somebody on Tuesday evening at a dinner. It was a very strange dinner because it was under the *Cutty Sark* and I have never, ever had dinner under a ship before. It's not something I would recommend, it was a bit unnerving. This gentleman had three children and he was in what he called a modern marriage. I couldn't have ever wanted to meet a happier person who was so effusive about his 3-year-old twins and his other child as well, and he said to me he was in a same-sex civil partnership. He thanked me for what I'd done, not for any other reason than it made him feel that his relationship could be valued as much as somebody who was in an opposite-sex couple relationship. So I think that is probably a good thing to have done.

When you spoke about it at the despatch box several newspapers pointed out that I think there was only one of your cabinet colleagues in the House at the same time when you were speaking on this.

Oh well, that's apropos of nothing. You know, whenever we speak there are usually very few people there. I wouldn't take that to mean too much. Unfortunately, as a cabinet minister, you are often out and about doing lots of different things. But you are right to say it is an issue that has been very difficult for all the political parties. It's an issue which I think you have to approach by respecting people's views, and respecting that people can have very different views. My approach has been that I will respect the right of two people of the same sex who want to get married, as much as I will respect the right of, particularly, the Church of England, Church in Wales, to not want to undertake those marriages. I think if you can come at it with that mutual respect then we have made a huge amount of headway. Nobody's trying to pull a fast one, nobody's trying to do something which is untoward. It is just really trying to make sure that the State, which I am a representative of, can value people equally and not discriminate.

What is the position at the moment? When is the law going to come in, if it is going to come in?

The law – it's not a Bill, it's an Act now. So we do have a law, unlike the French who seem to implement their laws within 24 hours of passing them. Apparently we can't do that, we have to do a lot more. So we are currently going through a lot of what we call an implementation plan, where we are looking at how we make sure our benefits system, and our pension systems, and all of the different things that need to be brought up to date, are brought up to date, and by the summer of next year the State will be able to undertake same-sex marriages. Then it is really for religious institutions and others to decide how they move forward, whether they wish to do that as well.

Wearing your other hat as Culture Secretary you have had another hot potato which is the outcome of the Leveson Inquiry, and the Royal Charter, because you were your party's representative, with Harriet Harman and Lord Wallace. Where are we on that at the moment?

Well, yes, every time I see the Prime Minister I say to him you've obviously got a mantra in mind here; if you've got a tough job you give it to a woman, so whether it's equal marriage or Leveson it seems to have landed in my lap, and when it comes to the Home Secretary's job, well, I think she is doing an amazing job, and we've got a female Northern Ireland Secretary, so I think I've proved my point. He does believe that women do the tough jobs in Cabinet. That's my story and I'm sticking to it. Where we are is, I think, that we have probably come to a good place. When Lord Leveson was asked to look at press regulation, you have to remember that the trigger-point was a dreadful incident where there was an assertion made that the press had gone in and deleted messages that had been left on Millie Dowler's mobile phone, leading her parents to believe that she might still be alive. I don't know if you can remember that, but that was the trigger-point for that inquiry to be set up. It has now been established that that never happened, which is interesting. There was never a point where those messages were actually deleted. The Inquiry was brought about because of the public outrage at that situation. Interestingly, all the things which created that public outrage are now in court, and obviously we wouldn't want to talk about those tonight, but are subject to criminal prosecutions, and therefore probably showing that there was quite a robust system in place to deal with that type of wrongdoing. The Leveson Report was never about criminality; it was about culture. I suppose the feeling was that criminality may have been brought about by lack of the right culture of regulation, of self-regulation and whether the Press Complaints Commission was working as it should. So the Leveson Inquiry looked at that in great detail, and Lord Justice Leveson came out with a very extensive report, and we have been trying to interpret that over the last year. From the start, the Prime Minister and I were very clear we did not want to have statutory regulation of the press; we felt that was not consistent with British democracy; it wasn't consistent with our belief that freedom of speech for the press was of paramount importance. What we did believe we needed to have was a standard set of principles that the press could look at and then self-regulate themselves. Which was really what Lord Justice Leveson was calling for. So what we have done, a bit like the BBC, we established a Charter which set out a set of principles and then it is for the press to set up their own self-regulatory body, which they are doing rapidly, and I applaud the work that they are doing there. They are calling it IPSO, and they have already set up an appointments committee, and the people are coming in place to show that the press can set up a more effective regime. That regime may decide to apply for recognition under this charter, this set of principles, or they might not. If they do, great – they will get some benefits, some advantages, when it comes to costs when they go to court. If they don't, then I guess they're taking a judgement on risk that they don't need to have those benefits of cost protections, and exemplary damages protections. It is really for them now. I have to say I think there's only about 12 people in the country who are interested in press regulation as much as I am. I can give you a much fuller answer if you need it. Suffice it to say, I am trying to get to a situation where there is a confidence when people read the newspapers. At the end of the day, newspapers are there to sell their product to all of us sitting here. If people can be confident that if there is an error or a mistake made in that newspaper, something that is said that is wrong, that they have got an independent way of having it sorted out. Ultimately, that is what people have been calling for, that is really what this Charter gives us an opportunity to put in place. And I think that is really what the press are already doing, through this new self-regulatory process. So I am confident we will see a better outcome.

Could we have two regulatory bodies, one set up by the press and one set up by the Royal Charter?

The Royal Charter will oversee all regulatory bodies; it's a legal service, a sort of commission over the top. You can have any number of regulators who can apply to be recognized. So you might have one from a certain section of the broadsheet newspapers, or from the tabloid newspapers, or from people who are national magazines. There are all sorts of different organizations who could set up regulators and apply to be recognized, or not, as the case may be. We are talking about self-regulation not statutory regulation. That is important because what nobody wants, I can guarantee you, is for politicians to be involved in the way the press is run. The way we set up the Charter is that it is completely and utterly divorced from the meddlings of politicians.

Is the public view of the press likely to change as the trial of Rebekah Brooks, Andy Coulson and the others goes on, as new sensations come out every day?

I don't know. I think most of us look at those trials and see that this is a certain section of a small section of journalists who were acting in a certain way, and it is not for me to pre-judge any trials. I don't get the feeling at all, I may be wrong and there may be people who disagree with me, but I certainly don't get the feeling that people feel that this was an activity or way of operating that was widespread, and it is clear that we have already got the laws in place to deal with it. So the self-regulation is really about, in future if people see things that are wrong, and mistakes are made, there is an easy way to address it. I think that is something people have been worried about in the past.

Fairly widespread in the News of the World, *though.*

That organization is no longer in existence.

One of your other main responsibilities, nearer to your heart perhaps and maybe more rewarding, is the whole culture thing. You wrote a very strong article in The Stage *newspaper about the importance of the arts. You managed to restrict the cut in your culture budget to only 5 per cent, which, compared with some of the other departments, is quite good, though I suppose the arts community screamed about that too?*

My job is the best job in the world. I get to look after all the things that people care about most: the BBC, arts, theatre, the culture of this country, the heritage of this country, beautiful places like the cathedral. How can we make sure that we have got enough funding to look after beautiful historic buildings like that? Sometimes I think we undersell the importance of arts, culture and heritage. We have got to value it for its own good, and of course we do. I went recently to the '50 years of the

National Theatre'. I don't know if anybody saw it on the TV last weekend. An astonishing evening, showing that we are not only the best place in the world for theatre, or have been for the last 50 years, but we will be for the next 50 years, because the talent is extraordinary. It is no good just saying we should appreciate Derek Jacobi because he is one of the best actors in the world, and that in some way that culture can never be linked to anything other than intrinsic worth. I think it has a very strong economic value for the country, whether it is the tourists who come into the theatres, whether it is the creative industries that feed off, in a very positive way, the talent that is created both in acting terms but also technical terms. And whether it is the ability of organizations like the National Theatre to go abroad and to take their wares abroad. Let's look at *War Horse*, which was a National Theatre experiment, which is now an international success. All of those things are hugely valuable, so my pitch to the Chancellor was very simple. It was, 'You have got to make sure that we continue to fund the culture and arts and heritage of this country, not only because it is the right thing to do, not only because it is part of our DNA, but because it is hugely important economically as well.' And, frankly, I won the argument.

Was the Chancellor more impressed by the economic argument than the cultural one?

If you had ever met him you would know that the cultural war would have won very strongly with him, because he is a hugely supportive person when it comes to the arts. But he is Chancellor and he wants to put his money where economic growth is. At a time when we are starting to turn that corner in terms of the economy of this country I think culture and the arts gives us a turbo-boost. As I came down here tonight I was thinking what a strange week I have had, but I think that's probably most nights and most weeks. But this week was particularly exciting and interesting. I was privileged to be one of the people hosting the President of the Republic of Korea, and signing a cultural memorandum, a memo of cultural understanding with my counterpart in Korea who is interestingly also Culture, Media and Sports as well. It was fantastic to be able to do that. Korea is one of the fastest-growing economies; if we want to have trading partners in the future outside of the EU, which we do, then Korea is going to be one of those countries. So to be able to use culture as a way of joining us together is extraordinarily important. I would like to point out that the President of Korea is a woman as well. So that's good.

One of your predecessors, David Mellor, used to refer to the Ministry as a Ministry of Fun. Is it all fun?

Well, after the first year, no. I don't think that the press self-regulation and trafficking through the equal management bill were enormous amounts of fun. Enormously important, but not enormous amounts of fun. I think it is much, much more important than that. I think my department is an economic powerhouse for the Government, and I think culture and the arts are an economic powerhouse for the future of this country. Yes, I do have a lot of fun. I was at the British Museum at a dinner last night, which was extraordinary and wonderful in the Gallery of Enlightenment. Tom Friedman was talking about what will make the difference between a successful country in the future, and a not successful country, and, as he rightly pointed out, it's ideas and it's that creativity that we are teaching our children, how to think and how to be creative. When I think about my own children and the jobs they may be doing in the future, you can see that is absolutely right. So, yes, it is the Ministry of Fun perhaps, but more importantly the Ministry of Creativity, and that is really the life-blood of this country.

I am sure I don't need to tell you that arts organizations can be the most tenacious fighters for their own corner. A lot of the regions complain bitterly that too much of the cultural subsidy goes into London. How do you cope with that charge?

Well, it's fascinating. That has been a story in the media this week a lot; I can understand the sensitivity. The first thing I would say is that local authorities have got a huge role to play and, even despite the pressure of finances, local authorities like mine in Basingstoke still continue to invest in a world-class concert hall, which we have got in the Anvil, and I know the theatre here is also hugely well respected. I was here very recently. So local authorities are supporting the arts in their own community. The Arts Council are doing a great deal to make sure that the split of the money that they give out to arts organizations on behalf of the government, on behalf of taxpayers, better reflects the need to support regional arts companies. Sir Peter Bazalgette, who has taken over recently, has already effected a change from a 60/40 split to a 70/30 split in favour of the regions. What I would do if you are looking at those sorts of figures is urge you to look at the basis on which they are being calculated. If you are looking at a per capita head funding, then yes you are right, London receives a disproportionate amount of money. But if you look at a per visitor funding level – how many people actually visit an arts organization – then you will see that London receives one of the lowest levels of funding in the country. Why is it important to draw that distinction? Because not everybody who visits London theatres is a London resident – far from it. As I said earlier, their role in creating a pull for tourism is hugely important. Also, many of us travel into London to see the great theatres and the great opera houses that we have there. All of those organizations also reach out to regions, including our own. I was at the Willis museum in Basingstoke very recently at a V&A exhibition, which was superb and five minutes away from where I live.

Is there anything you urge organizations to do that they are not doing at the moment?

I think my message very clearly to all arts organizations is that all organizations who are dependent on public money and the heritage and cultural sector is to realize that the pressure we are under financially now is not going to somehow magically change. I do worry sometimes that people feel that 'give it another year or two and it will all be back to where it was a couple of years ago'. We all have to remember that in 2010, for every £4 we were spending as a government one of those pounds was borrowed. That was unsustainable, completely unsustainable. So if we are going to put finances back on a sustainable footing for the long term and not simply return to the problems of the past, we've got to realize that the pressures on finances are here to stay, particularly given our ageing population. We want to make sure that we are looking after people well in their old age, and this isn't going to make the finances any easier. So I think making sure that organizations are sustainable for the long term is what I am talking about to every organization I meet.

You have children of your own, and you have also been a governor at four different schools before you went into Parliament. At a previous dialogue, Frank Field was saying that the knowledge of Christianity and the Bible in schools is nowhere near as much as it used to be. Is that something that worries you about the whole religious education thing, and some of the proposals that your colleagues in the Ministry of Education have brought in?

I am most fortunate in that my two boys are Pilgrims' boys and my daughter went to St Swithun's, so I never suffered from that problem. They were very, very well looked after, and continue to be so. I think that education has an important role to play in helping children understand so much about our society, including the role of religion. I was looking recently at the A-level syllabus around religious education. It is very philosophical, looking at the philosophies of religion as much as anything else; I think that is really interesting. I do think churches have an important role to play. I think that parents have an important role to play as well, and perhaps too often parents lean on the schools to do the religious education for them, when perhaps they have also got to take responsibility themselves. I have been really fortunate to be a governor of church schools in my time, a number of different church schools, including one right in the centre of London, right next to the BBC. Seeing the role of a Church of England ethos in the running of a school can make an enormous difference to all sorts of things, whether it's the discipline or just the focus or just the involvement of the parents in the school life. That ethos can be hugely powerful.

Do you think Frank is right, that the knowledge is not what it was?

I am not sure I can answer that directly; I suppose it depends on the individual school. I go into schools in my own constituency, particularly some of the Catholic church schools and also some of the Church of England schools, and I think they do have a very strong teaching focus on religious education. Within the state schools, I am not sure I would be able to answer that directly.

You mention the BBC, which is another of your responsibilities, and you gave a keynote speech at the Royal Television Society Symposium in Cambridge. I know it is something that matters to you. Were you embarrassed by the chairman of your party attacking the BBC and saying we should cut the licence fee?

I think the article that was written, perhaps some of the comments, were taken a little out of context. I feel like a politician saying that, but I think that is probably the case. I think the biggest thing the BBC needs to do at the moment is to focus on how it fixes the problems it has got. I think it is very easy to start creating the fog of saying, 'Well, let's start talking about the future and what might happen to the licence fee and what might happen at the next charter renewal sometime in 2016.' No, this is a major organization, I happen to think it is one of the most important organizations in our country; it is one of the organizations that make people abroad, when they get to know our country, more likely to love Britain – if they know the BBC – which is astonishing. It really is; it is an important way to shape attitudes towards Britain. I want the BBC to fix the governance problems it's got, which it clearly has got. I think that Tony Hall is just the man to do that, working with Chris Patten. Rather than starting to get into some debate about licence fees in the future, let's see that fixed. I think the BBC owes it to us to do that.

Do you think that Jeremy Paxman's recent outburst about all politicians being boring and he couldn't think who to vote for, would do him and the BBC more damage than the politicians?

I think about this a lot; one tends to get a lot of comments about the way one does things. I was reading an article today about the way I talked about a particular issue. I think all too often the media want politicians to be performing artists, but then when you are a performing artist they don't really want you to do that at all, they want you to be serious about the subject you are talking about. I think what the people who elect us want are individuals who care passionately about their country; they care passionately about creating a really good place for kids to grow up in, and they care passionately about having people who might have an ounce of experience in helping our economies thrive in the future. I don't think many of the people who vote for me in Basingstoke, or choose not to vote for me in Basingstoke, really care how entertaining I am. I guess they hope I really just care, that I feel passionately about our country. Certainly I do, and I think every single MP does, otherwise they would do something else. It is not an easy job to do, it is not particularly a job you always get a lot of thanks for, so you really have to have a drive from inside about wanting to improve your community.

You spent – was it 20 years? – in advertising and marketing and public relations, and you were in a very senior position in all those jobs. What made you decide to give up the rewards of that kind of profession to become an MP?

My husband asks me that a lot. Because I loved what I did before, it was a wonderful job and I sometimes wondered why I even got paid it was such a fantastic thing to do, absolutely wonderful thing to do. I worked with brilliant people in a very creative environment. But I suppose when you start to have children you start to think about what you want to do with the rest of your life. You start to think about how you can make sure that you have given something back. I think that is really what motivates most MPs. It is to take that experience that you have gained. I simply didn't think at the time, very arrogantly, that there were enough people like me in Parliament, who'd done 20 years in business at that point, who'd had two, almost three, children and had come out the other end and was able to give something back to the community. So I really felt very strongly that I needed to be there to give a voice to people like me, working mums who want to make the world a little bit easier for the next generation, particularly working mums.

You say you had young children; the hours of politicians are not exactly social. How did you balance that family/work time split?

The children had to get really interested in culture, media and sport! On Sunday my son is coming to Remembrance Sunday with me, because I have to host the Queen at the Foreign Office and then the Cenotaph. So rather than not seeing him for half a day he is coming with me. I don't think anybody's ever done it before, but nobody's said no yet, so he's coming with me. Putting joking aside, you do have to involve your family in what you are doing. I famously once took my daughter to a flower festival at a wonderful church in Basingstoke. Unfortunately my daughter has dreadful hayfever and it wasn't a great success. But usually it is a great success. I think it is about involving them in the life of the House and in your life as a minister. It is not easy, but I think they are a bit proud as well.

You say your husband keeps asking you that question too. How does he feel about your new career?

He's forming a Denis Thatcher Club. He was talking to a gentleman in a similar position to him last night who's married to a Baroness in the House of Lords. They have decided there is definitely a growing market for a club for men in their position.

You became an MP at a very interesting moment, politically, and you became shadow spokeswoman quite quickly. Did you expect at that stage that you would end up in a coalition government rather than a Conservative one?

No. I certainly didn't expect to be in the Cabinet either. My motivations for becoming an MP are that I love community politics, I love trying to make things a bit better on the ground in Basingstoke, I love nothing better than going wading in the River Loddon and counting fish, and things like that, and trying to make the River Loddon in Basingstoke a healthier place. Certainly when David appointed me as a shadow minister I was speechless, which for anybody who knows me is quite unusual. And then when he asked me to be a minister when we were forming the government, again it was not something I was particularly expecting. And suddenly when he promoted me to the Cabinet, although I was delighted to do it, it was not my original intention. I always felt we would have a majority government, and certainly that is what I shall be working hard to achieve next time.

A lot of the pundits are predicting it will be another coalition govern-ment, whichever way it goes at the next election. Do you believe that?

The website www.politicalbetting.com is always the best place to go to for looking for these sorts of data, and I think probably it's still early days for how the election might turn out. I think the way people will decide what they want next is how confident they feel about the future of our country, whether they feel that there has been enough done to put it back on to a track that is in the right direction for the future. They would want to have, I guess, a government that could continue to give them the confidence that we are going to have success in the future. I am not sure that we really understand how people have reacted to a coalition government. Sometimes my postbag would suggest that people don't like the fact that there is uncertainty about what it is that a coalition might be doing in the future. They quite like the idea of the having the mandate of a manifesto.

Harold Macmillan famously said that the biggest problem being Prime Minister was 'events, dear boy, events'. Do you think the events, or the material that has come out about the leaks from the spy agencies, is going to affect a political judgement?

I think it was interesting; I got to see some of the reports from the Home Affairs Committee yesterday, with some of the individuals concerned in front of that committee and saying very starkly that the information that had got into the public domain had already created significant concerns around security. So this balance between freedom of speech and security is a very real one, and it is not something that will go away. Again I think as residents and citizens of this country we do not want to see our security put in jeopardy. Whether it is in publications or individuals, responsibility has got to be taken on the sort of information that is put into the public domain. The clear evidence is that terrorists are using the information that is being put out there to modify how they communicate with each other in a way that will make it more difficult for our secret services in the future.

Is it too late now to put the genie back in the bottle? Now that it is all out like that?

I guess that has got to be the case, hasn't it? The information is out in the general domain. Of all things, for sure, the threat that we have in this country in terms of terrorism is something that is real, and something we all have to take extremely seriously. I think we owe it to our secret services to provide as much support as we can for the work that they do, and, as was reported yesterday, there have been a number of significant terrorist attacks thwarted as a result of their excellent and hard work. I have to say my money would always be on supporting them first and foremost.

The argument is that it is an interference with democratic freedoms, that there should be more transparency. You don't go along with that?

I very much go along with freedom of speech. I very much think that transparency in government is vital in this day and age where we can all go home and Google probably what I have just said. Somebody can be recording this now and we can be streamed live; there is no such thing as a private conversation. That is as it should be in the vast majority of cases. But when it comes to the security of our families, the security of our country, none of us can forget the horrors of 9/11 or the July bombings in this country, and all of us would want to support our secret services and the work that they do. But I absolutely agree with you there is a tension here between that and freedom of speech. It's a tension we have lived with for generations.

There is a lot of talk about sending immigrants home because a lot of them, particularly Somalis, have been caught doing jihadist things. Do you think that could whip up the wrong sort of feelings?

As an island nation we have always been used to having all sorts of people visit our shores. Again, going back to my British Museum visit last night, they were reminding me they were about to put on the most enormous Viking exhibition – if you want to think of people who have come to our shores and left their mark. So I think as a nation we are very used to having people visit our shores. I think what people want to know is that the people who visit our shores – perhaps the Vikings weren't a great example – are coming to add to our common good. So many people do, so many people come to our shores and do add to our common good. We have shortage professions where we don't have enough people to be able to do what we need to have done as a nation. We thrive on individuals coming in, whether it is to go into the medical profession or the engineering profession, areas where we might find it difficult to fill all the jobs without encouraging people to come from abroad. But we all want to know that those people are here for the right reasons. For too many years we saw individuals coming to our shores and managing to get in illegally and stay illegally, and I'm not sure those are the sorts of people who are going to be adding the sort of value that we want. We are a proud nation who have got a proud tradition of accepting and embracing asylum seekers. For centuries we have done that, but what we don't want to do is encourage people who are coming here illegally, potentially with motives which are not ones we would want to support, particularly terrorism.

Some of that feeling about immigration applies to a lot of the new Eastern European nations who joined Europe, and the feeling that they are taking jobs away from British people. Some of that seems to have generated a feeling that there should be a referendum. Do you think that is something that concerns you?

Well today was a very unusual day in the House of Commons; we had Friday sitting, which was attended by hundreds of members of Parliament because we were discussing just this issue. Whether or not there needs to be a further renegotiation of the European Treaty, and whether or not there is a better way forward in terms of our relationship with the rest of the European community. The overwhelming feeling in my party is that, yes, we do think that now is the time to look hard at what the European community is giving to Britain and what we are receiving in return. There is a growing anxiety that there is an imbalance here, and it is not only in terms of individuals coming to our shores, it is also about the cost and the bureaucracy, and the overwhelming feeling that Britain is being sucked into a political union, which is what people reject. That is not what we voted for back in the 1970s; what we voted for was a common market, something I absolutely support, and when I go and visit businesses in any part of the country, but particularly round here, that is really important and I don't think we can underline that enough. We were hearing that from some of the car manufacturers this morning; the common market is vital, but what I think as citizens we feel concerned about is that we never signed up for political union. We never signed up for the Euro; thank goodness the one good thing Gordon Brown did was not get us into the Euro. We didn't sign up for political union either, so I do think the time is right to renegotiate, the time is right to ask the people whether that renegotiation works for them. Today's debate was all about that.

Would the referendum, therefore, be before or after the election?

Well, it has to be after a period of renegotiation. I think that, particularly in the context of a coalition, is going to be best achieved when you have got a single party in charge. I think there is no hiding the fact that there are very, very distinct differences between the Conservative Party and Liberal Democrat Party on the issue of the future of Europe, and I think it would be very difficult as a result to do that referendum before the general election.

One of the other things you are interested in is the heritage, and your son used to sing in the Cathedral here. Part of these dialogues are to draw attention to the Cathedral Appeal. How important do you think the Cathedral is or should be to the country?

I think Winchester Cathedral is one of the big five cathedrals in the country; it is a thousand years of history, isn't it? It is astonishing. I can never go into the building and fail to be moved. Not only has it been a place that I have enjoyed Christmas carol services with my son singing, but also with my daughter's school, and my little one's end-of-term services are wonderful there. It is a magical place. But it is a huge place and it is a place that is, I would imagine, daunting to look after, because of its fragility, and I was delighted to see that the Heritage Lottery funding has been agreed in the summer. I know £10 million will hardly go anywhere, but will hopefully go somewhere towards mending the hole in the roof, literally. I really take my hat off to those who are running the Cathedral, for the way that they keep it in such great fashion. But whether it is Winchester, or any of the other churches and cathedrals around the country, they make up such an enormous part of our heritage and our historical buildings. We have to take a really hard look at the funding streams available. In fact my minister Ed Vaizey met with deans recently to talk about funding streams. We have got the Church, and the £40 million, which is to look after some of the upkeep. We have got the Heritage Lottery fund as well, which people can apply for, but we do need to look carefully at whether we have got sufficient in place to be able to support this amazing group of buildings in the future.

We are concentrating on the relations between Church and State in these dialogues. You have said that canon law and statute law are very different. What do you mean by that?

When I got into the Equal Marriage Bill I didn't become an expert in canon law, I just became an expert in knowing how little I know about canon law. It is the extraordinary relationship in this country between the Church and the State, particularly when it comes to marriage, because of course there is a legal duty on churches to marry people in their parish in England and Wales. Then you have canon law, which cannot conflict with civil law. We have to first acknowledge that canon law is very distinct and wholly British; I am not sure whether there are many other countries that have quite the set-up that we do. But canon law is something that, while it comes to Parliament, is very much controlled by the Church. The fact that it comes to Parliament is a formality, so when I say it is distinct, it is distinct, and it is not the will of Parliament to become involved in the setting of canon law.

There are people who argue for more separation. Only this week someone was saying the judiciary should not be compelled to go to cathedrals or churches, and if there is a case before them involving religion they should be standing back from that. Do you believe that?

I believe that we have got a very idiosyncratic way of dealing with things in this country, and we have no written constitution. I was recently over in the States, and I was rather taken by how certain they are about things, and rather jealous, I suppose, of a way that they can be so certain of things, but they can because they have a constitution. They can be very certain about freedom of speech and the overriding nature of that, with its drawback sometimes, particularly when you look at some of the things I am responsible for in the Internet. Freedom of speech on the Internet is important, but there are limits. In the States they find it much more difficult to deal with those limits than we do here, where we don't have that constitution which provides such a rigid framework. In not having the rigid framework I think you do end up with things being done in a certain way, and one has to accept that. I believe that being able to swear an oath on the Bible in court is as it should be, but equally respect people who don't do that as well. But there is inevitably a coming together of the judiciary, of the Church, of Parliament, of the Queen, in a way which is perhaps less formulated and formalized than it is in other countries.

Questions from the audience

Could I focus on the equality side of your job, with which John started this discussion? You were saying that it was important for you in the Equal Marriage Bill to allow the Churches, or rather particularly the Church of England, but perhaps the other Churches as well, to have their own views respected within the framework that you set up. I know from listening to your talk on television the other day about the Leveson Inquiry, how your soft approach to things can in fact change the way things work. You'll remember at the end of that debate the press who were present were really very impressed with what you'd said and I think changed their mind about how they were going to behave. Don't you think so?

I think so. Anyway, I wanted to focus on the equality, and perhaps on freedom as a broader expression of equality, and think about the position of children – you have three of your own, I understand – and come back again to the question of Church and State and particularly the Roman Catholic Church and the State. You may guess that I am going to talk about the 2007 Act, or regulations which I think were established by the previous administration, to do with sexual orientation and the particular case of adoption societies, the Catholic Adoption Society in particular, which had its own view about same-sex couples. If you are going to be able to accept that different Churches have different views about same-sex marriage, I wonder if you couldn't accept that some religious organizations have various views about the appropriateness of allowing adoption by same-sex couples? Because there are plenty of organizations that are very happy to welcome same-sex couples; there is just at least one, perhaps more, who aren't. If you talk about equality, not just equality as a word but equality of opportunity, there is equality of opportunity, for same-sex couples to adopt, there is no difficulty about that, but for some reason or other the previous administration was very concerned to establish principles very clearly and that this ...

(John Miller) Can you phrase your question, Sir? Please, if you would.

Yes, yes. This society had to close and in fact a lot of them have closed now, which denies the opportunity of adoption to a large number of children who are currently being cared for rather badly, I would suggest, in care homes. So could you tell us please what is your opinion, or the opinion of the coalition government, on that state of affairs?

You are absolutely right to say too many children can face long periods in care without finding a loving family to live in. I think in Hampshire we have got a council which does everything it can to support children in care, but like every other council in the country faces enormous challenges to get children who are in care living in the same sort of loving environment that they would live in at home. I have been to a number of other countries looking at the way that different countries deal with children in care, and I have to say I was very impressed by the way they deal with it in Denmark. It wasn't the main nub of your question, but I do think we should look around to see how we can deal with this issue much better. What really you are getting at is the provision of services that are funded by the State and how that deals with the Equality Act, as much as anything else, in terms of the way that we treat people equally. When it comes to adoption agencies I think this was one of the most difficult things, because particularly Catholic adoption agencies were helping some of the children who were finding it the most difficult to get placements with loving families. I think it was a very difficult decision indeed to say you have to; clearly if you are receiving public money, you have to treat the people who are approaching you equally, and the fact that they are in a same-sex relationship is not something you can discriminate on. I'm afraid that is the law, and if you are in receipt of public money in that way you cannot discriminate in the provision of those services. It is the same situation with regard to provision of other services in other areas as well. There are some other notable examples where people provide services and equally have to look at that law of equality to make sure they are not providing their services in a way which discriminates against people. So I understand the point you are making. I feel passionately about children living in loving families, but organizations have to be within the law when they are receiving public funds.

I work for a large financial organization – investment bank, I'm afraid – in the City of London, and women are woefully under-represented at a senior level. I have just formed a small working group to address the problem, and I am struggling with ideas of what to do. I would love to hear some tips from you of how to encourage the promotion of women to senior positions.

This is a really easy question. I had a bit of a seminar on it yesterday, supported by the Chancellor. I say it is a really easy question because now, due to the wonders of the world, more than 60 per cent of people who come out of universities in our great country are women. In fact more than half of the people who have postgraduate degrees in our country are women. This hasn't only just happened; this happened about 20 years ago. So around the late 1990s we saw the numbers of women and men not just equal numbers coming out of universities, but now more women are coming out of universities with good degrees than men. So to say there is a problem with the supply of women, there simply isn't; we have got fabulous women who are available, who are there. In fact, when you start to look at the pay that women receive when they go into work in their twenties and indeed into their thirties, they are not really seeing a problem with what we call in parliament-land the gender pay gap. Women are earning a bit more than men in their twenties. But then it all seems to go very, very sadly wrong. About the time women hit 40, and as they move forward into that later part of their career, not only are they not getting the promotions that you'd want, we are not seeing them hit the boardroom table, we are not seeing them on executive boards, and we are seeing them suffer a 15 per cent gender pay gap, so being paid less than the people who they are working alongside. So I think this is really easy: organizations are getting great women in, they are just not keeping them. I would say they are not keeping them for reasons of corporate culture. I can sit here and say we can pass lots of laws and legislation; indeed we did around pay – 40 years ago we passed the Equal Pay Act, and perhaps that is testament enough to say that law is not enough. You can pass a law, but if you don't change people's attitudes towards women, and the contribution they have in the workplace, then we will never, ever get to a situation where women are playing their rightful role at all levels of an organization.

I will be the first person to say that women have a vital role to play in bringing children up. But then so do men. There is some great research in Germany which shows that if men are really involved in the early years of a child's life, that child has a much better life ahead of them. So we have put in place a number of structural changes to try and modernize the workplace, around replacing maternity leave with parental leave, so that both parents can be involved in those early years, making flexible working the norm. I'm sure there are many people in this room today who work flexibly to fit around obligations they have got. They are producing as much if not more than those around them because they are motivated to keep those jobs. Also, making sure we have the right childcare, so that is why we have put in place not only more early-years childcare but also a tax break for childcare too to the tune of around £1,200. So government's done its bit. I think business now really needs to step up to the fact that there is a need for a culture change. I give you three very easy things to do. One is have a plan. Only 18 per cent of FTSE 250 firms actually have a plan as to how they are going to get more women at every level of their organizations. Second, I have just published my pay information, broken down by gender, for my department, 300–400 people, and I have shown that my department has got quite a lot of women in it, and we haven't got a gender pay gap. Do you know what? I have published that information and there will be huge pressure to make sure that there never is one in the future. So publish the information, be transparent. Third, identify the women who can be around the boardroom table in the future. Lord Davis did a fantastic report a year or so ago; he identified the fact that we want to get 25 per cent of our non-executive directors in this country in FTSE 250 firms to be women. Since he made that announcement we have doubled the number of women in FTSE 250 boardrooms. But there is still a lot more to do. So it's throwing a focus on it, having a plan, publishing the information, being transparent, and showing that the people at the top really care.

On the subject of the churches and heritage, the parish churches in this country bear a huge burden in keeping so many listed buildings up together to hand on to the next generation. The works to them cost a huge amount. Is there any possibility that VAT on works to churches can be zero-rated, please?

There are a number of organizations whom I meet with regularly on these sorts of issues, and as I said earlier the deans of the cathedrals got together with one of my ministers, Ed Vaizey, recently to talk about funding and funding streams. The Churches Conservation Trust does a fantastic job of work and are mostly funded through my department – just over £2 million a year, and we have also got a specific funding to try and help the conservation of churches as well as the Heritage Lottery fund. So trying to make money available, our heart is there, whether it is through particular tax breaks or whether it is through direct funding. Ultimately what you want to know is that there are ways of getting hold of the cash that is needed to keep this treasure trove of buildings in one piece. I think we have got a reasonable set of funding streams there. I am sure there are more things we can think about for the future, and certainly there is a very clear appetite for me always to be examining ways that we can support, particularly, historic churches if we are able to.

I just wondered, with your enthusiasm with same-sex marriage rights, might you have a concern as to how the children of the same-sex arrangements might feel when they are 10 years old, 15 years old, 18 years old? They won't have had the same upbringing or environment that you have with your family. There is no child to ask at this point; we are stuck with what we've got, whether it is with Elton John or whoever. It's an odd arrangement maybe, would seem odd, by these children when they become adults.

I think children thrive on love, don't they? They thrive on love and stability. I have friends who do not have spouses, maybe they've been widowed in tragic circumstances, but their children thrive. They thrive on love and they thrive on stability, and I think those are the things that every child thrives on. Going back to the earlier question about children living in a care home, if my children were ever in a position of not having parents around, my goodness I would love them to be in a loving family, and whether that was a couple of the same sex or a couple of different sex, then I would much prefer them to be in a loving environment, and I think that is what children thrive on.

What are you and your department doing in terms of making the arts more accessible for people with disabilities? And providing information in accessible formats and audio introduction for the opera houses, in cinemas, that sort of thing?

It is an absolutely critical issue and it is not just in the arts, it is in sports and is throughout everything we do in my department. I was minister for disabled people for two and a half years and you don't do that job without remembering for the rest of your life what you are doing has to be accessible to everybody. So the Arts Council have a whole host of programmes to support arts organizations in helping make what they do accessible to everybody. Whether it is people who are visually impaired, or people with any sort of disability at all, it is critical that our arts organizations are both physically accessible and also accessible to people when they get there too. Interpretations that are done in different formats are vital. It is also important for disabled people to be able to get access to our sporting facilities and I think this is one of the things that people have just realized – that disabled people really want to keep fit as well. The Paralympics taught us as a nation a huge amount. That is why Sport England are investing multi-million pounds in helping local football clubs, local sports clubs, to become more accessible, to be able to allow people who may have different incapacities to be able to come in to use the facilities, but also have training so that people can understand how they can help disabled people get more out of sports. This is one of the enormous legacies of the Olympics.

You have come into politics after a career in business. Do you think our particular parliamentary democracy, our style of parliamentary democracy, is made by people who make politics their actual career? We have a lot of people who come in very young to politics.

I think that Parliament is really strong when it is diverse. I was only 41 when I was elected, so I wasn't that old; I feel very old now, though when you look at the age of some of the politicians ... I think Parliament is served well by having a diverse range of people, whether it is people like me who have been in business before, who've got kids, whether it is people who are in their twenties when they come into Parliament. I don't think I would have had the confidence to go into Parliament in my twenties. These people are incredible individuals, somebody like Chloe Smith, who came into Parliament in her late twenties and makes a fantastic contribution. And, importantly, they can show to young people that politics and Parliament are relevant to them. I don't think we should have any organization which is homogeneous, going back to the gentleman sitting next to you on how do you get more women into business. Parliament needs to have a diverse cross-section of people who represent our society, and I think then people will feel it is something which really does have a voice which reflects what they want Parliament and government to do.

A question on your role of minister for women and equality. Do you get much demand from women in the Islamic community, seeking perhaps the same level of equality with the menfolk that exists in the Christian and other denominational centres?

Interestingly, in our government, the way we deal with issues is that we don't put all the equality issues into my department. When I talk about women and equality I deal with women's issues and the Equality and Human Rights Commission. Other equality issues are in other departments. So disability issues are in the Department of Work and Pensions, and racial equality issues are in the Department for Communities. I think that is a good approach because every department has to look on equality as something which is part of their day job. But to your point, and I do have quite a strong feeling on this, I do think it is important that as a nation we talk, whether to men or women about the role of people in our society, and I think women have got an important role to play. Whatever race or creed you are, if you are in Britain as a British woman from whatever background you come from, you have an important role to play. I think we should allow women to wear whatever they like. I know that wasn't part of your question, but it might have been. I sometimes find it quite scary when I see people wearing very short skirts, particularly if it is my daughter, but I respect their right to do that. It is for women to decide how they dress, but what I want every woman in this country to understand is that they have equal rights to men and they have a government that will ensure that the law of the land respects that equality.

Last word from the Dean.

The Dean

Thank you very much to Maria Miller for finding time to be with us tonight. When I wrote to you I knew as a cabinet minister there were enormous pressures on your time, we are really grateful that you have been able to be with us. There couldn't be a better base to be a Minister of Culture than to be chorister parent at Winchester Cathedral, that gives you a definite hidden advantage. I was interested you said you shouldn't do politics through polling. We all need to relax a bit and do our job well and not keep wondering how people are assessing us. I also liked your 'culture can give a turbo-boost to society'. One of the things I would hope about Winchester Cathedral is it's there for its intrinsic value, as a place of faith. It is also quite an economic generator in the community. and one shouldn't forget those two things. Culture deserves support because it is a significant economic force.

You have beautifully taken us in a way to the moral qualities of equality – how all of us are trying, and the Church is a part of that I hope. It is very good to have a politician telling us that we are working for respect for one another; having the integrity to do our own thing, but always to do it with respect for other people and with openness and honesty and transparency. For that message tonight, thank you also very much indeed.

4

Out of Africa

BISHOP OF WINCHESTER TIM DAKIN

It is a very great pleasure to welcome Bishop Tim Dakin. I would like to begin where you began, which was where you were born in East Africa, to missionary parents, and you were there through kindergarten and primary school before you came back here for secondary education. How formative an experience was that for you?

I think it was hugely formative for so many things that I have valued and learnt to appreciate. The experience of growing up in Africa gave me not only a sense of that whole African feeling for life, but also gave me a glimpse into what it might mean for those who have almost nothing to somehow survive. I was born and spent my first few years in a part of East Africa that was going through a major transition period. It was the period when colonialism was coming to an end and nations were being born. Once we had moved up from Tanzania to Nairobi we lived in a part of Nairobi where you had to live, or to have a pass if you were a white person, to travel through. If you lived in that part of Nairobi you had to have some sort of evidence as to the permission for staying there on a permanent basis. So living in that part of Nairobi was an amazing experience for a young child, because it gave me a sense of the vulnerability of life. This was during the Mau Mau, you see. I will never forget that sense of a background threat that there was at all times, for all of us who were living there. That sense that there was something to be frightened of that couldn't quite be named. I still have in my mind's eye the image of people coming to our front gate and me being not quite sure as to whether I was safe or not. But, on the other hand, I grew up with Africans not Europeans, and I spoke Swahili with my Ayah, not English. I grew up with people who I didn't know were Africans and I was a European; I just grew up with people. In that sense I was formed in a way that I suspect I didn't really understand, not as a single-culture person but as a multiculture person. So Africa has been extraordinary in all sorts of ways. As you can imagine, that led on to that longing you have when you've been born elsewhere and you are living in a place that isn't quite home.

So when you came to England, was that a culture shock?

The first time, I think I was a little too early in my growing up to realize, but I must say seeing snow for the first time was more than a culture shock. When we came back we lived with my grandparents for a short while. Our return was into the winter of 1962–63. I can remember being cold from when I first got off the plane. I still have images of my grandfather climbing up a ladder in order to pour hot water down a drainpipe that had frozen over to try and get the taps running again from the bathroom. That is how cold it was. So it wasn't so much a culture shock as a climate shock.

At what point did you decide to study theology?

My grandfather was ordained and my father is ordained, so in one sense I was attracted to something that was already part of the culture that I belonged to. But I was consciously aware of a growing interest in theology from about the age of 15. I did have an abortive attempt to study philosophy and Greek studies as an alternative, but I found my interest in theology to be so great that after two years I switched, and focused primarily on theology, with philosophy as well. I think once you have found the passion that makes you go, you want to keep going back to it and you want to get deeper into it, so I still study and I read nearly every day.

I was interested that once you were ordained the first thing you did was to go back to Africa.

Yes.

How did that happen?

You know how some things are planned and some things just happen? Well this is one of those things that sort of happened. It's a very strange story. By then I'd been selected for training to the ordained ministry; I had done a lot of theology by then, so my training was going to be very short. Given that my research was in the area of practical theology, I had done an awful lot of preparation that was really much more like ministerial training. So part of that research included helping a college in Africa to prepare a new course for training people who were going to be ordained, particularly those who were going to have a commitment to evangelistic and mission ministry. So I found myself completing my preparation for the ministry by becoming responsible for those who were being trained for the ministry. Like many people who get involved in higher education in some of our traditional colleges, you can be ordained into some of these academic posts. So I was ordained into a combination of being curate in Nairobi Cathedral, where I had worshipped as a teenager, and gone to school as a boy, and being principal of a theological college that was training people for mission ministry. I also began a business school in order to make some money to keep the thing going. So not a route that I would recommend most people to go, but one that fortunately was supported by my bishop, Bishop Richard Harries, and had the backing of my supervisor who happened to be Rowan Williams at the time, so that was quite useful really.

You had an interesting time at Carlile College in Nairobi. You wrote at the time about 'safari theology' having more of a loose-leaf approach. What did you mean by that?

Well, one of the interesting things I suspect that we believe about the Church in East Africa, or other parts of Africa, is that it is very conservative. Actually, the African approach to Scripture is not quite as conservative as people imagine. Because of the emphasis on life and what gives life, the Scriptures are very often interpreted in ways that are much more flexible and probably more Hebrew-like than by those of us in the West who want logic and clear arguments and outcomes that we are absolutely certain of. So the African approach to the interpretation of Scripture is much more in terms of 'What kind of outcome and impact does it have on us as a community? How does it bring life to us? How does it bring salvation that we recognize to be life-giving and life-transforming?', rather than 'What is the doctrine that we can draw up out of these texts and prove to be true because it coheres with a whole lot of other things that we believe?' So the loose-leaf approach I was referring to was the ongoing interpretation of Scripture that brings life to the community. That's a story that gets written in people's lives, rather than in books. It's much more generative than many people imagine. It is one I thoroughly enjoy being part of when I can.

You stayed there for seven years and then you applied for – or were you asked to apply for? – the job as General Secretary for the Church Missionary Society.

Yes, I was given hints that it might be an idea that I should think about.

Might you have stayed in Africa if that hadn't come up?

Yes; in fact as a family we thought we were there for the rest of our life. We bought a house there. I thought I was going to be Principal of Carlile College until I retired. I was committed to developing tertiary-level education in East Africa. It is one of the things that the mission societies didn't complete. They started primary schools and secondary schools, but they didn't complete the process, which the Catholics did, of setting up tertiary-education institutions. So I thought I was there for life, turning Carlile College into a university college. To do that in the East Africa context requires quite a lot of development work to be done, so we bought 250 acres. We began building; we worked out how to farm all that land; we plotted and planned in terms of how the campus would develop, in terms of the major highways. Sally and I had bought a house halfway between the Nairobi campus and the new campus, so that I could travel in-between. This was on a convenient road that was due to become the Cairo to Cape Town highway. We thought this was it: we worked out where the schooling could happen. And then one of those things that happen – does happen to you if you are listening and open to God: you suddenly get a 'Well why not go this way instead?' I went along to a conference and somebody preached a sermon, and I realized that it was directly for me. It was all about Elijah and Elisha and handing over the responsibility to somebody else. So I was shocked and thought, 'God, is this really right?' I put in my application; I did the thing that you should never do. I went to the airport on the very last day when I knew I could get someone to carry the post and take it to England and put it in a letterbox here. If asked, 'Has anybody given you anything to carry?' they would have to say, 'No.' Of course I had the most precious thing, which was my application form, and I kind of knew that as soon as I had sent off the form, I would get the job. It was one of those feelings, and I did. The only two times I could travel over for interviews were the two days I had free in my diary.

You said the purpose of the Anglican community is missionary. Was that something you believed before you went to the new job, or has that always been your view?

Yes, always. Again I think one of the odd things about the Church of England's experience of Anglicanism is that it is different from most other people's experience of what it means to be an Anglican. We took quite a while to get into 'mission mode'; we really got stuck. Once Henry VIII had got rid of all the religious communities and religious societies, there wasn't much left to generate new life in the Church. Movements were needed. And so one of the movements that had a big impact on the Church of England was the Evangelical movement generated by the Methodists and company. They produced mission societies, that along with others of the High Church tradition, began to take the gospel and the idea of the nature of the Anglican Church around the world. So that all the churches planted around the world, including those also planted from America, have this missionary character to them. They just know themselves to have that foundation. We do too; in fact, this diocese has got a missionary foundation, where St Birinus brought the gospel. We were founded by a Benedictine mission, but we have forgotten that some-how. So yes, most Anglicans know that they are missionaries elsewhere in the world. One of the great things to discover when you are part of that wider communion, and you are out and about, is how energizing it is to be among Anglicans who have got that vision. Because they are engaged with their society; they believe in their church, and the gospel they have got is alive. So it is very encouraging to get out and about, and to realize that is the nature of us as Anglicans. We are missionaries.

In the 12 years you were at the CMS you visited a lot of countries with a community there. You must have found the relation between those Churches and the State in those countries to have varied quite a bit. Did you draw any conclusions from that?

Yes. Obviously one of the things that influenced the development of the Anglican missionary movement was colonialism. There was an attempt by many of the mission societies to plant the Church in places where colonialism hadn't reached. So you could tell the difference between churches planted in a colonial context and churches planted in a non-colonial context. Those differences become fairly obvious in the way that the Church sees itself involved in public life. But of course the nature of English colonialism is not straightforward. It was much more of a prag-matic approach than a planned approach. So I am afraid it is not possible to read off English colonial influence, therefore this must be the Church/State relationship pattern. Because we did it in different ways and for all sorts of different reasons around the world. Sometimes it was economic, sometimes it was for defence reasons, sometimes it was an accident – because no one else was there and we wandered in. But when the Church deliberately got involved, when the Church found itself committed, because other English people had gone and made their home there, then yes, you did find yourself pretty early on as a church in getting engaged with political life and the ongoing debate about the relationship between Church and State, which is part of the Christian identity.

You went to Asia and the Americas, but it seems to me from reading some of the things you have written that Africa was always closer to your heart than anywhere else.

It is quite hard when you have been born somewhere to get it out of your system. I am African by background and African by foreground. When that is part of your life it is not so much a choice. It is just who you are. So given that I have got Africa under my belt, as it were, I had a splendid time going around other parts of the world. To go to South America in the latter part of my time at CMS was fantastic. The size of South America is just vast. I mean, Africa's huge; you can put South America, India, North America, Australia, New Zealand and Europe into Africa and there is still room. That is how big Africa is. So Africa's not a continent, it is continents. So to go to some of the other places was just wonderful. I went to northern Argentina and Brazil, and Asia is just … well, you can tell I am still feeding off that.

You clearly had a wonderful time when you were at CMS. So, again, you might have stayed there had this particular current offer not come up. Was that a surprise?

I might disagree with you there. I think I'd done my bit in CMS. I think there is a golden period between seven and twelve years when you know you are making a major contribution – because you have done all the donkey work. You have cleared out all the pre-changes that need to be done. You've got the thing honed a bit, and you are ready now to make some deeper changes or to make some broader contributions. I think I knew I had come to the end of my energy and my real contribution to CMS towards the end of my eleventh year. We had begun to make some major changes that I thought were pretty significant, because mission has changed in the postcolonial context. People not only don't like their country being colonized, people don't like their minds being colonized. The postcolonial, the Empire-strikes-back, response to the impact of colonialism, was something that mission work had begun to realize. So we planted CMS in former mission fields, and they were beginning to ask, 'Can we help you to do mission in Europe?' That is when I knew some of the work that I'd done had been completed. That is when I knew I ought to be offering myself to wider work within the Church, and so when I was asked to fill in the forms, and the mysterious nature of the way that people get selected to be bishops had got a grip of me, I found myself, yes, in this process that led to this appointment.

The Prime Minister has to sign it off, doesn't he?

Well, during my time – by the way, I was on the selection committee that used to appoint bishops, which is the Crown Nomination Commission, so I knew a little bit of how it worked on the inside – during my time, and during the period that Gordon Brown took over from Tony Blair, Gordon Brown made it very clear that he wanted less involvement, and he saw it more of a church responsibility than a prime minister's responsibility. So I think I was clear that by the time I got into the process I was going to be somebody who was going to be looked at under the new process. So the Prime Minister's involvement was pretty minimal in my appointment. It was more a question of whether those who were representing the wider Church were comfortable with who I might be and what I might do.

You said at the time that the important thing the Church needed to do was to get back a sense of mission, which is not surprising with what you have just said. How did you see that happening?

Well, last week there was a gathering of most of the diocesan bishops of England and Wales, and all the Catholic bishops of England and Wales. We met together for two days. The focus of our concerns was the re-evangelization of not just Europe but the world. So the Catholic Church is very clear that the re-evangelization agenda is not just something for us in Europe, who are experiencing some challenges, but something that is now global. There is a global challenge to the Church to communicate the gospel in a new way that connects with people in a day-to-day understandable manner. So what was great was that we had earlier on in the week, those of us who were in the Church of England and had been part of the General Synod, a debate about intentional evangelism for the Church of England in future years to come. So the combination of our interests in intentional evangelism and the Catholic commitment to re-evangelization meant that we had some very fruitful discussions. The gathering of the bishops of these two ancient Churches made a common commitment to make this a top priority. We had a sense that God was working among us in a way that really brought fellowship and depth and a sense that we were going to go forward in a new way together. This is not something about my personal passion, or about a slightly non-English way of looking at Anglicanism: we are talking here about two global communions recognizing that something needs to change, and something needs to move on. So I am looking forward to seeing what our two communions will be doing together, particularly with Pope Francis leading the Catholic Church – I think we are up for some very interesting times.

Women cardinals?

Ooh. Do you know you should never comment about other people's Churches?

Well, let's come to your Church. How about women bishops?

Wonderful.

That's a quick, sure answer?

Yes. It looks like it might perhaps happen. We only had eight votes against last week. To see some of those who had previously said, 'Look, I really don't think this is going to be right for the Church', or, 'This is going to question my place in the Church', standing up and saying, 'I don't agree with this, but given the new place that we have got to, where we have stated publicly that we want everybody to flourish, even if we disagree with one another about some of these things, I am prepared to compromise and go with where we seem to be moving forward to the point of making women bishops.' I thought that was great, and it has been embarrassing, hasn't it? In the last few years, it has been embarrassing; we do everything in public as Anglicans, all the dirty linen comes out, but it is great to see just how we have been able to work through some of our disagreements, to get to this new point. I think it has been good for the country to see that we have managed to come to a new place. Now I am presuming we are going to carry on going forward. Next, I am afraid we have got quite a few stages to go, so there will be a debate in all the diocesan synods as to whether we now agree with this development. It has got to come back to the dioceses, because it is such a significant change; it is a change in doctrine, which means that all the dioceses need to be involved; it's a change in doctrine, so all the bishops have to agree to it, before it can be put to the General Synod. We have a few stages yet to go, but I sense that we are in a new place, and we have a new way of doing things. Whereas before we wanted to say, 'Let's find a new way of electing the laity, who didn't vote the right way', well, the same laity elected to do the right thing this time, so we have now decided not to change the way that we were going to elect the laity, so they must have been the right people after all.

And then suddenly in today's paper there is a story about the blessing of same-sex unions. What's your view on that?

Gosh – who'd be the Archbishop of Canterbury? I think it will be very good to get the women bishops debate a bit further along the road before we take that one on. We can't avoid it. I think we will have to look at that in great detail. But it would be good if we learnt how to care for one another, as we have the other debate. We may have learnt how to do that in the disagreements that we have had over women bishops. We have realized that to have such deep discussions with each other about things that we consider to be fundamental means that we can hurt each other a great deal; we can confuse a lot of people in public. Perhaps we have learnt to do things slightly differently. I am hoping that we have. That is not going to make it any easier, and this one is bigger than the last one. So it is not going to be straightforward, and I do think that we are going to face some very difficult choices. I think that someone like me will have to be careful how I lead those for whom I have a responsibility. I am one of the members of the House of Lords who voted against same-sex marriage, so I have been very clear what I believe the Church teaches, and I have been very clear what I believe that means for how the Church should try to guide the government in the making of law. But I recognize the decision that has been made is now something that will be put into law, and I recognize that in the provision of the quadruple lock, as it's called, for the Church of England; we have the opportunity to maintain our understanding of what we believe to be the biblical and orthodox view of marriage. Now, within the Church of England, some people will say, 'Well, we are not as sure as you, Bishop', so my responsibility as a bishop is to both maintain the unity but also guard the faith. How I do that is something I hope you will be praying about for me. Because we are going to have to have the debate thoroughly, properly, carefully and with due consideration for all those for whom this is not a theoretical matter; it is a personal matter, it is something that affects those in their families whom they love deeply, it may even be part of their very way of life, and is therefore a very important matter to them.

It is important for this discussion about Church–State relationships because Maria Miller, who was here last time and made a claim that she has urged the government to support same-sex marriage, also made it plain that they have no intention of imposing that on the Church, and that's when the quadruple lock came up. Who do you think should take this decision? The Church or the State?

In 1668, I think it was, we had the Act of Toleration, which was in the Glorious Revolution when a Protestant monarch was put back on the throne, and James II was removed, and we all wondered how we were possibly going to survive together, with so many of us feeling against one another and some of us having been chucked out of the Church. Because only a few years before, in 1662, in the fourth Act of Uniformity, thousands of clergy were forced to leave the Church of England because they had not been episcopally ordained or because they refused to accept that episcopal ordination was necessary. So within just a few years there was both the determination that we should be an episcopal church, and yet a decision, led by the Protestants, that there should be toleration within our country for those who were not necessarily Anglican. We had a breadth of opinion. Unfortunately it took a couple of centuries before there was the Emancipation Act for Catholics. So it is not as though toleration suddenly burst out upon the English scene, and the Welsh scene and the Scottish scene. It was just that those two came together. What I am saying is that these developments that we have at the moment are part of the way in which the Church and the State have had to come to terms with their different responsibilities. The understanding that we have of what is lawful and what might be thought to be Christian doctrine has not always coincided in the way that some people would imagine or wished or could impose. On the other hand, our understanding of the nature of sovereignty in this country is still one determined by the oath at the coronation and by the presence of the Lords spiritual in the House of Lords. In other words, sovereignty is understood as being under God and that is why the Church must always be present and involved in the State. Nevertheless, the Church must abide by the law of the land except in those parts where it has the liberty not to do so. And it is in that area where you are trying to get me to give my answer.

How importantly do you take your responsibilities of being a member of the House of Lords?

I take them very seriously, so that I haven't been very often. I have a responsibility for higher education in the Church of England, and so what I would like to do is to slowly make a contribution in the area particularly of higher education policy. But to work up a brief in higher education policy, as you can imagine, is quite a tall order for somebody who has got a few other jobs to be getting on with; it is not my day job. It is the part-time voluntary bit that I am meant to be adding in. As you can imagine, the significance of higher education for the governments that have been in place in the past and the ones yet to come only needs to be gauged by the reaction to the imposition of fees and the threat of more fees. No government wants to say too much about higher education at the moment, so any bishop that wants to say anything about higher education needs to be very careful. Let's just say I am building up a portfolio of background knowledge and a little bit of a growing understanding of what the politics are, and who is important. When you realize that higher education comes under BIS, which is 'Business, Innovation and Skills', and the rest of education comes under the Department of Education, you know there is already a split going on in the government between how the policy in one department works and how policy in another one works. Education is stuck in the middle, in the sense that those responsible for the training of those who are going to be educated is in one and practice is in another. So I am learning about how all this works, who all the important people are, how many different sorts of universities, because we have five different sorts of higher education institutions that now call themselves universities in this country – how that all fits together.

Let's just say that I have made my maiden speech, I have been along to a few important debates, I respond when I can to requests to go in and vote and be present when all three bells are rung. There are no whips, by the way, with the Lords spiritual. But I am waiting to get my head round my portfolio before I try and make inroads into what I hope will be a significant area for the Church. I hope everybody realizes that we have 12 Anglican universities, and at any one time there are 75,000 students in those universities. One of them, of course, is Winchester University. There are lots of students that we have an Anglican responsibility for, so my focus is going to be in that particular section, but I hope to learn enough in detail for that to have relevance elsewhere. I have the good fortune to have different sorts of universities in my educational background, so that I have a love for each kind, including the ancient, the more recent and even the Anglican ones.

What is your view about the state of religious education in the schools?

Getting better, possibly.

*But not brilliant. Frank Field was sitting in that chair and was fairly with-
ering about the lack of knowledge of Christianity and the Book.*

Yes. He said a lot of what needed to be said. I think it was very good when
Michael Gove came to Lambeth Palace recently and met with a lot of
bishops and a lot of us who are committed to education – that he said he
might have got something wrong, in the area of not supporting religious
education to be part of the baccalaureate. I think it is deeper than that.
I think that religious education is so important for an understanding of
who you are as an English person, a Scottish person or a Welsh person,
that unless it is part of your education generally, unless you are taught by
people who understand the place of religion within our society, then you
will come out having a smorgasbord of 'Some faiths do this on this day,
and Christians might celebrate that on that day', but no genuine understanding of why people believe passionately about what they do, that
communities are based on traditions and those traditions have contributed
to the development of our society across Europe, shaping our societies and
our values. That really means there is a responsibility on the Minister of
Education to make sure that we understand religion thoroughly, and particularly the Christian religion. I think that is vital, and I say that not just
because my daughter happens to teach religious education to secondary
school pupils, but because I think that if we don't understand our history
we won't know where we are going. Just to add fuel to the fire, I think
the way we are going at the moment in politics is that we are very good
at the processes but we have no idea of the purposes. One of the things
about religious education is that it helps you to understand why you are
here and what is valuable, and why other people who disagree with you
are valuable, and how to live with them. That is what religion helps you
to understand. Social cohesion is created by religious people who respect
other people, even though they believe and think differently. So if we
don't have that at the heart of our society, if we don't have the kind of
toleration that enables us to live together, we won't understand why we
should tolerate each other at all. We won't realize that the purpose of living from our Christian perspective is to worship God and to share God's
love with each other and to do that in a way that reflects the Lord Jesus
Christ. We won't know how that relates to those who may want to do
something similar but to do it from another perspective. All that is vital.
To say that it shouldn't be part of our basic education strikes me as very
short-sighted, it is going to leave a society that is so economically driven it
will end up with people not understanding why they are earning money,
which is where we are getting to, I think.

You have said the Church must be passionate, pioneering and prophetic. What did you mean by those three?

As you can see, I am working up to being prophetic. I think being prophetic means that you have got hope, and we are coming into Advent, Advent Sunday is coming up. Christmas is the response to the hope that we have that the longings and the heartaches that we have can be filled but also cured. To be prophetic is to say that we have hope. We believe the Lord Jesus Christ can make a difference to lives. The Church can offer a pioneering way of being human. We can be passionate personally in our lives, our daily lives, so that people understand that this is something that is not done in church; this is something that you live. It is ordinary, it is what normal people do. It is normal people who have made a difference to this country and created it and made it what it is. I am therefore committed to a prophetic public faith. I believe that that is the nature of our faith. I think that means there is a possibility to go on having hope, because of who Christ is and what we are called to be as Christians in our everyday lives.

So you don't subscribe to George Carey's gloomy view about the next generation?

Well, Archbishop George Carey has always been misunderstood. It is always true that we are one generation away from extinction, isn't it? That's a truism. It is also right that unless we have confidence and belief in our faith, then I am afraid the age of our gathering tonight, which indicates that we are a little the other side of 30 – only just, I know; I am so sorry, for some of you I realize that was just recently – it does mean that we are probably in a little bit of trouble. I am fortunate to live with a teenager and somebody in their twenties, so I get updated on all sorts of things. I know what a selfie is. But I think we need a church that knows what a selfie is. A church that lives in that world isn't frightened of it, and is led by people who are from that generation. So I am passionate about re-evangelization because I think there are lots of young Christians who think that we ought to be making a difference and doing the things that I have been talking about. But we have got to do something to make that possible. I think part of my job in this particular phase of the Diocese of Winchester is to do something about that. I am going to try.

In fact, you said in the twenty-first century the Church has to refound itself. How do you see that happening?

There is a wonderful Catholic priest I have learnt from about the whole vision of refounding; he's an Australian Marist. You couldn't get somebody who is probably further away from my tradition; he lives in Australia; he's a Catholic; he prays through Mary and I tend to pray through Jesus. But we get on splendidly and I just saw him the other day. His vision is that if you know where you have come from, and you understand the vision that founded you, then the best way to understand what you are meant to be doing now is to get hold of that previous vision and update it. Now, we were founded by St Birinus, who had a vision for engaging with Anglo-Saxon society, and helping it get full of the life of Jesus Christ. I think that is what this Catholic priest is trying to tell me; we ought to be doing that. I am into a vision for refounding ourselves on the Benedictine mission that gave us life in the first place, and asking what it means today. So that the refounding is something that gives us life, by rediscovering the vision that brought us into being in the first place. If I have to learn that from a Catholic, Marist, Australian priest then that's good for my humility. Having seen him just recently it was so encouraging, and I have learnt a few more tips, including this one. You know when you are stuck when there is a lot of moaning and a lot of mourning. If we are moaning and mourning in the Church of England, we are just saying we are stuck. It is good if we just admit we are stuck, because once that energy gets going, once we acknowledge that we are stuck, by moaning and mourning, we might just reconnect with the vision that will lead to new life. So I am not for closing down the moaning and mourning. Let's moan and mourn, but let's get the energy going, so that we find the new vision and go forward, and make sure that young people come and cheer us up.

Are you encouraged by the young people's response?

Well, here we go. We don't have a lot of young people in the Church of England today, but do you know which diocese is number two in the numbers of young people that belong? Yes, Winchester. And we haven't got a lot. So I am encouraged that this diocese is beginning to attract young people. Let's get a lot more young people in, and help them to help us. In fact, help us to let go so that they can get on with it, and lead us into the next generation, and the next view of what the Church looks like. The Archbishop is right; it has got to be the next generation that leads us into the new way of being Church. But let's not get too gloomy – they are just there waiting to come in.

And the mission that you talked about – do you see that happening in this country or are you still talking about it in a global sense?

Why not this country?

Questions from the audience

Bishop, thank you for telling us all about where you would like the Church to go. As a parliamentarian, perhaps you could say a little more about where you would like Parliament to lead us.

Gosh. As you know, there is a sensitive relationship between the Upper and the Lower Houses. It is not quite the right thing for the Upper House to guide the Lower House. But the occasional threat does seem to have an impact, and so I think when the Archbishop of Canterbury and a recent former Chancellor decided to put in an amendment that suggested that the Finance Bill might benefit from a tweak or two, there were some changes made. I think leadership does primarily come from the House of Commons, and obviously comes from the government in power, but it is possible for the upper chamber not only to offer some revisions to policy, and obviously to legislation going through, but it is occasionally able to have some debates that it launches itself and make some suggestions for how things might go forward. I suspect it would be interesting to see how higher education is going to be tackled in the future. It might be possible for the Anglican Church – the Church of England – to sponsor one or two debates and have an impact on the development of higher education policy. After all, that is where the next generation is being educated at the moment. So we did have the Robbins Report 50 years ago that changed the nature of higher education in this country and opened up higher education, so that it looked more like a transition from primary to secondary to tertiary education with State-funded provision, and perhaps we need somebody to propose that we have a new Robbins Report, something that will make us all think again. I don't think the Right or the Left are prepared for having that debate at the moment. I don't think anybody's going to mention higher education at all probably, because they don't want riots on the streets. That is probably not going to come up over the next 18 months; but possibly, after the next election, when we know how the land lies, that might be an example. I am treading on toes here because I am still learning about higher education, and I haven't even met all the important people in it; that's therefore a little bit of a risky response, isn't it? But that is the sort of thing I would expect us to do. If you can see the impact the Archbishop has had by getting involved in the development of our Finance Bill, you can see there is still life in the 'old girl' yet.

Bishop Timothy, the Archbishop recently commented that to wear a cross you may as well wear a gallows or an electric chair. What do you think he meant by that?

I think he was pointing to the fact that crucifixion is probably one of the most painful ways that people can die, and therefore when Christians adopted the symbol they weren't adopting something that gave a sense of completing their outfit. It wasn't meant as a piece of jewellery; it was meant to be a statement for how they were prepared to live. They were prepared to die for the Lord Jesus Christ. It was really a statement about the nature of Christian witness, the adoption of the cross, and of course there was the fish symbol first. But when Christians made that transition it was all part of the whole process of Christians coming to terms with the martyrdom that was part of Christian experience for many centuries, up until Constantine's settlement of deciding that the Empire should be Christian. I think the Archbishop was saying that if you are a follower of Christ you can expect there to be certain aspects of life that might not be comfortable. I happen to wear exactly the same cross as the Archbishop of Canterbury, because we have both been part of Coventry Cathedral. I was canon of the Cathedral for 11 years, a canon theologian. Of course the story of Coventry Cathedral is one of reconciliation around the whole appalling experience of the city and the Cathedral being bombed in the Second World War, and of the ability of the Christian faith to overcome those things that would otherwise destroy the relationships between nations, never mind between people. It is therefore not only that sense of the cross being something that points towards the nature of the Christian life that might include an element of suffering, it is also the confidence with which we approach that commitment to live like that; knowing that because of that willingness new life is possible, that reconciliation is possible, that new life and new relationships between nations can come about. Therefore, one of the things that this reminds me of is the import-ance of the European communion. Because the European communion was set up on the basis of Christian principles. The aim was that never again should nation go to war against nation, never again should there be competition for the production of, and the access to, raw materials, coal, the production of steel, and the whole competition that led to fighting over resources that meant that nations really thought it worthwhile to go to war. So the whole move towards having common markets, having common policies, having common ways of developing a Europe that was really meant to be a wider community, does have some Christian founda-tions to it. We sometimes forget that and so this cross is a reminder of the power of those who are willing to follow Christ. So Church and politics cannot be separated.

Bishop, do you agree with me that the Human Rights Act seems to be taking greater precedence in the view of judges and the law than Christian belief is? And that people from other faiths seem to be getting a better deal in view of respecting their beliefs than Christians are? I am thinking particularly of the case of the two people who refused accommodation to gay young men and they have lost their business. It always seems that other religions are getting a better deal than the Christian faith is.

You are referring to the recent ruling this week. That is a complicated ruling. There were some minority opinions, expressed by some of the Law Lords involved, but there was a clear understanding by the majority that discrimination had taken place. There was a disagreement about indirect discrimination. I think that what you are pointing up is the unresolved tension that there is at the moment, about what takes priority. Is it, for example, sexual preference as something that you can affirm as your right, or is it a belief, a religious belief, which is something that you can affirm over against other people's preferences? I think what we are trying to work out is where some of those interact and which takes priority and in what way. It is obviously not a sensible thing for me to comment on the expertise of those who have made some decisions in the last few days, without having more time to reflect on it. But it does strike me that we are caught there in a deeper exploration of the nature of liberty, and the freedom that religious rights has over against personal liberty, than we have ever been engaged with before. I think we have got quite a long way to go on that journey. It is back to the act of toleration, and it is back to the limits on toleration and liberty. We are now in a society where people think that their human rights include their freedom to express their own preferences in nearly every way. I think we are at a stage now where we are beginning to ask, 'Is our government primarily there, and our legal system primarily there, to preserve the processes or to set the purposes?', as I mentioned earlier. That debate is something that I think we haven't yet taken all the way through. So I suspect we are going to have more cases like the one we have had this week. We will have more disagreements as to the meaning of those cases, but I don't think we have heard the end of this one. The relationship between human rights and religious belief is also something that needs to be reconsidered. Again human rights do have religious roots, particularly from the tradition of the Catholic teaching, social teaching, and that's one that many Anglicans would affirm. It is because humans have dignity in the eyes of

God, it is because people are made in the image of God, that they have rights. But in that teaching there are also responsibilities. I think that we will slowly, probably, begin to see the importance of responsibilities being considered in the development of the debate that is yet to be had further along the road, as to how these things are going to turn out when it comes to some much bigger cases, not that that particular one wasn't a difficult case; it was, a very difficult one. There are some details of that case that I would love to discuss with you. There were one or two missing jumps that would be interesting to explore, but probably best done in private, because of the whole complexity.

I wondered what you think about faith schools and whether you think they help or hinder social cohesion?

I think faith schools are important if you understand faith schools as schools sponsored by faiths. We have 100 in this diocese that we are responsible for, and so the tradition of the Anglican sponsoring of schools for the whole community is one that I would want to affirm. It was the Church that realized that many poor children were having no education, which led to the setting up of the National Society, which led to the establishing of most of the primary and some of the secondary schools in this country. So we have a whole wonderful tradition of such schools within our own Church. However, faith schools per se, that are set up with a perspective that includes a deliberate commitment to teach a particular interpretation of either the Christian tradition or another faith, I think are also going to be an important contribution to the rich diversity of our culture – so long as they are also set within the context that we have learnt and put together over the generations: a culture of pluralism that accepts people in their diversity and difference, and allows for that to be part of how it is that we will live together positively for the common good in a society that is always being made up of people who have come from foreign parts, turned us into something else and brought their faith with them. So I tend to be a 'glass half-full' type of person on this one. That doesn't mean we are not going to have some difficulties and some institutions that are not going to work, and of course they are the ones that hit the newspapers and they are rather embarrassing for all those concerned. But I would say, so long as there is a commitment to abide by regulations that are required, and those things that are quite clearly going to lead to people who are going to be effective and will be developed personally through an educational process that everybody can recognize as positive and part of the British system, then why not? I think I am very up for it. Again, you must remember I went to school with people who were Hindus, Muslims, Catholics, different sorts of Protestants. I don't have that sort of singular cultural background, so I think that is normal and good and positive. I like it.

Do you think that is what the Prince of Wales meant when he wanted to be a 'Defender of Faith' rather than 'Defender of the Faith'?

Gosh, John – you expected me to answer that one?

Not really, no.

Bishop, you have used the word reconciliation twice over the last five or ten minutes. I just wonder whether you could comment on how effective the Churches might be in developing reconciliation. One thinks of Bishop Tutu in South Africa, one thinks of suggestions the other day in Northern Ireland that we should drop all prosecutions against either side. Then you think of the 'Arab Spring'. Is it naive to think that the Church, Pope Francis, the Archbishop of Canterbury, yourself, could band together and make a real effort to form the basis of reconciliation, because all these wars seem to be economic or religious. But it is difficult to disconnect between that fact and what one sees happening around the world.

Yes, of course we don't always have a brilliant reputation, do we, in the Church for bringing reconciliation? We would have to start off by saying that repentance really begins at home; we have a few things to repent of, in terms of not always being a peaceable community. I think that is partly what I was trying to say in relation to women bishops. The odd thing is that reconciliation begins with disagreement very often. You have to be honest and recognize what your disagreements really are, and be open about those before you can learn to value someone else, and realize that if you are going to get anywhere then it is better to respect people and work out how you are going to live together in a common world. So I think the Church can make a remarkable contribution to that if it is prepared to be open and honest about how it has learnt to do that itself, and where it has learnt to do that to offer that to others. But it is no good coming in and saying we have got the answer. I think we can come in and say we've learnt this through some painful processes; we've learnt this because we have actually hurt each other; we've learnt this, but we've now learnt also that when we have lived together it seems to produce something wonderful. So reconciliation always has to be accompanied by truth – it is truth and reconciliation. The truth bit is the tough bit. I think it is going through the truth stages that so often is something that we are not prepared to do. We have had a very unfortunate history of not doing that very well, and some people would say that Europe has suffered because of the wars of religions, now many centuries ago. People would say that there is a root of atheism in our European culture because of the devastating impact which we experienced in this country too, because our own Civil War, some people would say, was fundamentally a religious war. I think until we have really understood how important it is to learn to disagree without destroying one another, then we haven't really learnt what the nature of truth is. So I have some hope that it is possible. I have some hope that because of who Jesus is, if we follow him through, that we can do that. But I am as caught up in that as anybody else. It is not easy to be honest and open with people when they disagree with you, and when they have hurt you, and when you have hurt them. Reconciliation takes a long time sometimes. Our new Archbishop is very skilled in this and understands the processes. Sometimes you have to get to such a pitch that it all looks as though the whole thing is going to fall apart, before you make the compromises that allow you to go forward. I think holding your nerve is part of the problem. Sometimes we compromise too early, and therefore we never really reconcile, we just put the weapons down for the next occasion when we can clobber others a bit better. I think there is more yet to come on this one.

I speak as an Anglican clergyman. I rejoice with you that Synod voted for us to have women bishops. I very much look forward to that day; I have been praying for women bishops since the 1970s. God has been a bit slow in answering my prayer. At a lunch party today I was asked if the Church of England should be disestablished. If you were asked that question, what would your response be?

At the beginning of the last century, I think it was the Bishop of Oxford who said that the Church is already disestablished except in the lunatic asylums. What he meant by that was that the only place where the government was sponsoring involvement in state institutions was those institutions which unfortunately had that appalling name. The Church is always getting disestablished. We are in the process of finding ourselves, having to invent establishment as we go along. I hinted earlier on that I think the key connection between Church and State is around the area of sovereignty, that our sovereign, our government, is under God. It is that which represents the key element of establishment. The coronation oath is a very important oath – under God our Queen serves – the government exercises its authority under God; the bishops represent that, and sit not on the government benches, please note. The Lords Spiritual do not sit on the government's side; the government sits on our side. It is the Lords Spiritual who are there representing the sovereignty of God over the government. That is the symbolic significance. We are only 26 in 800. I do not know what all the fuss is about. Why are 26 people so important? We must make such a difference. So I think disestablishment has been happening in all sorts of ways. I would be concerned if we ever lost that sense of how important God's sovereignty over our nation is. If we do lose it, then let's hope that we have a boldness and a willingness to speak out. One of the things I learnt from living in Kenya was where there was no establishment, there were bishops, who spoke out because they knew that God was sovereign, and the President and the government were under God's law. So whatever form of government or relationship between Church and State is present, I think what is important is that we are clear about what the Christian testimony is, about who God is. Disestablishment might come and I might no longer sit in the House of Lords, and other forms of disestablishment might take place, which will include, by the way, losing all the relationships that we have between our schools and local government and the relationship between that and the Ministry of Education. So there is a fifth element of establishment that we often don't talk about. The other four elements I have touched on already. I would be concerned if we disestablished without that witness remaining. Is that a thorough enough answer?

The Dean

Bishop Dakin, thank you very much. I think you have almost enjoyed being in the 'hotseat'. But hotseats are where bishops should be; after all, you have cathedrals and it's all about the bishops' teaching seat. So often you have had to delegate your teaching responsibilities and it has been really nice to enjoy you sitting in a seat and sharing, and doing what a bishop should do, which is teaching. Thank you for being willing to share something of yourself in the process – the insight of you growing up in Africa not Europe is a special part of your identity which you bring with you as Bishop of Winchester. I also thought we got a bit of that passion as well – I certainly didn't think you would be encouraging us to moan and to mourn. This passion for evangelism is something that we shall all be encountering and all be a bit changed by. I also like the idea of a safari loose-leaf approach – I think it does mean that sometimes when you turn the page, an unexpected page, you don't see what's coming. Thank you so much for being with us tonight. Thank you for sharing yourself, and thank you for allowing John to interrogate you.

5

Fixing things behind the scenes

LORD JOHN WAKEHAM

(The Dean) I have bad news and good news tonight. The bad news is that John Simpson, who was due to take part tonight, is at this moment in the air en route to Kiev, to report for the BBC on the Russian annexation of the Crimea. His dialogue will be rescheduled in the Autumn. But the good news is that Lord Wakeham has gallantly agreed to step into the breach tonight.

(John Miller) I echo these thanks to Lord Wakeham for stepping in at such short notice. We are enormously grateful to you. It is 40 years since you were first elected to Parliament – you were in fact in your early forties when you were elected. You had a very successful business career. What made you decide to give that up and move into Parliament?

Actually it was the other way round. I think I always wanted to be a member of Parliament, but I took the view that I couldn't be a member of Parliament until I had made myself financially independent. So I set to, to be a reasonable success at business in order that I could afford to go into Parliament and I am absolutely sure I made the right decision. I see the number of people who are in awful difficulties getting in there without being able to support their wife and family when they lose their seat; you have got to face all these possibilities when the time comes. Also, if I may say so, I had had 20 years or so experience in business, I perhaps had something a little bit more to contribute after 20 years in business, than I would have had if I had gone in straight from university. In fact, for the last 15 years I have been Chancellor of Brunel University, the only one in the country who never went to university myself. I left school at 17 and started work and got my first honorary degree just before my elder son got his first real degree.

Your first important job was Chief Whip. Looking you up on the various sources, you were described as Chief Whip as 'more of a fixer than a philosopher'.

I haven't seen it quite like that, but the role of the Chief Whip is quite interesting. It's not like what people say, that their job is to persuade people to vote with the government. The most important thing is to make sure you have no problems in getting people to vote. The government's got the story right, and got the story across, so half the time you are sorting the government out to make sure. In fact, *The Times* once referred to me as 'the minister for stopping the Government from doing silly things'. The object was to really get the government right, and to get the policy right, so you are sure that your supporters feel that they are being looked after and represented. Of course there is occasionally tension, but most of the time you try to avoid it.

The very title 'Chief Whip' implies that you have certain powers that you could use to whip people into line.

You certainly had more in the Commons in my day than I think there are now. You certainly have got very few in the House of Lords, because if people don't like it they don't go, that's it; there is nothing you can do about it. In the House of Commons traditionally, I suppose, if I was being absolutely ruthless, you say 'All right, well you don't stand much of a chance of progress in the House of Lords, up the ministerial ladder or something unless you toe the line.' In my day, you didn't get on to the Select Committee, you very rarely went on an overseas visit, because the Chief Whip might be consulted about what are you sending him away for when he can't even vote for us when he is here.

You were also Leader of the House. How different was that?

I am the only living person who has been Leader of both Houses, and there have only been five people in British history who have ever been Leader of the Commons and Leader of the Lords. I have often said – I am not going to deny it because I have a very wise audience – I have often said I would give a bottle of champagne if somebody could tell me who the other four are.

Disraeli?

Disraeli was certainly one. Lord John Russell in the nineteenth century. And there were two in the twentieth century – Willie Whitelaw, who was the person I learnt most of my politics from, and then a lovely Labour peer before him called Fred Peart, who was a great man. So there haven't been many of us. The Chief Whips never speak; you never make a speech, but you fix things behind the scenes, and you get the thing organized. The Leader of the House does the speaking part. If I may say so, the most difficult thing that I had to do when I was Leader of the House was that Mrs Thatcher asked me to stand in for her at Prime Minister's Questions whenever she wasn't there. And if anybody wants a nerve-wracking job, I can tell you answering Prime Minister's Questions is pretty high on the list. I went for a briefing the morning of it, with the No. 10 staff who dealt with these things, and I said, 'How many of these questions do you anticipate? Not the detail, but the subject.' And they said, 'About five out of six.' The very first question they asked, I hadn't the remotest idea what it was about. But fortunately a colleague was sitting next to me and he whispered the subject, and I got away with it.

Apart from PMQs, what was your most difficult moment in the House of Commons?

I suppose the most difficult moment, or the most controversial moment in a way, was when we brought television to the House of Commons. Television had been in the House of Lords, but the television companies wanted to get in the House of Commons. So they did everything in the House of Lords to please the House of Lords. They didn't begin to do anything that would upset the House of Lords because they wanted to get into us. Mrs Thatcher wasn't very keen on television, and nor was I. It was eventually going to come, and it did come, so then I said to the House, we have made the decision, we will set up a Select Committee to establish the rules, and I will be the chairman of the Select Committee. I set up the rules to do it, and the crucial moment was this – I took the view that if you were bringing television to the House of Commons, you wanted to have it reasonably under control in the sense you did not want to encourage members of Parliament to make antics of themselves, and so on. The control of the cameras – to where they looked, and whether they looked around at all sorts of people – was crucial to do this. I've never said this publicly before, but I will now say it, I decided the thing to do was to go and speak to Neil Kinnock who was the Leader of the Opposition. I said, 'Look, it must be in your interest to have this under control, and a lot of your people won't like this, but in my view it is in your interest to have tight rules for it and it is up to you to deliver your people in my committee to do it', which he did. The leading Labour Party man in the committee got frightful stick in *The Guardian* for having gone along with it, because they didn't know it was Kinnock's orders that did it. So we started with fairly tight rules, which could gradually be relaxed, and that was quite an upheaval.

Were you afraid that somebody might pick up the Mace and whirl it around?

Well, that's always happened. Once a very burly Labour member of Parliament punched Norman Tebbit in the chamber. We have a few of those episodes, but they are pretty rare.

Michael Heseltine made a great thing of that.

Yes, I was there then too.

You were Secretary of State for Energy. Was that very different from both of the other positions?

It was a very significant time because I privatized the whole of the electricity supply industry; which at the time was the biggest privatization that had ever taken place anywhere in the world. So it was quite a big job. But instead of dealing with members of Parliament, I had to deal with some quite strong characters in the industry. But it was interesting, yes.

You enjoyed that, did you?

Every single job I have done I have enjoyed. I have had a great range of jobs. I was 11 years in the Cabinet; I have enjoyed every single one of them. If I look back, being Chief Whip was the one I enjoyed the most.

One of the controversial periods of your career, from what I read, was when Mrs Thatcher was moving out of power, and you played a fairly crucial role in that. You took some stick for your role?

Yes, it is quite interesting really. First of all I was very much involved with Energy at the time, and I wasn't part of her campaign at all. When she lost the first – well, she didn't lose the first vote, she didn't get enough. She telephoned me from Paris and she said, could I get to Downing Street when she got back from Paris the next morning. I said I can't get there till 12 o'clock because I am having a great press conference to privatize electricity. Then I got there, and the crucial thing which some people criticized, but I'm absolutely sure I was right, is I said to her, 'You must talk to every member of the Cabinet to make sure they are going to support you. You must know where you are.' Some people think she shouldn't have done that, that she should have tried to steamroller them through. In my view it would have ended up in a mess down the road if she had done. I knew four of them who were not prepared to go along with her in the Cabinet; they thought she ought to retire.

Ken Clarke being one?

I am not going to mention names. He's perfectly entitled to say it, but I am not sure I am entitled to. Anyway, we had this great discussion and I said to them, 'Look, you owe it to the Prime Minister to tell her exactly what you think.' She listened to them all – this bit I will tell – in the middle of the discussion without any warning, without being invited or anything else the great Alan Clark barged into the room. He said, 'Prime Minister, you must fight on, it's a glorious fight, but you will lose', and off he went. Off he went into the blue yonder. Anyway, she decided at about 7 o'clock that evening that there wasn't enough support for her, and she went back to Downing Street. It was awful, because she was a great part of our lives and did a fantastic job, but I think it was the right thing to do.

One of the threads in national life that ran right through your time in the Commons was the Troubles in Ireland, and people forget how exposed cabinet ministers are. You suffered that in the Brighton bombing.

Yes. Roberta was killed and I was very severely wounded. I fell. I was on the fourth floor, in the next room to Mrs Thatcher, and I fell four storeys when the bomb went off, and they dug me out seven hours later. It wasn't a happy time.

That was an extraordinary moment, because the conference went on, didn't it? There was talk of it being cancelled, but Margaret Thatcher said, 'We must go on', and it did go on.

Yes, and rightly so. We certainly weren't going to be put off our stroke by a terrorist. It was absolutely right that we did go on. I was a long time in hospital and when I came back, which was a moment for me, I came back into the House of Commons on crutches, and I said to one of my whips, Archie Hamilton, big tall fellow, 'You walk behind me; your job is to catch me if I fall.' I went in and the whole House got up, and it was the first time it had ever happened since Churchill's eightieth birthday.

That was a most extraordinary experience. Did you ever think then that we would have the Good Friday Agreement?

Well, I was part of the cabinet committee that was working on it, and it was the only sensible solution that was there. But it was a very difficult job to persuade people to do it. Each of the leaders of the extreme factions had to control their more extreme members, and gradually it worked. But as you can see from today's newspapers, it wasn't easy to do. It was a long and arduous process.

In fact, probably the only way to do it was to have this amnesty which now people are objecting to.

Well, yes. I don't think it was ever thought it was an amnesty. I think what has been in the papers in the last day are two things that have got muddled up. There was certainly a man who would have been accused of some pretty serious murders, who got a letter saying he was not going to be prosecuted, and that was a straightforward mistake; it was never part of the agreement. But the judge said, if you have been given that letter, however wrongly given, that's it. The other was that there were something like 200 people who were on the run, who hadn't been prosecuted, they didn't know where they were. A lot of them were in Southern Ireland or in America, and there was no way they were going to get peace if they had to wait maybe 20 years before they caught up with these people. So they had to make a decision about which ones they were not going to prosecute. But the way it has been reported in the papers is as if it was all part of the same process. There were two quite separate issues there.

The other thing to the outsider – it looks as if it is a sectarian thing, a dispute between Catholics and Protestants. Was it just religious or was it something deeper, more political than that?

I think it was substantially religious, but I am not too sure how religious some of the fanatics on either side were; that's where they started from. And there were some pretty disagreeable people on both sides, and there were some very interesting people as well. Some of them were not as bad as they are made out, but others of them were perhaps worse, but I don't think I'll mention any names.

Were you keen to go to the House of Lords? Keen to leave the Commons when you did?

Yes. I decided that I had done enough in the House of Commons, and I didn't want to stay there too long. John Major was one of my whips when he started, and I was very much pushing up the ladder, and he became the Prime Minister – that's another big story. He asked me if I would be the Leader of the House of Lords after the election, if we won. I said to him it was a great honour and I would very much like to do it. But I only wanted to do it for about half of Parliament, because I really wanted to retire from politics soon and do other things while I still had my marbles about me. So I did it for half of Parliament, and I thoroughly enjoyed doing it. It is quite different in the House. The House of Commons you have to manipulate and keep the show going. The House of Lords – I don't know if it is still true or not, but it was certainly true in my day – what the members of the House of Lords wanted was to think that the Leader had a close relationship with the Prime Minister. So they couldn't get to bully the Prime Minister for what they wanted, but they could get hold of the Leader and tell him exactly what they thought should and shouldn't be done. There was a wonderful man, some of you will remember Sir David Eccles, Lord Eccles, who in the 1953 coronation said that he had the most wonderful leading lady, meaning the Queen. He was desperate to tell the Prime Minister how to reorganize education at some considerable length, and I didn't know how to resolve this. So what I did was to ask him to come and see me, and then I produced a secretary, one of the very bright male secretaries, a very senior man, and I said the Prime Minister sent him over, he wants to hear what you have got to say, and he will take a note and do it. And so he must have discoursed for at least an hour on the subject, so that satisfied him!

You were Leader of the House of Lords and Lord Privy Seal at the same time.

Yes, yes.

What does the Lord Privy Seal do?

Well, I was Lord President of the Council who organizes and runs the Privy Council. The Lord Privy Seal originally, if you go back into the Middle Ages, was the person responsible for the seal that the King used for those powers that the King retained following Magna Carta and all of that. In about 1890, there was an act passed to say that the Lord Privy Seal had no powers at all of any sort as Lord Privy Seal. Therefore, it was a sinecure job. Some very distinguished people have been Lord Privy Seal: Ted Heath, Anthony Eden, Clement Attlee. But it is always a sinecure job, meaning the Prime Minister has given you another job to do, and that's the title you get to go with it. So I was the Lord Privy Seal. The only job you actually get as Lord Privy Seal is that by tradition you are the Chairman of the Trustees of Chequers, Dorneywood and Chevening. That's not a full-time job.

You were in the House of Lords, you still are, you still go regularly. When Tony Blair asked you to chair this commission about reform of the House of Lords, did you accept immediately?

Yes I did, but only because I had a suspicion it was coming. If you look back at reform of the House of Lords, the problem has been that the process has got bogged down because people would say, 'What are you going to replace it with?' and it died a natural death. Nobody got it through. Blair's government said, 'We've got a new idea. We are going to get rid of hereditary peers from the House of Lords. That's all we are going to do, and then we will consider what we should do to replace them.' So it was inevitable he was going to have to produce something of this sort. I was sounded out by one of the people in the cabinet office as to where I stood on all this. Well, I wasn't born yesterday; I knew exactly what was going on. He asked me to do it, and I very much enjoyed doing it. It was an interesting job because I produced a solution which was a compromise, because I knew everybody had strong views and the only way we would ever reform the House of Lords would be if we all under-stood everybody else's point of view. The result of that was that virtually everybody said they didn't think what I proposed was right. It didn't meet their particular prejudices, but it was a compromise. Everybody said it was a wonderful reform, absolutely right, but I am not sure this or I am not sure that. But that was what I did.

You chose to recommend that only a minority of peers would be elected, the majority would still be appointed?

Yes, and this was part of the compromise. I don't think I'd have ever got an agreement not to recognize there were a lot of people who wanted the whole House of Lords to be totally elected. So I proposed a small number representing the regions who would be elected for 15 years, which was as long as you could be, not normally, and never able to go for re-election. So they had a lot of the advantages of being appointed for life because they were there for a pretty long time. I said to people who were dead against electing, actually they are appointed by the people; they are not really elected because they can never go back to their electorate. So the whips couldn't bully them, the electorate couldn't bully them. When they were there they had to express their own views as to what they thought was right for the country, which is what the rest of us do.

Why did you suggest they should be elected by proportional representation, which we have never had here?

No. Well, we have had it in Northern Ireland, and we have it of course now in the European elections. We suggested that it was with the same sort of constituencies as for Europe, but it was only meant to be a very minor part of the process.

One of your predecessors in these dialogues, Frank Field, last year ruffled a few feathers when he suggested that the bishops should be removed from the House of Lords since their attendance was so poor. Did you make any recommendation about this?

Yes we did. I am not sure he was right, either. At the moment there are 26 bishops and archbishops in the House of Lords, of which the two Archbishops, the Bishop of Winchester, the Bishop of London and the Bishop of Durham go into the House of Lords as soon as they are made bishops; the others go in seniority – I suppose that's 21, and they get there. We proposed something different, in the sense we said we thought it should be reduced to 16 instead of 26, in order that we should have 10 places reserved for people from other faiths. We thought that was appropriate. Now, it was in a way how my proposals became unravelled, because the government said, 'Well it's a good idea, but how do we choose the other 10 people from the other faiths?' I said there were plenty of ways of doing that; that was not the difficult thing. The bishops said, 'Reducing us from 26 to 16 is damaging for us because bishops are not there all that many years; they are not politicians, they don't come, and they normally take several years to become effective in the House of Lords. If you have only got 16 they will thereby on average be there much less time than they would when they were 26, and we think this is damaging.' To which I said – this was not in the report, but it is what I said to the bishops talking about it – 'We don't necessarily think the government would mind if you appointed people. I think they would be upset if the two Archbishops weren't there, but not necessarily the bishops in order of seniority. Pick the ones who are most able and feel that they want to contribute.' Because the other faiths were not ever let in in that same way, the government said they should be part of the cross-benchers. The cross-benchers said, 'Why should we have to have 10 more people from our allocation taken for religious leaders?' The Church of England said, perfectly reasonably, 'If you are not going to allow in the 10 other people, we don't want to be reduced from 26 to 16', and it sort of unravelled. Because the message they should have understood was that what I had proposed was a compromise. If you fiddle with one bit, you unravel the rest.

Maria Miller, when she was sitting in that seat before Christmas, was talking about advocating women bishops. Did you find there was much support for that in your colleagues in the House of Lords?

There are many, many different views in the House of Lords about that, but I think the majority of people that I talked to were simply dismayed that the General Synod frankly didn't deliver when they thought they were going to deliver on that, and it is difficult, but we absolutely think it is an inevitable process and you really can't stop it. It is going to happen. It is quite tricky. I wonder if I can tell you a little story about that? When I was Chief Whip in the Commons, when I was responsible for government, it was women priests that were the thing then. Bob Runcie was the Archbishop of Canterbury and I said to him, 'Do you want me to get this legislation through, or do you want to make a speech?' He said, 'What do you mean?' I said, 'The truth of the matter is I can get it through, but the more hoohah you make the more you will stir up trouble.' Of course, in reality he had to make a speech, he had to bring it in, and we got it through, but that is after the Synod had passed it to get it through Parliament. I would be horrified if the Church doesn't get it through next time. I will be very surprised, and horrified.

Do you think same-sex marriage will go through easily?

Go through where? I mean we have passed the law to allow it. I can't say I jumped around with joy at the idea of it. The only thing I would say is that nearly all the people I know, and I have to say including my children, tend to say, 'What is all the fuss about?' It is a generation gap. I find it very hard to get my mind around it, I'm afraid to say that I didn't vote for it, but that is another story. But it is a younger generation, and David Cameron's view is that he doesn't particularly advocate it but he thinks that the next generation are going to demand it.

When religious issues are debated in the House of Commons or the House of Lords is there a different tone in the different Houses?

Yes. I can tell you the most interesting moment in religious debates in my career. It happened very soon after I got there and I will never forget this. There was a massive great debate in the House of Lords when the Methodist Church wanted to merge with the Wesleyan Church, and the method was to say that Parliament had to approve this, and I couldn't understand why if these two Churches wanted to merge they should have to go to

Parliament to get them to approve. Of course they didn't, but what they wanted was it approved by Parliament, because if anything went wrong you would have to go back to Parliament to get it unapproved, and it was the parliamentary seal on it which was necessary. If you look back, a lot of these things are economic. The Methodist Church tended to be a large urban church; the Wesleyan Church tended to be much smaller and very rural, and there were people in the Wesleyan Church who felt that if we merge they will close down our Wesleyan chapels, sell off the property for weekend cottages for stockbrokers or something, in order to increase the stipends for Methodist ministers. So they wanted the agreement ratified by Parliament. There are sometimes big issues, but not often.

Do you think the whole Church–State relationship is stable?

I think it is reasonably stable. I don't see any signs of substantial change in the rules, although there will always be people in Parliament who have their own views about it, and most probably not in good form. There are all sorts of things. I tried when I was Leader of the House to get Cardinal Basil Hume into the House of Lords, and I have to tell you it was the Pope who stopped it. I had chats with the Papal Nuncio, and I said, 'The House of Lords would love to have him, an extremely wise and sensible man.' He said the Pope does not approve of the priests getting involved in politics. I said, 'Look, we have a Chief Rabbi in the House of Lords; he doesn't get involved in politics, he makes big and wise speeches when he wants to.' To which he said to me, 'Does the House of Lords pass legislation?' I said, 'Yes.' He said, 'Well, how can you say he doesn't get involved in politics then?' And they wouldn't budge.

Donald Soper was a member of the House of Lords, and quite a significant member too.

And I'll tell you a story about that too. A bishop comes to do prayers every day. They do a week and somebody else comes, and they are all very nice people, and they have a nice week in London. They do five minutes of prayers, and I hope they have a nice time the rest of the time! What they are allowed to say and what prayers they use are laid down by the House. They are not allowed to use their initiative and put something else in, although we have just recently allowed them to have one colleague of their choice. There was one extremely good man, the old Bishop of Lincoln, Bob Kirby. It was Donald Soper's hundredth birthday, and he was sitting up there on the Labour benches. He said he would like to be able to say something to recognize his hundredth birthday, and he went to ask the clerk who said, 'No way, you are very lucky, you now get a choice of which psalm you can use.' But the House of Lords will not allow it. I think we are moving a little bit.

You do have older members of the House of Lords than the Commons. I remember Denis Healey telling me when he went to the House of Lords he bumped into Manny Shinwell, who was just celebrating his hundred and first birthday, and Denis said, 'Manny, you look wonderful', and Manny said, 'Oh, yes, Denis, but you will find out as I did you slow down a bit in your nineties.'

I had a chat with Denis Healey about two weeks ago. He was at the same party as I was. He is 96 now. He is an old man and he didn't stand up for very long, but his brain was as sharp as can be, and I had a very good chat with him. For all reforms of the House of Lords, one thing that is very difficult to get the House of Lords to agree on is the age limit, because some people go on for many more years than others. When I first got there, you might remember, there was a man called Douglas Houghton, who used to often broadcast, and he was 84. He was bringing private members' bills in to deal with stray dogs, and all sorts of things, and he was as vigorous as can be, and miles more vigorous than people 30 years younger than he was. So the idea that you should suggest that he should be thrown out because he was 84, and somebody of 54 could stay in – no way – they wouldn't agree with that. So it varies; the older ones tend not to take much part any more and they don't come that often.

There is no retirement age?

No. There is a bill going through the House of Commons at the present moment, which is coming to the House of Lords in about two or three weeks' time, which is a very small bill, and we have had several attempts to get it through. It's doing two things, it is not a total reform, but it is doing two things. It is first of all saying that those members of the House of Lords who commit criminal offences of a serious nature can be pushed off, and that there should be a right for people to retire from the House of Lords. Now, you might think, 'Why do we need an act of Parliament to do both of those things?' I will tell you why we do, it is very interesting. The first thing is, each of us is there not because we are elected or have been appointed; we are there by virtue of the Queen's summons. It is only the Queen who would have to decide not to summon us to get us out, and that is very unfair on her to have to choose. So we are changing the law on that. The second thing, which is a total anomaly that happened when the Labour government changed the tax laws for British people, so that if they went to live overseas and become non-doms, then they could live abroad and they didn't have to pay English taxes. If you are a member of the House of Lords, you are ineligible to become a non-dom. You can go and live overseas, but you still have to pay income tax in Britain as if you lived here. That was a straightforward mistake. Things didn't happen which should have happened.

But MPs who go to jail are automatically disqualified from standing for the House of Commons ever again. Why should that not apply to peers, some of whom have been to jail?

Because they are there by means of the Queen's summons. So you are going to have to say to the Queen, you must give the summons to one or not to another. What are the rules for the Queen to choose which to give a summons to or not? Therefore, the only way we can get over that is by passing this law, with the Queen's agreement.

But she takes the advice of her government. If they recommended that, would she not agree?

Of course she would. I tried to do this with the clerks in the House of Lords. I said, 'Look, we don't want these people back, we just don't want them back; get rid of them.' And they said, 'We are not allowed to do that. What we can do is suspend them for a session.' I said, 'Right, we suspend them for a session and at the beginning of the next session we have a list of those we suspend on the next session from day one.' They said they thought that wasn't the way the House of Lords behaves. I tried very hard to get it, and we have now got this bill coming and, like everything in politics, something tricky has come up. What has come up is, in my report, the Royal Commission Report; if you have been a member of the House of Lords and leave the House of Lords, you can't stand for the House of Commons. I wanted it for life. The lawyer said that would be an infringement of their human rights. So I said, 'Make it 25 years', and they knocked me down to 10 years, and then the bill that Nick Clegg brought in, which was defeated, reduced it to four years. If you are elected to the House of Lords and then left, you shouldn't be able to go back to the House of Commons. If you are appointed to the House of Lords, or you are hereditary or something, then I don't think it is quite so serious; you are less likely to go back.

Lord Hailsham and Lord Home and the young Lord Stansgate renounced their peerages and went into the House of Commons.

Yes, they did. Absolutely right. What we were concerned about was, if you had elected members of the House of Lords, you would find a young man who wanted to get into the House of Commons would somehow get himself elected for the same district of the House of Lords. As soon as he could disrupt things in the constituency, get rid of the member of Parliament, he would then stand as a member of Parliament himself. We didn't think that would produce the sort of stability that we wanted. There is absolutely nothing to stop, or nothing wrong with, a hereditary giving up his peerage to go to the House of Commons; that's an entirely different situation.

Before I throw this open, apart from what you tried to do with the House of Lords reform, is there a particular reform that you would love to see for either House?

I'll answer it two ways. The thing I would like Parliament to do is to take a bit longer when they are making reforms and think about the implications of them beforehand. Therefore I am a great believer in there being a pre-legislative scrutiny committee to look at the bill and try and understand what it is about. My dear friend Ken Baker brought in a Dangerous Dogs Bill some time ago. I don't think it was very good, but he did it in very quick time and everybody said how efficient and quick it was. That's what happened. But there is another side to the story. When I was Chief Whip in the Commons one of the problems that we had were private members' bills. (I am being very indiscreet tonight.) We had private members' bills which the whips are not supposed to have anything to do with. People sometimes produce the most difficult private members' bills, and sometimes the whips manage to intervene by per-suading a backbencher to put down another bill, which is then debated for a considerable length of time in order to stop them. In fact, we had one in my time. We had a Hairdressers Registration Councils Bill, which was to stop an anti-hunting bill getting any time in the House of Lords. We discussed that quite a long time and got rid of it. So I did say to the proposer of the bill, 'Don't you think it is all a bit of a waste of time, this bill you've done here?' 'Ah no,' he said, 'in two years' time I'm going to have the Hairdressers Registration Council Abolition Bill'! I had one of my whips, a very distinguished and senior person who actually died very recently, say to me, 'We never want to allow any private members' bills through.' I said, 'Why can you come to that conclusion?' He said, 'Most of them are bad and should be stopped, and the good ones we want to have on the stocks to put in to stop the bad ones.' So I am in favour of better legislation and less legislation. That is my official answer.

Questions from the audience

Going back earlier when you said you were involved with privatizing electricity, whether that is one of your prouder moments I am not sure. How do you feel that has gone, compared to your original vision for it?

I will tell you exactly. I don't approve of what's happened. When I privatized it, there were 17 distribution companies when I had finished across the country, and no electricity company was able to generate electricity and distribute it. We had to have a proper market. I had generators and distributors, and they had to be a proper market, and I am afraid the subsequent government allowed these things to merge. Now I saw a woman on television the other morning saying they are going to have very strict rules as to the prices between the generation and the distribution. That was exactly what I had and we weren't allowed to do it. They weren't allowed to be the same company, and that is one of the major things that has gone wrong. It was very important to do it, and there were all sorts of reasons – one about why, one about efficiency, and one of the reasons is this. You really do need to encourage the building of power stations in the places where they are needed to be built in order to provide the electricity, so that you don't have massively expensive grids and overhead wires. You are still going to have a lot of them, but you don't want them unnecessarily, taking electricity from one part of the country to another. The efficiencies were enormous when we did it, but I am afraid some of them have disappeared now, and I am pretty critical of what has happened in the last ten years or so.

Can coalitions work?

The answer is yes, they can, and by and large they do. They have got strains, but if you look at politics, certainly the Conservative Party has always had an element of coalition within the party. There are always some people on one end and some on the other. The Labour Party very much so. So a coalition with a coalition agreement was absolutely the right thing to do, based on what the electorate decided they wanted us to have, and I think it has worked better than people might have expected in terms of the improvement in the financial situation, the dealing with the deficit, and all the things that have gone on. Of course there are tensions, and there is also, if I may say something a bit unofficial really, if you look at the present situation the Liberal vote is way down on what it was as a result of it. The evidence is that about three out of every four people who voted Liberal last time, who have now decided not to, have gone to vote for the Labour Party. Consequently the one thing that the Conservative Party needs to do between now and the general election is try and boost the Liberals. Because if they got some people back it would help us enormously!

But the serious part to your question – coalitions can be made to work. Of course they have tensions, and of course there are the difficulties we have. The difficulty is, in a sense, that the members of the Liberal Party who are most in favour of the coalition, this coalition, are ministers in the government, and the ones who are least in favour of the coalition are not in the government. So we read all sorts of stories from that element, but, you know, I think we just have to get on with it; it's not as bad as all that.

It is probable, would you agree, that the reason we have a coalition government is because of a television debate in which Nick Clegg did quite well. Had he not done well in that debate, we would probably not have a coalition government. Do you think, therefore, there should not be such televised debates?

Oh no. I don't think the fact that somebody does well in a television debate means we should ban it. That is not a solution I could reasonably advocate. I think he did do well; how much difference it made I just don't know. People hadn't seen him really, he was new on the scene. The problem is with what is going to happen next time. UKIP, the Greens, Liberals, Labour, Conservatives – I don't think that you can have five in a debate. It is not because of one doing well or not, it is just not possible to have a sensible discussion with five different party leaders, and I think therefore there's a fair chance agreement won't be reached.

(John Miller) Or Alex Salmond as well?

Yes, I know Alex Salmond very well. Oh yes, I've got something else to tell you. I have never been a great sportsman, but I do have a record. I have thrown more people out of the House of Commons when I was Leader than any other Leader of the House since the war. When a person is thrown out of the House of Commons it's not the Speaker who throws them out, it is the Leader who gets up and moves a motion, that the honourable gentleman no longer be heard. And I have the record; I did more, including Alex Salmond when he tried to disrupt the budget one year. And of the ones I threw out …

(John Miller) Name a few.

Tam Dalyell. The serious thing about it is, of the ones I threw out, eight out of nine knew exactly what they were doing. They did it deliberately;

they caused trouble; they knew they would be thrown out, and they decided that the publicity of being thrown out was what they wanted. The one person lost his cool, and we didn't want to throw him out. We just wanted him to calm down. I was trying to signal to his friends, 'Calm him down, calm him down, I don't want to throw him out.' But we couldn't; I couldn't get him to see sense. So out of the nine only one of them didn't go under his own free will. So there we are, human life. It is a very human place, politics, the House of Commons, very human.

What is your view on UKIP?

I can't say anything too complimentary about them, as you wouldn't expect me to. I think it is an interesting phenomenon. The interesting thing is this, I remember when I first got into the House of Commons (1974), the Labour government had a referendum on British membership of Europe. All the opinion polls, all my political life, if you ask them, say Britain is not a very enthusiastic member of Europe; that has been the position. Except once. When they had a chance at deciding, when they decided to have a vote. So I have absolutely no doubt in my mind that when the vote comes the British people will vote to stay in; there will be changes in the terms, and so on. But UKIP is cashing in on the general feeling that they think things want to change. If you analyse why people want to vote UKIP it is mostly about immigration, it is not about Europe. It is supposed to be about Europe, but it is about immigration, which is a big problem. Almost certainly a vote for UKIP is to bring in a Labour government, and you may want to, but I don't think most of the people I know who vote UKIP do it because they want a Labour government.

Lord Wakeham, I think most people would agree that a better representation of women in Parliament would be a good thing. How would you feel about a single-sex selection list?

Having worked most of my political life, certainly in office, for Mrs Thatcher, she would be horrified. She very much took the view that she wanted more women; she would encourage women whenever there was the opportunity. But most women that I know of compete pretty well, and I don't think it is the right way forward to have special selections or special lists. I am very, very much in favour of promoting women and encouraging them. Of course, the practicalities of being a politician and having a young family – there are very real problems. But if they can put those together and get there I'm all in favour of it. But I am not convinced that a special list, a special candidates list, is the way forward.

(John Miller) Mrs Thatcher wasn't very keen on promoting women ministers, was she?

Oh, she was, if she could find them. I have to tell you in my five years as Chief Whip there was nobody, except in the Cabinet, there was nobody who got a job in any position which wasn't as a result of me talking to her. I won't say everyone was my choice, but I was involved in every single one. And I know perfectly well she wanted to promote women wherever she could; she was in favour of them, of the good ones. But we didn't have that many; we didn't have enough. A lot of them were very happy to be a member of Parliament, but they really didn't want the grind of being a minister.

Just leading on from the last question, my question is really what has to happen to enable Parliament to have more women in it, because it does seem ridiculous in this day and age that there are so few women who can become members of Parliament.

Well of course there are a lot more than there used to be, and in the House of Lords we have a lot of women, and very capable as well. The men find it difficult to get a word in edgeways sometimes. Plenty in the House of Lords, and extremely able. We have had many Leaders of the House of Lords that have been women, and many Chief Whips of the House of Lords, and if a committee was set up and has to come to the House of Lords for approval, and if it didn't have women on it, the House of Lords wouldn't pass it. It would go back to the committee of selection to do the job properly. So we are very keen. Of course, the House of Commons, whatever numbers they are, the one people who don't choose the members of the House of Commons are the House of Commons. It's the people in the constituencies who choose their candidates, and there seems to be in some parts a reluctance to choose enough women, although I don't know why, but that is nothing to do with Parliament. We would be very happy to have them if they came. But if the constituencies don't choose them as candidates, then they don't get there.

(John Miller) I remember Barbara Castle saying that she fought very hard that there should be at least one woman on a short list to become an MP in her constituency, and then she got the nomination and got into Parliament. That seems fair.

Yes she got into Parliament, and I speak with great affection of Barbara Castle, she was my pair for many years, and one night it was about 11 o'clock she put her arm around me and she went up to the Labour whip and she said, 'John and I want to go home to bed. Isn't that right John?' I said, 'Well Barbara, yes I do, but I am not quite sure I would have phrased it like that.' She was capable of dealing with men, when I was Leader of the House of Lords, and she was in the House of Lords, she did put a question down as to why in the House whenever anyone got up to speak they said 'My Lords'; she wanted it to be 'Members of the House of Lords' or 'My Lords My Ladies', whatever it is, she put this question down, and I had to answer it. It was quite difficult to answer because you couldn't answer it by saying well she's wrong, because she wasn't wrong, it's just a tradition and so on. I thought about it and I said to myself, what I have to say is: in a way you are right, but is this a big deal to make a great fuss about? So in reply I praised her for all her achievements, all she had done, and I just said I wonder whether this issue is worthy of the noble lady. She went 'HMPH'. That was the end of that. Strangely enough we had a very similar question in the House of Lords this week, it came up, there may have been a better answer, but it was the same answer in a sense. You can't defend the business, but is it the biggest deal? I think women are doing better, they will continue to do better, and they certainly are very dominant in the House of Lords and I hope they continue to do it in the House of Commons, but I can see the difficulty.

(John Miller) I think that's a wonderful moment on which to end, and I know the Dean would like to express his thanks.

The Dean

What I want to do, Lord Wakeham, is to express huge and warm appreciation on behalf of all of us. It has been quite a privilege and quite memorable for us to be with you on the fortieth anniversary of your election to Parliament. Thank you. We have all felt taken into your confidence and you let us eavesdrop on what you really think – I am thinking of your wisdom, your humour, and just a touch of parliamentary gossip, which we all like to have as well. We have had a glimpse of a career of considerable stature, moral authority and astuteness, and insights into crucial moments in the corridors of power which have affected our nation. We love to know what goes on behind the doors of Westminster.

I think as well it is really important that there are people who understand the place of faith in the public square, and you have been one for 40 years who understood that, and helped to interpret it. Very often people don't understand the place of post-religion and how it is possible to be part of the great landscape and still contribute something that is significant from a faith perspective. So I wouldn't say you are more of a fixer than a philosopher; I think there is quite a bit of the philosopher there.

I wonder if I can say thank you in this way. Some of us are pretty ancient, and some might remember there was a very famous salacious trial in England of Madame Cyn many years ago. When the case was heard the foreman of the jury was brought in and the judge said to him, 'Have you reached a verdict?' He said, 'Yes m'lud, we find the defendant not guilty, but we would like to hear the evidence all over again!' That is my way of saying to you, I have thoroughly enjoyed coming, and if you have a speaker who unfortunately doesn't arrive, just give me a ring. I have got plenty more stories to tell you.

6

The importance of language

P. D. JAMES

It is a very great pleasure to welcome P. D. James, Lady James, as part of these Winchester Dialogues. It is two years since Lady James was last in this hall, so it is very nice to welcome you back. I said I would begin at the beginning. When you were a child I was intrigued to read in your autobiography that you and your childhood friends played church, and you always played the parson.

Yes, well I was the eldest of three so I got the best part, and of course the best part was the parson, because I could preach a sermon, and that was very gratifying to me. So the other two had to be the congregation. Yes, that is absolutely true. May I just tell you while I am here what a joy it is to come back, a joy always to be in Winchester, where I was baptized and my mother was born.

You say in your book that you were the child of unhappy parents. Was that a problem for you when you were growing up?

Well, I think my father and mother were mismatched, they were totally different people, and I think that caused difficulties in the marriage. My father was very, very intelligent and very musical, not easy to get on with. My mother was very warm-hearted, she loved other people. She did a great deal of public talking on women's rights; she would sometimes take me with her. She gave little talks about journeys in the Bible, or something like that, and she was a great churchwoman. I think she would have been ideal as the wife of a country parson who had a large family.

She would be very good with people; she would love that life. But I think she didn't meet any of my father's wishes in a wife, and I think he was very sarcastic and not always very kind to her. So it was not a very easy upbringing. I think it was easier for me because I was the first child, and they were delighted to have a child after some years of waiting. I think they tolerated me more, and I think my younger sister in the middle had a rather tough time, and my brother who was number three did. But I don't think we can complain in a way, because there were so many children in the world at that time, and now today, who go hungry every day, and don't get schooling and don't get any medical care. Saying you didn't have an ideal childhood is being a bit difficult really, but we didn't; it was not the happiest time of my life; I loved being at school, but childhood was not particularly happy.

The National School which you went to was very influential on you?

We were at Ludlow at that time, and there were two schools. I think they were founded in the Victorian age by the British Association for the Provision of Schools, and the National Association. The British was secular and the National was Church of England. First of all I went to the British with my younger siblings. I was very happy there. I so remember the headmaster whose name was Mr Milne, and he was very kind. He loved poetry, so he really fostered my own instinctive love of poetry. Then when I was 11 – this was the time when you took the 11-plus – my parents got a letter saying I had passed, and the school came round with a uniform. Then they got a second letter to say that I couldn't go, and I had to give the uniform back. I think there wasn't quite enough money, and I fell off the bottom of the list. I was certainly at the bottom of the list, because although I'd been able to do all the rest of the things, I had never been able to do mental arithmetic, and there was an awful lot of mental arithmetic, so I think that stopped my getting the 11-plus. By then we moved to Ludlow and I went to the High School.

You talked about remembering the particular odour of Anglicanism. What did you mean by that?

Yes, the smell of Anglicanism. I suppose it was prayer books in some churches, but not others, a vague smell of incense, and very much furniture polish, and polishing of brass, and flowers, especially of course at the festivals. We were very regular going to church. My father sang in the choir; he had a very good alto voice. Sometimes he was carrying the cross, the huge brass or gold cross. This was a big job and we were terribly proud to see him carrying the cross, but we were agitated in case he dropped it; of course, there was never any suggestion that he would. That I think is what I meant by the odour of Anglicanism. I was very much brought up in that, I think on both sides of my family; certainly the churchgoing was very regular. We went to Evensong. It was certainly quite class-ridden in those days, but I suppose many of us would say that class is still here in one form or another, but where churchgoing was concerned if you had servants on a Sunday you could go to morning service, because they were preparing the Sunday roast. If you hadn't any servants, then mother was coping with the Sunday roast, which was the big meal of the week, and therefore you went to Evensong. So it was Evensong that I grew to love. Father, as I say, was usually singing in the choir, and Mother would take the two of us, and my younger brother would go to sleep against her for almost the whole of the service. I don't know what Monica did. I think she sat very still and quiet. I started reading the Prayer Book. I had all sorts of wonderful stories from it, because when I got to the Holy Communion it said that if there was a disease in the town, or the plague, and everybody had fled, and nobody would take Communion with the sufferer, the priest only could take Communion. I pictured what that meant, what a sacrifice that would mean. Almost certainly, sharing the chalice he would have got the plague, so I could picture him walking through the streets, empty streets, everybody having fled, with his cloak on and carrying the sacred vessels with him to this Communion. Then, of course, there was all the excitement of shipwreck in the Prayer Book, and the prayers getting more desperate when there was a bad storm; and then, when the storm got worse, 'Oh please, God, do something about the storm.' When the ship was sinking, everybody got together and said the Lord's Prayer before the ship went down. I don't somehow think that would work today. I'm not sure everybody would know it. Anyway, I could picture all this desperation. It was a very lively book really, so I quite enjoyed, while the sermon was on, having these mental pictures and making up these stories for myself.

Sermons did go on for a very long time, and they were not easily comprehensible to children. There were some people who were brilliant preachers, and then they did go on quite a long time, and I expect that the adults were rather pleased about this, but I had my head in the book of prayer, the Book of Common Prayer. I remember also that there was one wonderful copy of it. It was bound in brass, I don't know whether you have ever seen that, with a brass clasp, and I loved that book. It was always in the pew where we sat, so I used to use it, and I longed to have it, and I thought, well, it wouldn't really matter if I took it home, it is always just here, it can't belong to anyone. That was a great moral temptation to take it home, and then I thought, no, if somebody owns it, the day I take it home may be the day she comes back to church and wants her prayer book, so I left it there, and as far as I know it is probably there still.

Did you know what you wanted to do when you left school?

Oh yes. Well, I knew I wanted to be a writer. I don't think I felt that I would earn my living necessarily by it; I thought I would have to earn my living in another way. I took exams and went into the Civil Service. That is not what I would have liked to have done; I would have liked to have been a lawyer, very much liked to have been a lawyer. I am an honorary member of the Inner Temple, so I am addressed as Master James. It makes me think of a seven-year-old little boy with short trousers, Master James. Anyway, that is what I would have liked when I went into the Civil Service. But I always wanted to write. I remember having an exam at school. It was the oral examination before school certificate, I should think, and the French discussion, a conversation we had in French to see how much I knew. He asked what did I really want to be, and I said in French that I wanted to be a writer, and he said, in French, that wasn't going to get me much money. Well, actually, he was quite wrong!

I am glad to hear it. In fact your first book was published relatively late, I think you were 31 when Cover Her Face *first came out.*

It was, it was very late, and I think the trouble was by then my husband had come back. He was a doctor, and he came back from the war mentally ill, so I had to support the family. I went into the Health Service, which was then in its infancy, and I worked at the London Skin Hospital. It was an outpatients hospital and I was an administrator there. Then I realized that he wasn't going to get any better, so I needed a senior job. So I went to the City of London College, and took all sorts of classes and then I passed an exam in hospital administration and then medical records, so I did get a promotion, and quite a considerable one. So there I was in the Health Service, and I stayed in the Health Service until my husband died. When he was alive I felt it was so important to keep the job, a job that I was right on top of, and had no worry about. After he died I thought I would like a change. So I took an examination, and entered the senior grades of the Civil Service. I must tell you, this is me being conceited, this is absolute conceit. I put in my application for this and I got a reply back saying they wouldn't consider me; my education was nothing of the kind required of the senior principal grade in the Civil Service – I had to have a first-class honours degree in two academic subjects. I hadn't even been to university. So they didn't want me. The next year they had made another alteration; they said if you haven't got a first-class honours degree in an academic subject, you can take an examination of that difficulty, which will be competitive. So I went in for that. And I passed it. But the funny thing is that I was number three in the country out of about 8,000. Anyway, they sent me a letter saying I was successful, and it started 'Dear Sir'. The 'Sir' was crossed out in ink and 'Madam' was written at the top! I have always kept that; it's part of my personal memory. I sometimes think I may have it framed and put up in the lavatory or somewhere. I went into the Home Office. I had a choice of the department I went into and I went into the Home Office, and I was very happy there. I was in the Police Department, so I got a lot of information, very necessary to me as a crime writer, which I was then, and I sometimes had to go to meetings to clerk them, which were meetings of senior detectives, and they would talk about methods of collecting evidence, and I was always tempted to say, 'Well, it wouldn't do for Dalgliesh' – but I resisted the temptation. I was certainly there, and I stayed there until I retired, but by then I was producing a book every two years.

When your first book came out, you wrote in your autobiography that you discovered that people do literally jump for joy, that you ran down the corridor jumping for joy.

Oh I did. My husband was in hospital, he was in hospital most of the time really, and I had come home quite late from the office. The children were in school – they had to go to boarding school, because their father was ill – and the phone rang, and it was the agent I had sent it to. Someone had advised me to send it to her, and she said Faber and Faber are taking your book. It was absolutely one of the great moments of my life. I did a little jig up and down the corridor. I was terribly pleased. I think it was a more exciting moment than when I actually saw the book. It meant that I was going to be a published writer, and that was so important to me.

Your young daughters were rather surprised, which made you rather cross?

Oh yes, I said the daughters that didn't have faith in mummy's talent would not get new bicycles out of the proceeds! And I think a couple of rather nice bicycles were about as much as we got out of the proceeds. Still, we did, and it was a beginning. After then, book followed book.

What made you decide to use your initials rather than your first name?

Well it certainly wasn't that I wanted anybody to think I was a man, because I rather like being a woman, and I've never particularly wanted to be a man. I thought that P. D. James was rather enigmatic and rather good. I think I wrote down Phyllis D. James, and I didn't like that, and then I thought P. D. James. I wrote not under my married name but under my family name, because I thought that, after all, my genes were not the genes of my husband or his family, they were the genes of my own family, and I should write under that name. I think most women do. They separate their married life, as it were, as far as describing themselves, from their professional life, and they write. But I never thought of writing any other way. People do think that I am a man occasionally, but you couldn't pretend that, because, as soon as a book is published, there are photographs, as you know, so everyone knows who you are. So it wouldn't have worked. I do hear people sometimes say 'P. D. James', and they think it is a man.

You said about your ideas for writing a novel that you begin with a setting. Why is that?

I am not sure why. One could begin by having a wonderful idea for a better plot, or a wonderful idea for a character, or in fact a new idea for a new kind of detective. They would all start you off. It is always with me that I have a very strong response to what I think of as the spirit of a place. When I am there it might be a very old house, perhaps one with a rather bloodstained history. It can be a lonely stretch of beach; then I think, this is where it happened. It is quite extraordinary. It is a place I would love to describe and I want to describe. Also, of course, it is very useful if you are a crime writer, at least if you are a detective writer – and there is a difference, which we can go into if you like – if you have a society of people, a forensic science laboratory, a publishing house, a school, a hospital, where people are thrown together through their job, not necessarily because they like each other. I have been in all sorts of institutions like that, and it is like being in a committee, when you see people reacting around the table to each other, and that's fascinating. So often a community is a very useful thing. But even so, it will have an interesting background, and I have in fact set them in a forensic science laboratory in *Death of an Expert Witness*, and in a theological college.

I was going to ask about Death in Holy Orders. *What gave you that idea?*

I loved writing *Death in Holy Orders*. Always there is a sense that the place must really come alive. It has to come alive for my readers, it has to come alive for me, it is tremendously important.

How important was it to continue having Inspector Dalgliesh in so many of them?

Well, I suppose in one sense, if you have gone to the trouble of creating someone who is popular, you may as well keep on with him, and you can learn a little more about him each time. Because readers get to like him. It is extraordinary, isn't it; we don't say we must have an Agatha Christie, must have a Poirot, or a Miss Marple. I must say I prefer Miss Marple to Poirot, I like Miss Marple. People have a loyalty to that person. You can develop the character more. You do not have to have everything about him in one book. You can learn more and more about him. I hope that that happens with Dalgliesh. I wanted to suggest that what was really important to him in his life was his poetry, but that he needed a job. He always felt he needed a job, which brought him into touch with the real world; he didn't want to be a professional poet. He didn't want to go round literary societies and literary festivals reading his poetry. He wanted to be there doing a man's job, preferably one with some element of danger, which brought him into touch with lots of different people. So in a sense his job fuels the poetry, and that's why the job is so important to him, and of course he is very good at it. But that is how they are related. That's why he is a poet, and having gone to that trouble with him, I have stuck with him. I think he will die the very same day that I will. He won't die earlier. I am not going to do a 'Morse' on him, I can tell you, never do a 'Morse' on him.

Were you happy with the TV adaptations, which were very successful as television adaptations, but the author often isn't?

Well I think they were much better, funnily enough, at the beginning, when they were done at much much greater length by Anglia Television. Then drama became so expensive that they really couldn't afford to do it in five or seven episodes, you have to have it in one or two. On the whole, there has always been something that's been irritating, there really has. They made changes which they think are important, but they are not really true to the book, I think that I have been much luckier than most, much luckier. So I really can't complain. It is true that the television adaptations do bring people to the books, and people like the books. I get far more letters about the books than I do about the television, much more, so it means people do read the books and love the books. Dalgliesh and I are stuck together now for life. He will appear in the one I am trying to write now, marginally. Well, he's never quite marginal is he? He's not.

You were reputed to be initially unhappy with the casting of Roy Marsden as Dalgliesh, but then you changed your mind. Is that true?

Well, I suppose in a sense one is always unhappy because you never get anybody who is your own idea of the character. I think I upset Roy, who would keep standing up and interviewing people with his hands stuck in his pockets, elderly ladies, he never seemed to have very good manners, which upset me a bit. Then I realized that that is his idea of Dalgliesh, and it was a very popular one. I think Roy was the most popular of all Dalglieshes, and he had a lovely voice, and he had the sense of a still presence at the centre of the book, which was very, very good. I think he was a very good Dalgliesh. So if I did say I was disappointed in him I was probably critical on one occasion, but I came to believe that he was in fact very good, and he was certainly immensely popular. He is the Dalgliesh most people remember, I think.

One of your books that surprised me most was The Children of Men *(They have copies here which you will be signing later.) Totally different from all your other novels – really about the possible end of the world. What gave you that idea?*

I was reading the Sunday papers – I think it might have been *The Times*, or maybe the *Telegraph* or *Independent*. There was a review of a book, a new science book, which dealt with the extraordinary fall in the fertility of Western man, that said young men today are about a quarter as fertile as their fathers and grandfathers were. In some countries, like Italy, it is almost as if the human race will die out. People are just not able to have babies – they are not arriving, or people are not choosing to have them. That made me wonder what life on earth would be like if in fact the human race did start to die out; if no baby was born and no baby had been born for 20 years, anywhere in the world, nobody had had a baby; if there were no children, no children's hospitals, no schools, no playgrounds, and nobody bothered to invent anything because everybody was dying off, very young, dying off at about 25. So everywhere, particularly in England, they lived entirely for pleasure, just getting as much out of this brief life as they could. There was no point in inventing anything or writing anything, or doing anything, no point in planting a garden or a forest or a tree, because it was all ending. Then England was ruled by a rather awful dictator called the Warden. The Warden put down any sort of objections to his rule, and he gave people exactly what they wanted. If there was any work to be done, you imported the people who were still under 25 from poorer countries so they could do the work. When people became old and couldn't look after themselves they would have mass suicides, with decorated ships putting them out in the North Sea and sinking them. It was a terrible world. There is this young group of people, idealistic, one of them Christian and the others not. They started to feel they would get shot of the Warden and change things. So it was really an adventure story, but it was also a crime novel. It was made into a film.

It was made into a film and directed by the man who directed Gravity. *It was shown on television quite recently. They changed your ending.*

They changed the ending, absolutely. In my book, a baby is born and hope starts again. There is always the point at that stage – they have conquered and killed the Warden of England, and the hero takes the wedding ring of England from his body and puts it on his own hand – when we just don't know if he is going to be just the same as his predecessor was. He is also looking after the newborn baby. It's a very exciting story, but they did change it a lot, you are quite right, they really did. But I think the sense of a modern society in decay as a horror of the cities they showed, that was very well done, wasn't it?

It was indeed. I was intrigued – what was the reaction of your faithful public, who were more used to your detective novels, to something you call this dystopian novel? Very different from your other work.

Well, it was different, absolutely different. But there have been others that have been different, like the one about the adopted child, *Innocent Blood* – that's different too. Occasionally I might get an idea that isn't suitable for a detective story, but which does excite me and I do want to write about it. In that case I wouldn't contort it and mess around with it, and try to make it suitable; I would write another kind of book. And I did that. But other ideas have fitted the detective, like the one set in the theological college; it said quite a lot about the Church of England at the moment. But it was a proper detective story. It did have a murder in it, it did have a solution, and of course once again the setting was terribly important.

You obviously have a very strong work ethic, because when you were working at the Home Office you had a full-time job all day and you managed to keep writing novels. Then you retired from the Civil Service, and instead of devoting all your time just to writing you were on the Board of the British Council, the Arts Council, the BBC. How did you manage to combine all this?

With difficulty. I suppose I had always felt that women were not represented enough on the really important committees. I am not a mad feminist, but I am a feminist in the sense I think things should be fairer, and they are much fairer now than they have ever been before. I felt, therefore, that if I was invited to be a governor of the BBC, and felt I could do it, and I must say, perhaps I have been a bit conceited, but I felt pretty confident I could do it, then I should do it. I thought it was important, and I love the BBC. I thought I should accept. Then if you do one, and you don't cause any trouble to the chaps, then you tend to get invited for another one, so in the end there you are on all these various committees, 'Committee Woman'. Of course, because you are such a strong committee woman, and you haven't offended anybody very much, you suddenly find a letter in your morning post from the Prime Minister saying he has it in mind to recommend to the Queen to make you a Baroness. So that is how life changes.

Were you very surprised to go to the House of Lords?

Very, absolutely; it really was an astonishing surprise. I almost wrote and said some mistake here surely, but anyway there it was.

Your maiden speech was what one might expect?

Yes, it was on the importance of language. I think we do neglect language, in our schools and in our lives generally. We are so privileged to have English, which is not only a world language, but I think is the most beautiful, certainly the richest, language in the world. It has got more meaning in its vocabulary and it has produced some, if not most, of the world's great literature. And it has produced the world's greatest poet in Shakespeare. It is a huge heritage, and somehow we rather neglect it. I don't think it is taught very well in schools, and it's a pity. But to love language and to use language is a huge privilege.

And the King James Bible and the Book of Common Prayer are very important to you?

Oh tremendously important. Yes, I love the Prayer Book, and it has always been a consolation to me, because I have known it from childhood, and I think it's a book of great comfort. It brings one closer to an understanding of God, but it is a very personal matter, and I do agree that for a lot of people who come perhaps late to religion that they don't really take to it, they can't really quite understand it. They want something more in their language, that they can understand. So I think that *Common Worship* probably provides that. But I can't quite see why people find the Prayer Book so difficult, because if you think of the Evening Prayer 'Lighten our darkness, we beseech Thee, O Lord, and by thy great mercy defend us from all perils and dangers of this night', that would be just as much of a comfort to an elderly lady a bit frightened, living in a not very nice area, as it did in times of war and pestilence. It has got one prayer which I hope the priest who is now here who will certainly be burying me, or rather taking my service, will say: 'Almighty God, the fount of all knowledge who knoweth our necessities before we ask and our ignorance in asking, have pity upon our infirmities and those things which we dare not and for our blindness we cannot ask, vouchsafe to give us for the worthiness of thy Son.' The idea of knowing our necessities before we ask, and our ignorance in asking, speaks to me, and that is what the Prayer Book does over and over again, it just speaks to me in that kind of language, which I love, and of course the King James Bible too. There again, I think that the problem probably is that there are better translations and, of course, the translation is very important, but I think some of the changes are unfortunate. I mean, the expression that God was in this 'still, small voice', 'still, small voice' doesn't really mean anything. He wasn't in the thunder, he wasn't in the air, he wasn't in the fire. He was in the still, small voice. But we know what it means, and to have it translated into a 'low murmuring sound' – that's a vacuum cleaner as far as I'm concerned. I just like to have my still, small voice. But I can see there are problems. I think in the spiritual life we have to individually go to places and books and people who are helpful to us. We are all individuals and we have different needs. I find that I can worship in all sorts of churches. I have been in very simple chapels where there has been a sense of real worship, and of course I think one does have a wonderful feeling, in the great Easter celebrations in our cathedrals, and the wonders of the music, and of course in the Church of England, dear old C of E, which most of us belong to. I was talking to my PA, who doesn't really have a religion very much, and she says, well, the C of E is so useful, you are always filling in forms that say religion, and you can put 'C of E', and everybody knows what that is. But there is a sort of openness, there's a sort of a tolerance, there's a kind of accessibility about the Church, and I think it should be in the national church, and I think it should be there for everybody who wants it. I personally disapprove of the idea that you can't have your baby christened if you haven't been to church regularly. I think if you want your baby christened, the Church should christen your baby. If you want to be buried according to the rites of the Church, it should be done; why not? I have an affection, I have a great affection for the Church of England. Naturally I have, because I was born into it. If I was born into Roman Catholicism I would have a great affection for Roman Catholicism. If I was born Nonconformist I would have a great affection for that, I have no doubt. We are so influenced by our childhood, and the words that I have heard from the age when I could understand words at all are the words that I read now today and hear today, so in fact, I suppose, it suits me, and I think our religions should suit us, the way in which we individually try to search for knowledge of God, and I have never, ever doubted his existence. I have never found anything in the least convincing when I read what the atheists write. Apart from anything else, I thought that they believed that matter can neither be created nor destroyed. So in other words there must have been something before the Big Bang. Anyway, I don't go down that path, I just try and keep in touch with God as far as I can.

You have also said, however, that youth is a time for certainties. As you grow older, you are less sure of things?

Yes, I think I am like very many people. I find the dogma quite difficult to believe, and I think a lot of people do. And some of the miracles are extremely difficult to say I believe in, because I find I probably don't. But I find as I get older that, although I believe less of the theology and less of the doctrine, what I do believe in, I believe in more strongly. Which really, I suppose, is the existence of God, the love of God, and the fact that I can communicate with him, and he communicates with us, that he is there as a present force. I can never change that, you see, because through a long life I have so many instances when he has been there for me. When I have prayed in desperate circumstances and have had an answer. I'm not going to start denying him now. It's my life. I think we just have to find our own way to a kind of faith, and some people seem to lead very good lives without the need of it. They do lead good lives; they care for other people, they care for their families, they are good people. There are other people who are absolutely amazing to me, they often have very difficult lives and they show a degree of courage and fortitude and love which is really redeeming of our race, in a sense. But I think we have to find our own way – that's the only thing. Our need is greater in some people than in others. I certainly have friends who are not religious and do live very good lives, kind, generous lives. I don't think God overlooks them. But they don't seem to find the need for anything else, and we are all made differently. I know I do feel the need to believe in God and I do believe in him. Absolutely.

You've said that your most meaningful religious experience was in King's College Chapel in Cambridge. Why was that?

Well, I suppose it was the combination of great beauty and music, and

I used to go there when I was a girl at school. They had, I remember, Evensong at 3.30 in the afternoon. You could go in. It used to be if you hadn't got hats you were issued with black veils to put over your heads. It was superb music, the Book of Common Prayer and that chapel – what a combination. There was the poem by Wordsworth about the Chapel, because it is very easy to have a feeling that you are really having a religious experience when you are having an aesthetic experience, that in fact you are worshipping beauty, in a sense, or responding to beauty, rather than responding to religion. But then I think that this kind of beauty is in a sense a manifestation of God. So I think one should be able to respond to it, as one can respond to great music or great poetry, and this is in a sense a religious experience. If God is the supreme creator of everything that is good, one is getting in touch with him by listening to his music. Certainly in King's it was just so perfectly done, no flamboyance, just the choir coming in quite quietly, everything quite quiet, people sitting there quietly, and this supreme singing and wonderful liturgy. Yes, it was a great privilege to have it there to be able to go into.

On your last day as a BBC governor, after five years serving the BBC as a governor, you gave an address to your fellow governors in which you said, 'The pillars of society are cracking, and is it the BBC's job to defend that?'

Yes, I don't think I gave that, I think I wrote it. It's in the back of one of my books, my feeling about society and the BBC. Yes, I think what I was trying to get at there was that when I was a child, although there were great differences in richness and poverty, as there are differences today, then somehow the country was together, was bound together by common allegiances, usually the Crown, the Church, the Book of Common Prayer, the Bible, the Empire to an extent: you felt British in various different ways. You had these things, and on the whole they were not questioned. So it was very much easier for the BBC, or for anybody else, to operate from this common understanding that we might criticize them but they would just accept it, they were there. Now I think we are a sort of multi-racial, multicultural society, it is difficult to know what does hold us together really – but, still, there it is.

Tomorrow the first gay weddings happen.

I am not going down that one.

I thought it was worth a try.

If you press me, I think there's a difficulty with language here. To me marriage has always meant, in every society that I know anything about, the union of one man and one woman, with the ultimate aim of producing the next generation. I don't mind if people say they are married and they feel they are married. Apparently, it is now going to mean the union of a man or woman, who feel they love each other and want to call it marriage. Well, who am I to object to it? I don't think I can object to it if that is what they want. I see a certain illogicality about it myself, but if they feel they are married, there we are.

What is the biggest change you have seen in your long and very productive life?

I think the huge technical developments, in medicine particularly, but in everything else. It leaves me behind really, it is more for the young than it is for my age. After all, in August I shall be 94, and 94 is old by anybody's standards – you are on your way out, let's face it. Even my daughter's not young at all, but she has got this wonderful thing – everyone here will know what it is called – she just puts her finger over it and there are all her pictures of all her grandchildren, and they are in Australia, and she can look at them as they are in Australia on this thing. All these marvels of the technological – I can't understand them, and they go wrong as soon as I touch them, so I try not to. No machine made by man is user-friendly to me, I can assure you. It's changed our lives. And of course medicine too, though not so much, because there are still awful diseases we haven't conquered; but we have done a tremendous amount with contagious diseases. I remember when I was at school, the school used to be closed when scarlet fever came. It killed children, and children died in large numbers from diphtheria. Those have all been conquered. So there have been huge scientific and technological changes. The worst of them has been the atomic bomb. That has changed everything. We now know that we can destroy this planet – we are slowly, as far as I can see, attempting to destroy it. But we can destroy it by one act. We have never been in that position before, we have never had that hanging over us. So it is a different world. But the changes have been scientific and technological, atomic energy and the rest of it.

Are you basically an optimist or a pessimist about the future?

Am I an optimist or a pessimist? I am not all that optimistic, but I suppose basically, by a narrow margin, I am probably optimistic. A lot of my friends say to me, and it is not a very optimistic thing to say, and perhaps we shouldn't say it, 'I think it is time we were on our way; I think it's a good time to go.' That is not an optimistic thing to say! Then I tell myself, as far as I am concerned it is never a good time to go, but there we are. I think we are going to have different feelings about this. We have got so many advantages, so much on our side that we now know; if we can only conquer Alzheimer's and cancer, for example, and I think we shall in time. So I suppose, yes, on the whole I am an optimist.

Questions from the audience

Is it fair to ask how the Church of England can be expected to pay its way in today's world when the politicians who hold the purse strings seem so indifferent to it?

I think with very great difficulty that the Church pays its way. Certainly the politicians are pretty indifferent, but then many of them may not belong to the Christian faith. They may not feel that this is a high priority compared with tackling poverty or something else. But I do think the government, out of taxation, should do something about helping with our great cathedrals, because they are magnificent, and they are so important to us and to everybody else. It is almost impossible to keep them going, they are immense. I think we do very well with our village churches. I always go to look at the village church, because I love churches. There is always somebody cleaning, or doing the flowers or polishing something. The villagers do care about their church, and they do raise money occasionally, which some of us contribute to in various ways. They manage to keep going, but I don't see how the cathedrals can possibly keep going unless they have some central help. The task is too big. But of course we are not now, so we are always being told, a Christian country, and I like to think we still are. After all, the Church of England is the national church, and I think we should be glad that it is. But it is difficult for a member of Parliament, who may be a non-believer of any sort, to start making a great agitation to give to the cathedrals. It's tricky, but it should be done. They belong to everybody. Everybody enjoys them, everybody feels different when they go into them, everybody can listen to their services, everybody benefits from that particular holiness that is there over the centuries. Compared to what it costs to buy helicopters and weapons of war, it would be a very small amount that would be necessary. But it would make a lot of difference. So I hope that one day that might happen.

*Lady James, you have had a lot to do with the police and the Home
Office. There is an awful witch-hunt on at the moment over police corruption. Do you think this has any basis in truth, in your experience?*

I think, unfortunately, there must be truth. There is a great deal of
evidence that there has been police corruption in certain parts of the
Metropolitan Police. I am very, very sad about it, because I have a huge
respect for them. I think there are great temptations put in their way.
They often have to use 'bad' people and crooks to get evidence, and so
on. I sometimes think, why should we expect them to be better than
the society from which they are recruited? But we do expect them to be
better. And I think we are entitled to believe that. So I am sure that the
Met will be very vigorous in trying to deal with this problem. It is not
new in the Met; it was there several years ago, and it was dealt with then,
and I think it will be dealt with now. We just have to remember that the
great majority of police officers are not corrupt. You asked if I believe
it exists, and I think I have to believe the evidence that it is there at the
moment. There is or has been corruption.

*Baroness James, you didn't make any mention of the House of Lords. But
it has been reformed – so-called reformation, I think. In the view of many
of us, we seem to have ended up with far too many Lords and Ladies. Do
you have a view on this?*

There are, unfortunately, far too many, because there aren't enough seats
to go round! I think it is generally accepted that there are too many of
us, yes. The House should be much, much smaller, but the difficulty is
knowing how you make it smaller. You get a situation, when for example
the government of the day, now it would be the Tories, find they are
outnumbered in the Lords. They can't get any of their business through.
Everything is stuck there, because the opposition has the support of the
Lib Dems, who are supposed to be supporting the government but aren't.
And then there are the cross-benchers who do just what they like. The
poor government of the day feels that unless they make more Lords they
will never get anything through. So they make more Lords and then the
other side make more Lords, and so it grows. It is generally accepted now
that it is too large. It does need reform, but the difficulty of reforming it
is that no one can agree on how you are going to reform it. The general
feeling is that it will have to be democratic. We are supposed to be a
democracy in this country, and therefore it must be elected. But surely to
God we do not want a second elected House of Commons in there. So
who is going to elect it? Who will the candidates be? And if it is elected,

then it will have as much authority as the House of Commons. That will not please the Commons very much; at the moment the authority is definitely with the Commons. The Queen opens Parliament. She cannot open it in the House of Commons, because, when Charles I stormed into it, the House of Commons passed a resolution that the Monarch cannot enter the House of Commons. So she has to open it in the Lords, but it is the Commons who write her gracious speech, it is the Commons who have the power – because they are elected. And if we were elected too then there would be a real old muddle. So nobody knows how to cope with those problems. In the meantime we should jolly well cut down the numbers. That would be much better. Anyway, yes, there are too many of us, quite right.

I was very depressed, Baroness James, when I read your Children of Men, *by the description of the Quietus, which was a very vivid description of one means of disposing of the excessive ageing population. Do you see a better solution to a problem which I fear many of us are fast approaching?*

I certainly would not have this awful way of killing off the old or encouraging the old to kill themselves off. I think there is a very unhealthy attitude, about saying when people retire and they get very old that they make huge demands on the Health Service, which is true, and it would be much better if they died a great deal younger. I think that many of these old people are war generation. The majority are war generation. We have lived through a war, and survived it, and it is very discouraging in your old age to feel you are not much wanted on this earth. But as long as you keep working, like me, you are wanted. Perhaps I am exaggerating, but there is a sort of anti-old-person feeling going about. I think that is unfortunate. I think we know that we can be a trial. I know I am a trial to my family because I am so deaf. But here we are, and we do enjoy life on the whole, and I think it would be sad if society begins to neglect its old. The Health Service have ditched us already; there is no doubt about it. Some of the things we have read about what goes on in the care homes and what goes on in hospitals is absolutely appalling for a civilized country. Absolutely appalling. Something ought to be done about that. So things are not rosy for the old. And we should be rather ashamed of much that we read and hear.

(John Miller) We are much encouraged to hear that you are still working. Two years ago when you sat on this stage you weren't at all sure that you were going to write another book. But now you are.

I know. Probably it is foolish. What I really dread is reading a review which says, 'Considering Lady James was 95 when this book was published it is commendable, but hardly vintage P. D. James'. It's going to be quite difficult making it vintage P. D. James, I can tell you.

(John Miller) I think the last word should come from the Dean.

The Dean

Baroness James, P. D. James, you are a national treasure, and it is so good of you to be sporting enough to come on the adventure to Winchester and allow John to interrogate you for all this time. We are enormously grateful. We do think of you, as well, as a Winchester treasure, and as you reminded us you were baptized at the lovely font in the Cathedral, and your grandfather used to be the headmaster of the choristers. In those days I think the choristers had a little school of their own, which was a forerunner of Pilgrims. I remember you telling me on one previous occasion how you ran into a class once when you were a child. This is not what your grandfather thought his granddaughter should be doing. Thank you for returning to Winchester and sharing so much with us today.

Baroness James died on 27 November 2014

7

How to interview a tyrant

JON SNOW

We welcome Jon Snow with that music by the current cathedral choir, since he was a very illustrious member of it during his youth. In fact, Jon, I'd like to start with that. What effect did your five years at Pilgrims, and a chorister in the Cathedral, have on you?

Absolutely formative, an amazing, amazing experience. I think to become an organic part of a building, a place like the Cathedral, you felt like part of the stonework, and you felt incredibly privileged because you were elevated above anybody else who came in there. I mean, the rest were congregation, and it was great! But to be part of the delivery of that music in those circumstances was unforgettable and something which has stayed with me every day of my life ever since. I knew on the last day I was there, as I walked down the nave, that it was the last time I would matter there, that after that I'd be nobody. Amazing. I was very conscious that day after day we had been in there, day after day we had walked past the Deanery, looked at the slope running down to his door, wondering if he was in there or if he was going to come chasing out after us, looking up Dome Alley, remembering going to see a Bishop Lampure of Southampton, definitely the funniest bishop we've ever had, and that's without my having managed to listen to any others. But there is another one. He was an amazing character, and I remember going up there one Easter and knocking on the door and going in. He had a lovely wife called Lorna, and she said, 'Oh, come in', and there was the Christmas tree still up. Marvellous. It was Dickensian, but lovely. The school was very spartan too, gorgeous but spartan, and good.

It was your father's idea to put you in for the voice trial?

No, no. It was my mother's idea. My mother had been to the Royal College of Music and had been taught by Herbert Howells – taught composition by Herbert Howells – which was a pretty amazing thing. In fact on my 'Desert Island' I made sure we had Howells' 'Collegium Regale' Magnificat, which is [singing], 'My soul doth magnify the Lord, and my spirit', and so on. A really beautiful, moody piece.

Interestingly, I have two brothers, one either side – one older and one younger. My father, who was eventually a bishop himself, was very technically minded. He was a bodger, but he was technically minded. He had a workshop, and my two brothers were constantly in the workshop with him, soldering solenoids and transistors and building absurd apparati, but I wasn't interested at all. I would be spending the time with my mother, who would be playing Brahms. When I was about six she found that I could pick out some of the harmonies, and I would sing along with her without her asking me to do so. She said, 'This boy can sing', and she said to my father, 'He ought to be a chorister.' My father said, 'Well I was at Winchester when the Lady Chapel parted, you know, he'd better go there.' Then I came down for the trials in Dome Alley, and there was Alwyn Surplice – what a great name. Dickens would have loved him in every dimension, from name to actuality – he was a mythical figure because not only did he train us absolutely beautifully, he was a wonderfully caring and good and brilliant musician. He had been at Bletchley during the war, code-breaking, and in some way the code-breaking involved him tapping a lot, and every time there was a duff note in an organ voluntary, people would say 'Bletchley'! Because apparently his fingers were slightly clustered together as a result of constantly tapping – whether it's true or not, that's the sort of myth one grew up with.

Your father offered you a reward if you won the voice trial.

He did, yes. My goodness, you have been assiduous. He was fairly parsimonious. He was not a man who threw things at you. Life anyway was far less materialistic in those days, and he made this amazing statement. They were so overjoyed when I got it. I was told on the same day – everybody went in on the same day, we all went in and sang and came out, and then waited for about a couple of hours, and they'd say, 'You've got it, you're all right.' Then my father said, 'You can have anything you like. What would you like?' I thought, 'Good heavens, what does one want?' And I didn't want anything except to become a chorister. Then he said, 'You can wait; you can spend it another time.' But no – joy deferred is not an interesting joy. You want it right now. A reward deferred is not interesting either. So I think it was twenty past five and there was a toy shop near the Buttercross, and we ran up to the Buttercross and across to the toy shop and in, and I saw this Dinky toy car transporter in the window. It was 15 shillings and sixpence and my father was horrified, but anyway I got it. My mother said, 'Of course he can have it, come on.' And so I had a Dinky toy transporter. I have lost it now.

Your father was a bishop, which meant that you met some quite important people.

Yes, people like Trevor Huddleston.

Harold Macmillan?

Well, no, that wasn't through that. No, my father was the headmaster of a boarding school in Sussex, Ardingly, and when I was about six we had to go to chapel on Sunday nights with the rest of the school. We'd be in the back row of the chapel – which was one of those classic Victorian places – and I was aware, across the aisle but in the same row, of an old man in an oversized grey coat, who looked awfully unhappy. I asked my mother who he was, and she said, 'Darling, I'll get daddy to tell you next week, when he's here.' And so I said to my father, 'Who is he?' and he said, 'Well, I'll introduce you.' And he introduced me, and said, 'Jon, this is Mr Harold Macmillan, he's the Prime Minister.' [In Macmillan voice] 'Do you know what a Prime Minister is young man?' I said, 'Are you married to the Queen?' He said, 'No, no, no. I am a Conservative politician, and I run the country.' I thought, as he got into his Humber Super Snipe and purred off to Birch Grove, which was on the edge of our village at Ardingly, I thought, 'My goodness, if you get an oversized greatcoat like that, a car like that, and a house like that, why, I'd like to be a [Macmillan voice] "Conservative politician".' And until I was about 16 I really did want to be a Conservative politician.

You also met the Queen at one point.

I did meet the Queen in 1958. She'd gone to open Gatwick airport – that dates me, doesn't it – and Ardingly was just close enough to be able to row in on the back of it. It was the centenary of the school – whether it really was or it had been fixed to coincide with Gatwick airport, I have no idea, I never checked up on that. But anyway she came with the Duke of Edinburgh, and, boy, was there a kerfuffle. I mean, for example, the hallway had to be redecorated, the loo had to be redecorated, and cleansed in all sorts of ways it had never been cleansed before, in case there was a requirement for a call. My mother went to Harrods and bought a new set of two beautiful cups and saucers for the Royal tea – they didn't get new, they got old bone china, but the couple got the two. Anyway, I and my two brothers stood on the steps outside the house and were introduced, but all I can remember is she didn't say anything and the Duke said an awful lot. I didn't really get anything from either of them except that it was an event.

Before you went to university, you decided to go with VSO to Uganda. What prompted that?

The truth of the matter is, my father had a rather dim view of my capacities – beyond the singing in the choir, which gave him great pleasure, but that had rather worn off by the time I was 17. I was not a spectacular success at school. The other day I was on the *Today* programme after the A-level results, as an A-level failure. I was the last item in the morning, at five to nine – and just before the pips were going. Naughtie said, 'Thank you very much, Jon', and I said, 'Jim, remember there's life after A levels.' The idea really was to reassure people who had done A levels that there was a life after A levels, and there is a life after A levels, although my life after A levels was to go to Scarborough Tech, and clean up with another couple of A levels to try to get myself into university. In fact I couldn't get into university, so I thought two things: one, I would please my father by doing something like that, though I had no idea what was involved; and the other was that it might persuade a university that I was the right sort to have – it had no effect on any university, that's for sure, but it had an absolutely monumental effect on me. I remember going to the garden gate with my knapsack on my back – I really took very little to go away for a year – and my father coming down to the gate. I was going to hitch to London to get the plane, which was ridiculous from Yorkshire, but in those days one did. I remember looking at my father and thinking, 'Heavens, he might be dead when I come back' – he was much older; he was 50 when I was born. I shook his hand and realized it was possibly the only physical contact I ever had with him. Fathers were much less demonstrative in those days; it was a distant business, and I was still a bit of a shambles, and not the ace classicist that he was – he'd read Classics at Oxford; he'd been a scholar at Winchester, and all the rest of it. I think also the fact that I didn't go to the workshop with him, and that I'd spent my time singing with my mother, didn't really go down very well either; it was all a bit wimpish.

So I went to Uganda. It was an absolutely transformative experience. If you can imagine, never having been on an aeroplane, which was possible in those days – everybody's been to Spain by now – but I hadn't, the furthest I'd been was Swanage in Dorset, and Yorkshire to home. But the thing of looking north from the south was utterly transforming. To be in a place with kids who were so able, and yet there was no resource. The library was a sort of breezeblock shed called the library, but it had no books. It was a Catholic mission school. Two old Catholic priests and me – we were the only mzungus, the only white people. Seventy kids to my class. I remember in the third week I was there, I was standing in front of the blackboard and I had my back to the class, and somebody made a rude noise. I turned around and said, 'Who made that noise?', and a rather pretty girl in the front row said, 'That black boy at the back, sir.' I said, 'But you're all black', and she said, 'Ah, sir, some of us are much blacker than others.' And I looked, and he was a beautiful blue-black, Nilotic boy, up from the Sudanese border, and she was down from the south-west, close to the Rwandan border and was a sort of capuccino. And I realized suddenly, when the scales fell from my eyes: everybody was really completely different; they were not 'all black'; they were red-heads, blondes, in just the same way as any class in our country, but different in a different way, and it was amazing. Up until that moment I had been rather homesick. There was no telephone. A blue aerogram would come from my mother once a week. That was really the only contact you had with the outside world, except for the blessed BBC World Service – it was very difficult to hear, but it was enough. It changed my life, and I only became a hack, I think, because I wanted to go back.

You took the church services there.

Well, there was a problem. It was a Catholic mission school, but most of the kids were Protestant. I was in no position to take any service at all, but there was a problem because the padre, who had to come from about 30–40 miles away, which is a long distance in Africa, was often, shall we say, 'overcome' by the previous night's activities, and didn't turn up! You'd have 200 children in the sports hall, because of course the church was occupied by the Catholics, expecting a service. What could I do but deliver it? I had been in the presence of Dean Selwyn and Dean Sykes; I would certainly know how a service went. I wasn't very sure how to find out what was supposed to be going on; there were not many prayer books or anything. There was a Bible, so I devised services and preached as well. It was ridiculous, but they didn't seem to notice. I was white, I was tall, and I got away with it, and I think they enjoyed it, and I enjoyed it, and we sang lots of hymns. It was a funny business because about once a month the proper padre turned up, but the rest of the time it was me.

This was the first time you met Idi Amin, wasn't it?

It was, because one of my jobs was to drive the kids around in the lone school minibus. We were 220 miles from Kampala, on the banks of the Nile, and there were school boxing championships in Kampala. I had to drive the boxing team – I had no interest in boxing whatever – but I had to drive the school boxing team to Kampala for them to compete. We arrived, and, well, what should we discover but that Idi Amin – who was then head of the army but not President – was in the boxing ring. He was a boxing fanatic and was one of the referees. He noticed me immediately. He said, 'You're very tall for a white man, your mother must have eaten much paw-paw.' In those days, there was no Waitrose, and there was definitely no paw-paw, so it was absolutely a biological impossibility for my mother to have eaten much paw-paw. But of course I had no idea how mendacious and desperate he was going to become. I went several times, and he was always there, and he always told me my mother had eaten much paw-paw. It was a fairly limited relationship.

When you came back, you went to Liverpool University, and you were, I would say famously, or notoriously, one of the Liverpool Ten.

Yes. It was a revolting time, everybody was revolting, and I was particularly revolting. We were rebels in search of a cause. At every university somebody had found a cause – the Sorbonne was on fire, Essex University was closed, even Cambridge University had trouble. Everywhere there was trouble. These were the end of the revolting 60s. There'd been massive change and it manifested itself in attitudes: there were collisions between the attitudes of students and staff, and this, that and the other. But our dispute – we were thrilled to find it; we did search for a cause – we were really extraordinarily excited to discover that the University had vast investments in Tate & Lyle, which was the biggest company in Liverpool, and they had huge investments and rather notorious sugar plantations in South Africa. We said, 'This is absolutely unspeakable, you can't possibly have investments in Tate & Lyle with this record in South Africa. You've got to disinvest.' There was a tremendous move to try and liberate South Africa, even though it was a fruitless thing for a long, long time. But in that moment, Peter Hain was out with the 'Stop the Seventies' sporting tours business, and we said to the University,

'You've got to do this', and they said, 'You're here for five minutes, we're here for the rest of our lives, leave it to us to finance the University.' So we said, 'That's not good enough. Unless you do negotiate with us, we will occupy some element of your operation', and we seized the administrative block, which was a substantial block, and must have been a real pain to have been seized, and we held it for six weeks – about 2,500 students – and we set up an alternative university. There were various appalling characters, like a guy called Blackburn, and all sorts of characters came up from Leninist, Spartist experiences. I'd never read a page of Lenin, still haven't – and I was not really part of any political scene, I was a totally pink-liberal, fuelled entirely by what I'd seen in Africa. At the end of it all, they just picked out ten of us, and decided we were the ringleaders. I was a bit of a ringleader, so they had a kangaroo court of seven professorial staff, found us wanting and chucked us out. Which would be unthinkable nowadays. Somebody would talk about natural justice, for a start. We weren't represented, they were; they had a barrister, a QC. We had a wonderful man in John Griffith, who was Professor of English Law at LSE. He of his own volition – he'd read about it in the *Telegraph* – came up on the train, slept on one of our floors and represented us in the appeal, and did get some of the sentences reduced. Mine was reduced to one year, because I'd ensured that the building was handed back in the condition in which we'd found it. I'd said, 'Look, the greatest political coup we can have is to hand it back as we found it, because they'll say that we're animals and the rest of it, and we're not', and we did.

It couldn't have helped your cause in the University, though, that you succeeded in persuading the Chancellor to resign?

Well, that's true, but I suspect they just thought he'd handled it badly and got rid of him. You know how these things are. We claimed responsibility, but I don't think it was.

I thought you asked him to go.

Well, we did ask him to go?

But you were deputed to do that?

I was. I think he'd already had the bullet before I got there. But I think he didn't like to offer us the olive branch. I got an even better olive branch, though, two years ago. I, who was reading Law and have no degree to this day, got an Honorary Doctorate in Law at Liverpool University. A very sweet man, who is now the Vice Chancellor, and simply couldn't begin to believe it had ever happened, apologized, formally. I thought that was quite a coup.

I'm glad you now have your degree, in that case.

Well, you know how it is. It doesn't really amount to a row of beans, does it?

What drew you to broadcasting?

I couldn't get a job after being thrown out, so that was a pretty grim situation. And what I really wanted to do was simply escape on another burst of VSO, but VSO didn't take you twice in those days, and so I thought I'd do VSO in Britain. Voluntary Service Overseas in Soho! You know how life is, it's full of connections, and my cousin, Peter Snow, had been at Oxford with Lord Longford's secretary – somebody called Angela Lambert, who later became a journalist herself. And she said to Peter that Longford was looking for somebody to run a day centre for him for down-and-out 16–21-year-olds, and so somehow I found myself being interviewed. Not only by Frank Longford, but by Jack Profumo, of the Profumo affair, and Rear Admiral Sir Matthew Slattery, who was chairman of BOAC. This was a slightly daunting thing, particularly as it took place in one of the alcoves, in the day centre, with stoned addicts and drunk teenagers, and people rambustering around. But anyway, Longford said to me, 'I've just completed, on behalf of Hornsey College of Art, an investigation into their sit-in, and your predecessor was indeed the head of the student union, and he was thrown out of there, and I think, given that he was thrown out of there and he was a success, as you've been thrown out, I think you'll be a success.' So it became a qualification, and the reason that I became a broadcaster was simply because I stayed there for three years. I meant to stay there for six months and try to fiddle my way into another university, because I was obsessed with getting a degree, proving to my father that I was a brighter boy than he thought. I was now still in the slipstream of failure. But I stayed there for three years, and over time I started to write articles for the *Guardian* about what I was seeing, what I was witnessing. I was in a very acute position, it was a very troubled time in central London. You couldn't go to the theatre without stumbling over somebody young and in pain and suffering. So there we were, doing that job, and I began, as I say, writing about it, and speaking about it on the radio, and the rest of it. Then one day there was an ad in the *New Statesman* for journalists to go and work on commercial radio. Radio, until 1973, was entirely the reserve of the BBC and some amazingly seasick-making pop ships.

Radio Caroline.

Radio Caroline. There were all sorts of them. But they were illegal. Well, they were legal because they were out in non-territorial waters, and therefore as a result they were very rocky and bumpy and sick-making. But here was the first legal commercial radio station, LBC. And I went along and applied for a job, showed them my few interviews I had done, and articles I had written, and I remember this awful, awful statement: 'Well, his cousin seems to be all right, so we'll appoint him.' It really was nepotism of the worst water. Peter was at ITN then as quite a well-known correspondent at that time. So I was taken on. The wonderful thing was – no, the terrible thing was – the IRA were at that point bombing their way across London, the Old Bailey and all sorts of places. I rode a bicycle, and I had a Uher, a reel-to-reel portable tape machine, on my shoulder – there were no mobile phones and very few of the phone boxes worked. So we had huge brick-shaped walkie-talkies, which, if you were very, very lucky, might work from wherever you were, within a mile of an aerial which was on top of the Shell building. It was amazing, you would ride along on your bicycle, and there was the man from the *Daily Express* stuck in a cab. People had tried to get there some other way, but of course you got there first. And if you ran the tapes fast enough, you could get under the police tapes and get to the seat of the bomb, and once you started broadcasting on this brick, they didn't really like to disturb you. So you were in there, doing this stuff. There'd never been 24-hour news of any description, but LBC was on 24 hours a day, news every half-hour, and basically if there was anything like that it just went on and on and on, and I went on and on and on. So people at ITN heard it, and the rest of it. They then approached me about three years later and I refused to go because my cousin was there. Eventually, it was very interesting, they sent me a letter saying, 'You don't need to come for an interview, all you have to say is yes.' Wasn't that nice? So I said to my cousin, 'What can I do, it looks like nepotism?' He said, 'Well, I don't know. I'll be off to the BBC pretty soon, so why don't you come anyway?' And he was, so that was it.

And you moved around a lot. You spent a time as Rome correspondent. Weren't you the first person to interview the Pope in English?

Yes. He spoke, of course, something like 40 languages – whether he really did, I don't know. What I did discover was that he took time to get into a language, and therefore I positioned myself right at the end of the whole thing, in the hope that we could sort him out in English, and in fact it was great.

This was John Paul II?

John Paul II, yes, and he did speak English, and he was very charismatic, but he was also extraordinarily reactionary. He was socially very, very reactionary. But a wonderful man. And to be a saint on Sunday.

You have a quote in your book about him saying that he didn't like the confusion between Church and State. Could he elaborate on that?

No, he didn't, but what a contrast from the present Pope, who is a Jesuit, and my reporting experience in Central America, where I worked – the Jesuits were absolutely at the front of defending the poor, in a civil war which effectively pitted the oligarchs, together with death squads and the rest of it, against the poor. The Jesuits really struggled to defend the poor and they were very, very, very active, and of course they were practitioners of liberation theology, which was an extremely attractive activity. People think liberation theology was about taking up machine guns, but I never saw a Jesuit with a machine gun. We now have a Jesuit Pope, and I do believe that his 'Jesuitiness', or whatever you have, the fact that he's a Jesuit is an absolutely structural element of why he is such a remarkable character. I think a much more remarkable character so far than John Paul. John Paul was great because he did things no pope had ever done before; he broke the mould, he was interesting and fun and all the rest of it, but unfortunately not very progressive.

But you say he took the first brick out of the Berlin Wall.

Unquestionably, but that wasn't because of him in a way, it was because he was Pope and he was a Pole. I've always believed there was a bit of a conspiracy to get a pope from behind the Iron Curtain. It was great fun, you know. The choosing of John Paul II was the most political event I've ever been to in my life; I mean deeply, deeply, deeply political. If anybody was waiting for the Holy Spirit, the Holy Spirit was spreading into political gullies, the like of which I have never seen, and there were power blocs. Basically, there'd obviously not been, since the fourteenth century, a non-Italian pope, and the great thing was there were three Italians desperate to be pope. They were all three great barons. There was Turin, there was Naples, and there was somewhere else, I don't remember, but there were three of them, and they all knocked each other out. Nobody got a majority and nobody got enough to go on into the next round – they were sort of 30–30–30. So they were forced to extend it to lower-rank Italians. The first time round they got the Archbishop of Venice, who wasn't even a cardinal, and that was John Paul I, but he lasted 16 days. He was, I believe, pressured to death by the Curia. I mean they wheelbarrowed documents in. Paul was gaga by the time he died, and an enormous amount of stuff hadn't been dealt with on his watch, and as a result there was an enormous amount to do. A friend of mine, another Jesuit – in fact he was the chief of the Jesuits in Rome at the time, Father Vincent O'Keefe – said he'd met John Paul I in the Vatican garden, crying, and within ten days he was dead. I don't know what happened. There is a book by a chap called Yallop, saying 'Who killed the Pope?' and that sort of thing. It's quite well argued; I think he actually died of natural causes, but pressured to death. I'm going on about this a bit, but really it was such fun. The next thing was that all these Italian blocs splintered, and they really had nowhere to go. They didn't know who to vote for in the international field because they didn't know any of them, they all talked to each other. All these other-country cardinals were irrelevant, and suddenly they had to find one. There were nine Americans. That's not a very big bloc, but they caucused together in a very solid way, and they had a guy who was a Pole, also came from Krakow. He knew exactly what to do, and he first of all said, 'Who we want is Cardinal Wyszyński.' Wyszyński had had a heroic Second World War, an amazing role in the pogrom, and all the rest of it – saving Jews – he'd been absolutely terrific. And so they said, 'Let's have him.' But he was 81, and when they went to see him and said, 'What do you think?', Wyszyński said, 'No way, no I couldn't possibly do it, but I tell you who could; there's a bishop down in Krakow, he's your man, you should go to him – Karol Wojtyła.' And the Americans moved very fast, pushed everybody else – I believe Cardinal Kroll, who was the Pole in question, the American Pole, I think he was a CIA agent. I mean, it was so much in the world's interests that a pope should come from behind the Iron Curtain. There was the effect of having a Polish pope on Solidarność, which had huge Catholic roots. There is no more Catholic country than Poland, and to go there with the pope, which I did, was absolutely unbelievable. Here was a communist country turning out a million people to see the pope. The authorities were absolutely terrified, and of course they couldn't really do anything about Solidarność, because they were hiding behind the skirts of the pope. So they overthrew the government, and that was the end of communism. That was the first brick out of the Wall. So this guy, who I don't think was particularly political – John Paul II – did actually count for tremendous change.

We mentioned the bricks in the Berlin Wall. You were there when that really started to come down. You were at the key Gorbachev–Reagan summits.

I was. I went to every one – there were an awful lot of them. They really liked each other. It was so amazing.

That's unlikely, isn't it?

It was incredibly unlikely. I'd been in Central America where Reagan was an absolute brigand. He supported the death squads and they had American instructors and all sorts of ghastly things. The war in Central America was truly awful, and so I didn't have any great hopes. Of course, I went to interview Reagan before any of this East–West stuff, and I went prepared to really do him over. But he came into the White Room at the White House, and we'd set up our lights and all the rest of it, and there was a canvas – one of those things they put out in boxing matches to protect the carpets – and he came in and tripped over the edge of it and said, 'Goddammit, you'd have thought I'd have been in enough B-movies not to do that', and of course suddenly we were completely endeared. He was charming, and much brighter than he pretended to be on television. He was a very bright cookie, but expressed it in very simplistic ways. He was no intellectual. But anyway I did a very sort of useless interview, really, completely taken in by him. But these summits – the first one in Geneva was absolutely incredible. The idea that the head of the Soviet Union and the head of the United States should sit down together and talk was beyond belief. We were born into a world that was divided. The war was it, and never anybody, none of us, no diplomat, no military, nobody – ask any British General, 'Did you ever expect to win the Cold War?' – none of us ever thought it would be done; we thought the world would for ever be like this, and it was rather stable actually, it was quite a jolly place. Not too jolly if you lived the other side of it, but it was all right for us. Anyway, they got together in Geneva. I think all they talked about was where the next summit should be and what date, but I mean they formed some kind of relationship. As I say, I went to all the others and ended up in Iceland at the Höfti House, which is a little wooden house down on the seashore in this wooden, barren place, with geysers going on out there and all that, and all his aides had to be outside the room. They just met together, and they reached this extraordinary moment when they decided they would get rid of each other's nuclear weapons. They would all just get rid of the lot! There was a guy called Richard Perle who was mad as a hatter and extremely right-wing ...

The Prince of Darkness.

Yes, the Prince of Darkness. He was the Navy Secretary – banging his head on the wall, trying to attract Reagan's attention. 'You can't possibly do this' – because of course they had the whole thing bugged. Anyway, we were outside, standing on tiers of wooden benches, waiting for them to come out. And three hours passed, four hours passed, five hours passed, past the take-off time for the presidential jet taking us back to Washington. The pilots were revving up their engines. We realized something had happened, something really amazing must have happened. And they came out and, rather disappointingly, said that they hadn't agreed. Subsequently they did agree, but not of course to get rid of any – well they got rid of some – nuclear weapons. There's still a good number out there. But it was a privilege to be there, absolutely amazing.

And that was more fun and more rewarding than interviewing Idi Amin?

Well, interviewing tyrants – I had to interview Gaddafi as well – is not an easy process. There's just no point having yourself killed, you know. With Amin I think it could have well ended that way. But the funny thing is that, somehow, he remembered me, as this long streak of human effluent, whose mother had eaten paw-paw, and he kind of favoured me. I did a couple of interviews, and of course they were exclusive, but people thought it was all probably a bit compromised, that I'd managed to get him. Then one day he said, 'I'm going to take you to my village.' His village was miles and miles away. The French had given him a presidential jet – you executives out here who fly around in these things all the time, you'll know that they're rather small, one seat on each side, a bit cigar-shaped. And Amin had in some way indicated that he was going to fly the thing himself, which of course would have been a terminal experience. But fortunately, when we got into the plane, there was a Swiss pilot. Behind me there was a burly-looking air hostess, and otherwise it was just me and my cameraman. Then, suddenly, all the light in the plane drained away as the door filled with the vast bulk of Amin, and he plonked himself down next to me. Every time you ever saw Amin he was in a different uniform, and that day he was in a Texas Rangers uniform, with a Stetson. It was almost very difficult not to laugh, and to take him seriously, and to realize that you were sitting next to a mass murderer. But the thought that he was a mass murderer certainly dawned on me in that moment, because soon after take-off he fell asleep. It was pretty clear he was – there was a lot of heaving and the Stetson had fallen down over his face. And I looked down and there was a pistol on his belt, in the holster, and I thought, 'Should I shoot him?' and then I thought, 'I'm not sure it's the done thing for a hack to shoot a President', added to which I started to wonder, if you shoot a very fat man in a very confined but pressurized circumstance, does the bullet go straight through him, through the fuselage, and then shrink everybody in the plane to the size of peas? This is what I thought probably did happen – and then you go out through the bullet hole yourself, as a dead pea. Or does the bullet ricochet around inside the great girth, constantly battered by the flab and eventually come to rest and kill him? And then I thought, 'Is the gun loaded?' I mean, what sort of moron would allow Idi Amin into a plane with a loaded gun. And then I thought, I'm not left-handed and I've never actually shot a gun – I have now, but I hadn't, not as a result of this – so, no, I thought, this is not a good idea. I'm afraid my courage failed me, and it was down to me that 20 years later he died peacefully, beside a swimming pool in Saudi Arabia. I could have shortened it, but I think I probably would have shortened myself as well. And probably missed.

You confess you had the same temptation when you interviewed Milošević.

Yes, that was really sinister, in Paris, in a very high, windowed, attic sort of room, strange. He was there for negotiations; I don't know how I got in there. But he was looking out of the window in a Napoleonic stance, looking out, and framed by the window, the window was open. My thought was that I could charge him, and push him through the window, but it also struck me that he was very bulky, and (a) I wasn't sure he'd fit through the window, and (b) I thought he'd probably give me a pretty good duffing up. You see, I'm a rather pusillanimous character.

You were nearly killed, shot, in Kosovo. Was that scary?

Not really; these things are never scary until afterwards. I went in with Mike Jackson on his armoured personnel carrier. He was a great general, and a very nice man. There was this amazing convoy of armoured personnel carriers and troop carriers, troopers, troops in trucks, light guns and artillery pieces – it went for miles. How we got into his armoured personnel carrier I don't know. I think he fancied having a camera with him, and I had to go along as an adjunct. But halfway through the journey he said, 'I don't suppose you've got any whisky', and I said, 'Well, I think we do carry a little bit' – we use them as bribes at roadblocks. We have those rather beastly third of a litre or half a litre Bells plastic bottles – I'm not a whisky lover but I imagine most whisky lovers would faint at the idea of drinking the stuff. He said, 'Yes, that would be very good, let's have that on arrival', and I said, 'Fine', and he said, 'Do you have any more?' I said, 'I think we could possibly rustle up three or four, but we do need to keep one at least for a roadblock.' I said, 'You only get it, General, on condition you promise to give us your first live interview out of Pristina, into *Channel Four News*', and he arrived literally about twenty minutes to seven, British time, and we had him live on air at seven o'clock, which was a great coup. So I have a fondness for the General.

But on that occasion I think you were not wearing body armour, and afterwards you went on the battle survival course.

Yes. There were many occasions when we didn't have body armour – now you wouldn't dream of it, now you're not insured unless you go on a battlefield training course, which we have to go on every three years. I was on one last year, so I'm all right for a bit. Though, actually, the thing you really learn is the first aid, which is fantastic, but the rest is slightly Boy Scouts. In the end, you do what you can do, don't you?

Did you feel you needed a flak jacket when you interviewed Mrs Thatcher?

Not really, because there was something more sensual about the experience. If you've been to a public school, or indeed even if you've been to the Pilgrims, Matron was a very big and formidable figure. After all, it was our only touch with the opposite sex, particularly in public school. I mean, there were no girls in schools then, we were all boys, and it was a very non-feminine, anti-feminine, circumstance. So Matron could become quite a sweet creature, strangely, although fierce. Fierce and sweet, which is sweet and sour really, a rather tasty dish.

So meeting Mrs Thatcher – I had an enormous lot to do with her, I became a diplomatic correspondent before I went to *Channel 4 News*, before ITN, and that meant I had to go to every European summit. Well, the one thing Mrs Thatcher absolutely loathed was a European summit. I remember talking to her in Madrid, just after she had signed the Single European Act, and every time you ever interviewed Mrs Thatcher on a European summit, it happened at quarter past two in the morning, because they would go on and on and on, she'd get angrier and angrier and angrier, but she would want to be home for bed, even if it was only an hour. So the poor old pilot would be out on the tarmac waiting, and the meeting would break up at half-past one or quarter to two, and then she'd come in and demand to be interviewed. You would go into the room where she was being held, she'd have a glass of whisky in her hand, and another one on the side there. I remember going in, in Madrid, and she said, 'Oh, Jon, how perfectly lovely to see you', and I thought, there's one thing I know, it's not perfectly lovely to see me at all. There is no question but that Bernard Ingham, who is standing there, has leant over and said to you, 'Jon Snow, Prime Minister – frightful bastard. Channel 4!' So she said, 'How are you?' and you knew perfectly well she didn't want to know, so you didn't tell her. But she was sweet and perfectly pleasant. And then the whisky would be taken away, and we'd all be there together, and I would say, 'Prime Minister, here we are in Madrid. You've signed the Single European Act, and yet we're at loggerheads with every single European leader' – there were 11 of them then. I said, 'Is this really a sensible way to do business in Europe?' And she said, 'What a perfectly stupid question.' And I thought, 'Stupid boy, what have I done?' I thought, 'Matron's told me off.' And of course you were floored, every answer and question, the whole experience, was trying something, then [sound of slapping wrist], 'Stop it, silly boy, don't do that, I've told you that before.' 'And have you washed behind your ears, what about those fingernails?' Then you suddenly think how life must have been in Cabinet; all men, just her, and they'd be sitting around the table and she'd be looking at them, and she would never say anything, but she'd look at Kenneth Clarke and she'd say – it was unspoken, but you'd be hearing it – 'Kenneth, those fingernails, oh dear, Anthony really.' So I think people found it very, very difficult to deal with her. She got away with what no man would ever have got away with, and some of it worked fabulously, and some of it was slightly disastrous. But it was fun.

You also went to Ground Zero after 9/11, I think.

Yes.

Eight weeks later, and you described it in your book as being 'close to hell'.

Yes. The ground was still warm, there was still steam coming up, and they were still retrieving bodies, and the carcass of this vast set of buildings was everywhere. Some people will know Coventry Cathedral. In those early photographs of Coventry Cathedral, if you just expand that, after the Nazi blitz, where there were stakes and things everywhere, and they made a cross out of them – and they made a cross out of them at Ground Zero. It was such complete destruction, and there was such a sense of spirits and death. We got in because a friend of mine who was a panoramic photographer – in other words, he still had one of those extraordinary squeezebox cameras with a black cloth and big tripod – had got permission from the Parks Department to chronicle the evolution of Ground Zero, and he's still doing it now. I knew him because we go on holiday to Cape Cod, and he had a little cottage near us. He called me up and said, 'I think, although the press are banned from here' – there was a complete exclusion zone – 'I think I can get you in. I think I can get you in as my assistant, I have an assistant every day; he can be ill and you can come as him.' But I said, 'What about the camera?' He said, 'Why don't you have an assistant as well.' So there were the three of us, and for some reason the fact that we were British didn't seem to shock anybody, and we had free run of this place. It was a completely shattering experience. I was live on Channel 4. I was having lunch with somebody from British Telecom – they were trying to flog some idea to us, get us to report on it; that's what corporations do, they never win – in a restaurant in Soho, and I got a call on my early mobile phone and somebody said to me, 'Jon, you've got to come back, a plane has hit the World Trade Center in New York.' My imagination was that it would be some small single-engine Piper or something which had gone in, and I thought, 'Sod it, I suppose I'd better go. Anyway, this is a very boring lunch.' I got on my bike, I hurtled back, and I was on-air in time for the second plane. Those early hours – there is some footage that went out live, which will never be transmitted again, bodies falling from the buildings, people throwing themselves out of the upper floors, because there was no hope, because the fire was below them. And that's very difficult to commentate on and handle, because no one really knows what's going on, and really all you can do is share the ignorance with everybody and be the same. I mean, not talk too much. If there are things that you perhaps understand from having been there before that you can add, if somebody's telling you something on your earpiece which they've managed to garner from something else, you can weave that in, but basically the most dignified thing is to be quiet, and let people work out what's happening and absorb it. Little did we know that it would be such a world-changing event, and that we'd find ourselves now in an extraordinary contrast to the way it was in the Cold War; uncertainty about what the threat is. You heard Tony Blair the other day, not somebody I necessarily listen to biblically, but who said he thought this great threat of militant Islam was something we should be working on. Yeah. Big.

Sorry, that's a bit gloomy. Let's do something funnier. Do you know what I did this afternoon? Can I tell them one thing? No, you go on.

Something more hopeful. You were in South Africa when Mandela was released.

Yes. Can you imagine – you've been thrown out of university, you've been banned from South Africa because you helped dig up a rugby pitch that Springboks were trying to play on, and BOSS, the secret agency, had me on a blacklist so I couldn't go to South Africa at all, ever, until the night before he was released. I was on a plane going south, reading a biography of him, and the thought that having had that traumatic experience as a youngster, being thrown out of university for that cause, and now being deputed to handle for ITV – it was before Channel 4 – live coverage of him walking to freedom was absolutely amazing. Absolutely amazing. And to be there, outside the gates – and of course none of us knew what he looked like. There were no photographs of him. But they were very clever, the South African authorities, nobody had anything to rally round. All there was was an old picture of him as a heavyweight boxer – swarthy, that centre parting and the very dark hair, and real substantial body, quite unlike what he ever looked like in older age. That's all we had. There was no good looking for that, that was at least 30 years old, 30 years before. The other thing was, of course, we were live on-air, on ITV, and he didn't come out, he was an hour late. And they'd booked the whole hour to have Mandela come out live. So what do you do? He might come out any minute. So we had to stay on the air. I had no guests; I had nobody to talk to at all. There were a few other press people around, but there were no genuine people, so you couldn't dash over and talk to someone. In any case the whole thing was tightly controlled by South African broadcasting. We didn't have our own cameras there; you had to share their cameras and their microphones. We had our own dedicated one, but it belonged to them. At one point, about 45 minutes into the broadcast, I became aware that the camera was showing pictures of shoes, and feet, and I looked round, and I saw that the cameraman was asleep and the camera had drooped down. So I went over and I said over the commentary, 'You may well wonder why we've been looking at shoes and feet. I have to tell you that this amazing event isn't quite so amazing to some of the people who are here, and some people are really very bored. So bored that they've gone to sleep while filming this amazing moment.' But we didn't know what he would look like, and when he did emerge, his hut was 300 or 400 yards away. But when he came out, there was a swarm of people there, a swarm of ANC supporters. It was completely evident that it was him. In a funny sort of way, I don't know whether one looks back on it in some kind of a mystical way, but, rather like the Red Sea, it parted, and the people parted, and there was just him, and Winnie, and their hands clasped, and they walked towards us. I wept, I didn't have to say anything, just let it happen, it was just fantastic. Unbelievable. And to come out, and then go down to Cape Town, and to make that speech from the balcony and say, 'I forgive, but I won't forget. We forgive, but we won't forget', was seminal. This is just the most amazing moment in history. Sadly, it's often been let down since, but there hasn't been war. There is terrible corruption, there is difficulty, but there is a multicultural society there. I had to go down four times, each time Mandela threatened to die. I went many times, and interviewed him a good number of times. The funny thing is the first time I interviewed him, which was very soon after he came out, he'd never been interviewed on television; nobody had ever really interviewed him before. There had been a couple of other interviews before me, but most politicians you talk to have been processed, and so when you ask them a question they give you an answer to a completely different question, they think of something else they want to say. Or they've come in ready to say something else, so they say it anyway, whatever the question was you asked them. But he was quite different. He engaged in every question you asked him, and then he started asking me questions, and I had to keep saying, 'Mr Mandela, I'm here to interview you.' 'No.' But he said, 'I want to know, just tell me, how nowadays does the BBC World Service work?' Or whatever it was. There were all sorts of practical things he wanted to know, and I just had to keep saying, 'I must get this interview out of you, because nobody in Britain is going to want to hear me telling you how the BBC World Service works', or whatever it is. A very normal man, that's the extraordinary thing. A very normal man, with all the frailties of normal men. He would look through this audience and he would see an attractive woman, and he would look at her, no question, but that's what we all do, and he's like us, he was like us, but exceptional, beyond anything. But naughty. Not naughty in a criminal or even immoral sense, but wicked sort of thoughts and things, and normal, normal, deeply normal. But wonderful. Special, the most special person I've ever met.

Questions from the audience

Could I preface my question with an observation first of all? I've just started to read your interesting book –

And you've found some mistakes, serious errors.

I'll talk to you later about that. I've got to Chapter 2, and I note with interest that we seem to have something in common, in that back in our student days we were both members of what were 14, in the end, Commonwealth overland expeditions to India.

Yes! Gosh, which year did you go?

I was on Comex 2, two years before you, in 1967. Yours was rather larger – two years later in the summer of 1969, Comex 3.

Just to fill you in, it was an amazing, bonkers, mad, expedition, which was run by Colonel Gregory, who was bonkers too. But you'd have to be bonkers to do it. He convinced Bedford Duple, or someone, to provide the buses, and universities all over Britain sent buses in which there had to be – in our case anyway – a cultural element. And because I was at Liverpool University, we had a four-part close-harmony Beatle band, of which I was bass. We also had Sheridan's *Rivals*, a rather indigestible play to take to India, but they were doing it for A level, or O level, I can't remember which, and they wanted us to do it, so we did. But, sorry, carry on.

You mention that VSO in Uganda was a life-changing experience. I was going to ask to what extent, if at all, the Comex experience was life-changing?

The Comex thing was, in a different way. First of all, I was one of the two drivers. Driving to India is a megalithic experience, but it is the only way to visit India, if I may say so. There's no culture shock when you arrive there because when you get there, you've got there gradually. The bread, which starts at Hovis, ends up flat – it starts off erect and ends up flat as a chapatti. It's amazing, it's a very gradual experience, not like flying in and you're suddenly bowled over by the enormity of the crowds, and the noise and the joy and the colour and the rest of it. So I did find it informing, but not quite the same way as living in Uganda was. On the way, we stopped in Iran, and I formed an immediate and very strong and life-lasting love for Iran, a gorgeous country, and a country which has been, from within and without, badly sorted. But, they are our potential allies. I tell you, they are very like us. They look West, they are not remotely interested in the East. And if you want a form of Islam to live with, there's nothing like the elasticity of Shia Islam. I see it as very akin to the Anglican Church, except for the flagellation! The flagellation, I think we in the Anglican Church got rid of possibly a few centuries ago. I don't know if we ever did flagellate – did we, Dean? I don't know, who knows. Chaucer has a bit of flagellation. Sorry, I denied you the question, but that is my feeling, yes. It did have a big effect, not quite as big as actually living solid, for a year, among a different people.

Just a simple question. What was it you did this afternoon that you wanted to tell us about?

Well, I think you might be young enough to know what I'm talking about, because there is a television phenomenon which is called *Game of Thrones*. In *Game of Thrones* there is somebody called J-O-N Snow, Jon Snow. It has mystified me as to how the author got hold of this name, and I wondered whether I had anything to do with it, essentially. Well, I interviewed Jon Snow himself today. The guy who plays Jon Snow. Very, very nice guy called Kit Harington. Ostensibly I was there to interview him about *Pompeii*, a slightly overdone special-effects movie which is coming out soon, which has everything to do with the capacity of special effects and not a great deal to do with Pompeii – but never mind, it's full of explosives and experience. Anyway, suffice it to say that I interviewed him, and I am conscious from my own Twitter-feed that young people associate the name Jon Snow with two things: one of the things, which is said to Jon Snow, 'Jon Snow, you know nothing' – actually he's one of the good people in *Game of Thrones*; and the other thing is, he's also called 'The Bastard', and so I get 'The Bastard' and 'Jon Snow, you know nothing' on my Twitter-feed, from people either thinking I might be him, or alternatively wanting to use it as a term of abuse, which I might fully understand. Anyway, it was enormous fun interviewing him, because he turned out to be a very bright, clever, nice boy, the actor, Kit Harington, and we got on like a house on fire, and we took lots of shots of us – facing off, and all the rest of it – and I tweeted it and it went absolutely viral. It's going out tomorrow night at 6.45; it's a hoot. Kit Harington told me a very funny story. When he was at acting school – he's only 27, but he's a huge star – in his first year, he worked for an events company in his spare time to try and get money to keep financing his studies, and he was dressed up as a bellboy at the Royal Television Society Awards, which involved a red carpet. For some reason I had got an award that year. I walked up the red carpet, and he told me – I didn't remember this – that he called out. He said, 'John Simpson!' And I said, 'No, Jon Snow, but he's much better than I am.' And he remembers this vividly. And then when I came out I said hello and we had a little chat. I had completely forgotten this. It turned out that he was the right generation to have grown up with this moronic Jon Snow doing *Channel 4 News*, or whatever, and therefore we both respected each other for who we were. And needless to say, at the end of the interview, I said, 'Jon Snow, you know nothing', and he said, 'Bastard.' Whether they'll run it – I hope they do. I'm sure Ofcom will let 'bastard' through.

Mr Snow, of all the amazing people that you've met and interviewed, and the many interesting countries that you've been to, who does your heart desire to talk to now, and what country do you still want to visit?

Well, I'll tell you something. First, I'll answer it backwards. Amazingly, I think I've been to 110 countries, and I've never been to China. China is such a big thing to do, and I was so steeped in Africa – I mean, I've been to practically every country in Africa, and Latin America, and done a bit of Russia, and a lot of Iran, and a lot of Iraq, and a lot of Afghanistan. There just hasn't been time to bite off anything as big as China. I've been to Hong Kong; I went for the hand-over, but never to China. So I would like to go to China, but I'd like a lot of time to do it, which may be difficult to achieve, but I'm going to try to do it.

As to who? Do you know something, the most interesting people are the people you meet by accident. Somebody may have read an account of this, but it bears retelling. Some of the most interesting people I meet are on trains. Trains are great places for meeting people. Well, Winchester station knows it better than any other; *Brief Encounter*, gorgeous, sumptuous experience. Anyway, I was on a train the other day from York to King's Cross, and I sat down at a table of four, and there was a man, a woman, and a woman – that seems to suit me quite well, I thought. And I suddenly realized the man was making signs at me, and because his mouth was moving but there were no words coming out, I realized that he was deaf and couldn't speak. He was making hand gestures. And we tried a bit of this, and then the woman opposite spoke, she said, 'He's telling you you're on Channel 4', and I said, 'I know I am.' And she said, 'I'm deaf too.' So here were two deaf people in their sixties, and I thought, before I go any further, I'd better check who this is, and she was a Mongolian economist from Warwick University. So I had this very interesting trio, and I realized, at a very early stage that, with my laptop, if I went into 25-point, I could start asking the questions, and he could give me answers, and she could give me some of his answers. And suddenly we set up this most amazing conversation. Other people in the carriage began to get interested too. It turned out they were going down to a convention of deaf and non-speaking people. They were going to some sort of event, party even, I don't know; it was going to be in Sussex. Then they told me they were both deaf, and he was non-speaking, as a result of meningitis. Both of them had meningitis at the age of six and five, and they were now in their middle sixties. I learnt so much in that journey about being deaf and having no speech, and what full lives they lived. The amazing thing is, though, I never could write, in 25-point,

'What is your relationship? Are you brother and sister? Were you in the same family, or are you married, or are you lovers, or are you friends?' Very interesting. I was shy about writing it down, I don't know why. Then the Mongolian was absolutely fascinating. She got off at Newark, and a Tamil social worker got on. So I don't know who I'd like to interview, perhaps whoever I meet next on the train. You perhaps. I'm sure we could get a very interesting conversation.

I'm a fellow journalist. You come across as a very confident man, but have you ever doubted your own abilities, and, if so, how did you overcome them?

I doubt them every single day. Every day I try to live to try and prove myself to my father, although he's been dead since 1977. Literally, I mean I think I'm still battering on now because I think I can get better. Inevitably, every day you think, 'I've got to talk about what? The public sector borrowing requirement?' There's a challenge every day, to your intellectual capacities, even reviewing the bank results, Barclays Bank results, trying to read a balance sheet – I can't read that stuff. And in the end, I genuinely believe that it's a good thing to have a limited intellect if you've got to do the job I do, because you don't ask questions that you can't answer yourself, you stick to what you know, you don't try and be somebody intellectually that is beyond who you actually are, because that really would be trouble. What are your roots, darling?

I was born and raised in Scotland, but my mum's from Ghana and my dad's from Nigeria.

Wonderful. I once made a film, a Millennium film in 2000, and I made a journey from Tamur, which is where the Greenwich Meridian ends up before it reaches the bottom. There was a great fuss about the Dome, and I thought, 'Why is the Dome there?' Of course, it's there because of the Greenwich Meridian. 'But where is the Greenwich Meridian? Who does it link? Who else lives on the line with us?' And it's gorgeous. Ghana, one of the great countries of Africa, and most likely to achieve the next level of economic development. Ghana, Togo, strange little French outpost, weird military situation, but interesting. Togo, Burkina Faso, the poorest country in Africa, and yet utterly vibrant and wonderful, with the greatest music festival the world has ever known, in Ouagadougou, absolutely sensational, with all the great West African singers. And then Mali. Oh! What heaven, Mali! Mali, where they were trading books in the thirteenth century, where the university is older than either Oxford or Cambridge; it stands history on its head. And then Algeria, troubled, interesting, post-French. And then Spain, France, Britain – three post-colonial and five developing. Could you ask for a better union? And so we sent a Ghanaian down from Spurn Head, which is where the Greenwich Meridian meets land, and me from Tamur, where it meets land, and we met on the roof of the central mosque in Timbuktu, and we reviewed what we'd seen. He was shocked by the boar-hunting in Spain, and I was amazed to have met a man, a chief in a village in Burkina Faso, who didn't know the world was round, but he knew he was somewhere important, because whenever he looked up at night, at a certain time he would see lights going across the sky. And they were British Airways, and South African Airways, who, in Johannesburg, set the old dial to zero; Bob's your uncle, you're at Heathrow. Well, you might land at City by mistake, but should be Heathrow. Amazing, amazing. Again, a life-changing experience. We made a wonderful 90-minute film, with Oxfam, all sorts of other partners, and we got schools to team up on the line, all the rest of it. Anyway, I've gone mad now, sorry.

The Dean

Jon, almost a last question really, but I'm just so in awe of your interest, love and zest for people. You've had a lifetime meeting people, and you've never wearied of them. In just two sentences, what would you say about human nature?

Well, it's a delicious thing. I think somewhere in everybody, even in Idi Amin possibly, there is something there. Human nature, given a chance, is extraordinarily generous and ready. And we haven't talked about God, Dean. We haven't talked about the Church. I'm somebody who does go to church; unfortunately they only come to our church once a fortnight, although we've had a feast over Easter because our fortnight came either side of Easter so we got three services in succession. It's one of these parishes where the priest is looking after six parishes, six churches, and I go – I mean, I'm in trouble if you really want to pin me down on theology, completely in trouble – but I love the coming together with other human beings to do the same thing, whatever it is, to go through the rote together. You see, my heretical view of God is that it is the coming together of the human spirit, to aspire to do better, to do better by each other, and somehow live in a better world thereafter. But as to whether 'Is there anybody up there?', I leave it to the Dean.

8

Pilgrimage in the blood

DEAN OF WINCHESTER JAMES ATWELL

It's a particular pleasure to me to be introducing the Dean in this dialogue. When we first discussed what we would do with this series I suggested that we opened with the Dean. He was far too modest to do that, and has taken some persuading to take part in this series, so I'm delighted we finally cornered him. To begin – James, you grew up on a farm; that was quite important to your decision to read theology, wasn't it?

Yes, I suppose it was. Being brought up on a farm had all sorts of effects. When you are a youngster, you don't realize how lucky you are, and that everybody else isn't being brought up on a farm. In some ways you're in your own world; it's more isolated than a lot of youngsters. My father was a tenant farmer in Wiltshire, and I was the younger brother, so I was always brought up with, 'You're not going to farm; your brother is going to do that, so you've got to find something else to do.' My mother always worried I'd get too interested in the farm, so she'd hoped I might be a lawyer, and Dad always thought that an auctioneer would be good because an auctioneer in the family would be very helpful. We had a mixed farm. In the days immediately after the war, my father felt that quality was what people wanted, so when he decided to work up a milking herd, he chose Channel Island Guernsey cattle. He imported them from Guernsey and from Sark. We had quite a relationship with the Dame of Sark, who had been such a legend during the Second World War, making the Germans attend her house, and not going to them. So we had this lovely golden Guernsey herd, which was fantastic; the Guernsey bulls are quite tough animals. I do remember on one occasion when my brother had tethered the bull in the field, which had just been imported from Sark, and it obviously didn't like being tethered, it just pulled the tether up and walked straight through the barbed wire, snapping it, and up the road. We had some rather terrified people ringing us up.

One of the things about being part of a farm is it's realistic – you know things die, and people eat and all that. But also there is a great mystery to it. As well as having the Guernsey cattle, we had poultry: hens for eggs and turkeys for the Christmas market. We bred our own turkeys. We had old-fashioned incubators, in which Dad would hatch out the eggs laid by our own stock. He put little blue marks on the eggs and placed them in the incubator. They were paraffin incubators, so if the flame went too high, then you cooked the eggs and you'd end up with boiled eggs, which was not what you were supposed to do. If the flame went out, your poor old turkeys never got out of their egg. If you were really careful, and Dad turned the eggs twice a day, you suddenly would hear all this tweeting from inside the incubator and see these little animals pecking their way out of the eggs. A real moment of mystery. I was also lucky enough to have a horse, which was something of a 'Champion the Wonder Horse'; it would have done anything with a sack of potatoes on its back! On one occasion I did persuade my father that she could have a foal. You go to bed with one horse out in the field, and then you get up the next day and there's mum with its little foal – foals have very slender legs, but within hours they're walking – and you see this lanky little creature stagger-ing after mum, and proud mum with a great instinct for motherhood. It is quite mind-blowing. So you can't be brought up on a farm without a sense of mystery – that's why, I suppose, I've always been keen on creation theology. My reason for faith in God is something to do with the grace and giftedness of the world, and that if the world really is a gift, then the question arises as to who's the giver.

One side-story, which I was quite proud of. I trained a Concorde pilot once. I had a younger cousin whom I was supposed to be looking after, and we were out with the horse, and he asked, 'Can I ride the horse?' He hadn't ever ridden, but I put him on without asking permission from my parents – so I was in a bit of trouble anyway. Now, saddles have leathers with stirrups on the end. It was a bit of an effort to adjust them. So instead of pulling the stirrups up, I just stuck his feet in the leathers. He then decided he wanted to trot, and I said, 'I'm not sure this is wise.' But anyway he started to trot. Of course, the stirrups went 'bang, bang, bang', and the animal bolted. It galloped round and round this large field, and I eventually shouted to guide it into the hedge. Well, it was going at such a speed it went straight over the hedge and the ditch, and my cousin flew through the air and landed in the hedge, and I thought, 'Oh God, he's died.' Amazingly, he crawled out of the ditch just a bit dazed, and the horse went on to the local town and I caught it on the A4. The rest of the day I remember my eyes misted over and I could hardly see anything, I was so fazed. Anyway, he went on to pilot Concorde.

And gave up riding, I take it?

Well, I don't think he rode again.

Was Oxford what you expected when you went up to read theology?

Yes, it was interesting, both that I applied to Oxford and to read theology. I think my mother was very driven, because she'd left school at 14, and so education was something she prized enormously. I think she always felt Oxford was something one should aim for, and so I did have a go. I had decided by then to read theology, so I must have been fairly serious about ordination at that stage. I can remember my headmaster at boarding school calling me in when I said I'd like to read theology. The conversation was something like this. Headmaster: 'I don't think it's a good idea at all, because if you read theology you're committing yourself to a particular path. You ought to read something that's much wider, then read theology as a second degree.' I said, 'I'm not sure I want to spend six years doing two first degrees; I'd rather get on with some theology.' Anyway, Michael Ramsey, who was then Archbishop of Canterbury, luckily wrote an article about why more people should read theology as a first degree. I went back to my headmaster and waved it at him, and he relented: 'Well, I won't argue with the Archbishop of Canterbury, then.'

But, why did I read theology? I think the farming background made a huge impression on me in terms of the created order and what the world is about, and why it has this mysterious and wonderful quality. Also, my father was ill when I was a teenager and he died at the end of my first term at university. I think, particularly at that age, with life ahead of you, it does challenge you as to what life is about. How are you going to use it? What do you want to do with it? I think it did make quite an impact upon me. I was called home from school to go and help with the baling at crisis moments – so I was aware of Dad's illness, and I suppose also aware that he was a tenant farmer. His death meant that we lost the tenancy anyway, so my brother didn't farm in the end. So it was challenging enough to make me soul search and feel I was looking for some sort of meaning in life.

But the opportunity to go to Harvard must have been irresistible?

That was incredible. I graduated from Oxford in June of 1968, and I'd fixed up to go to Boston for two months to work with the Episcopal Church in downtown Boston, in the black areas where there had been a lot of riots and lots of challenging issues. I managed to persuade a friend, so we went together and shared this experience in Boston, which really was incredibly challenging and exciting. We arrived in a clergy house in the middle of Roxbury, a downtown area of Boston, and we were told, 'Whatever you do, draw the curtains at night, because people might take a potshot at you.' We'd drawn all the curtains, as advised, and suddenly on our first night there was an almighty commotion. We thought, 'There's a riot', so we plucked up courage, after about five minutes, to look outside. In fact, the old priest who was staying in the house had arrived in his enormous vehicle and knocked all the tin dustbins over, which had rolled down the hill. My friend, who is now an archdeacon, was placed in a Roman Catholic parish, and I was placed in an Episcopal parish, but we both slept in the Episcopal parish. The RC parish had a festival one Saturday. He was helping out, and was allocated the candy floss machine. There was a little kid who'd worked out that if you put your finger in the candy floss machine, it didn't go round the stick at all, it went round your finger! My frustrated friend, after asking him politely to remove his finger, gently cuffed him. Back he came with big brother. There was nearly an incident!

During our two months in Boston, one of the things we did was take the Boston subway out to Harvard Square, and the seed was sown: 'Wouldn't it be lovely to study here?' When I returned to the UK it was to my first term at Cuddesdon Theological College where Robert Runcie, who later became Archbishop of Canterbury, was the principal of the college. He was quite an enabler. On the college noticeboard was an announcement: 'World Council of Churches Scholarships to American Universities'. But then it said the date by which they had to be in and it was the week before I saw the notice. I said to Robert Runcie, 'Oh gosh, I'd have loved to have applied to an American university, and it's a week late.' 'No, no, don't worry too much – I know the secretary who processes the office work in London and it's her deadline, but the important deadline relates to Geneva.' So he rang up and I got my application in late and luckily it caught the tide in Geneva. You could put down which universities you thought you'd like to go to, so I put down Harvard first. And amazingly it worked out. It was one of the most rewarding years of my life. Truthfully, I had never before worked so hard at my studies. At

Oxford my tutor, who was Eric Kemp of blessed memory (who became the long-serving Bishop of Chichester), would say, 'What are you doing besides work?' and I would say, 'How do you mean?' and he would reply, 'It's all very well, all this work, but you want to do something to relax.' So I took up rowing, and Eric Kemp also organized borstal camps in the long vacation, for undergraduates and borstal lads to mix. So we used to go and camp on the Yorkshire moors in the summer. At Harvard, they didn't tell you to go rowing. It really was tough and they really made you work hard, but it was very rewarding. I managed to sign up as a seminarian in a parish, Salem, where they burnt the witches. So one evening a week there was a course at the Episcopal Theological School, and then on Sunday I had a placement in Salem parish. They really spoilt me; they had a big chart in the parish hall as to who was going to have the seminarian for lunch on which Sunday. If you're English they just love it, so I was looked after incredibly well. It kept my sanity, because it was really hard work – late at night and everything – but I could look forward to having a Sunday, which was a bit more relaxing.

Your first curacy was rather a change, wasn't it?

I suppose it was a bit like downtown Boston rather than what I was used to in the countryside. I got back to Cuddesdon and had to finish my time there – in fact Robert Runcie by that time had gone to be Bishop of St Albans – and the Vice-Principal decided where he'd like to send me. I won't say where it was. I went to have a look and came back and was so depressed, and thought I don't want to go and work there. At Cuddesdon in those days, although I was an ordinand in the Diocese of Salisbury, the college placed its own students, not your diocese. The college has the patronage of two parishes in London, one St John the Divine, Kennington, and the other St John the Evangelist, East Dulwich. The Principal was going to the induction of the new vicar at East Dulwich and said, 'Why don't you come with me, because you never know, he might be looking for a curate.' So I went to St John the Evangelist, East Dulwich, and thought, 'Wow, I'd love to work in South London; it's completely different from my experience growing up in the country.' So then I cornered the vicar just after he'd been instituted and said, 'Are you looking for a curate?' In those days the parish had two curates, and he said, 'I shall be looking for a curate, when are you available?' So it was that I ended up in South London, in Southwark Diocese, and had a fantastic four years there as a curate.

That was where you ran the reggae club.

Yes, and that's what got me my subsequent job in Cambridge. East Dulwich was a very interesting community – in fact, the curate lived in Peckham and the vicar lived in East Dulwich! It was an amazingly mixed community; the PCC had on it the stationmaster of the Elephant and Castle, a lovely West Indian lady, who had been in my confirmation class, who was a conductress on the number 63 bus, and the Clerk to the House of Commons. We didn't even know it was the Clerk to the House of Commons who lived up on Champion Hill until I once turned on the one o'clock news to hear Robin Day say, 'We're going to talk to Sir Barnett Cocks, Clerk to the House of Commons', and I thought, 'That's funny, Barnett Cocks is the chap I gave those stewardship envelopes to.' Lo and behold, he was indeed the Clerk to the House of Commons. So what he made of the PCC at St John's, East Dulwich, I cannot imagine. We did have a problem with the youth club, in that we couldn't attract any black children at all. It occurred to me, 'Why don't we have a reggae club, that might do it?' This very nice West Indian lady, whose brother became the Dean of Barbados, offered to come along and give me a hand. In fact, she and her husband both helped out and we set up a reggae club. We started off in the vestry, would you believe it, but it got so popular and so big we had to move down the road to the parish hall. One problem was that they would kick the Coke cans along the street at 11 o'clock at night, which did not endear us to the neighbours. But the club was popular and worked very well.

The other thing that I remember about St John's, East Dulwich, was setting up a Children's Week. There were a lot of children at the local schools who never had a summer holiday, so we devised a holiday week in the summer. We could take 200 children, and we put them in groups of 50 and had various activities. We hired one of the Inner London Education Authority playing fields; we twinned with a parish in sunny Sussex by the sea, who would take children for a day and give them a seaside experience; we took over a hall and did an art group. There were four different activities and during the week they swapped around. We raised several thousand pounds from livery companies the first year; the event pressed the right button. We were able to do this Children's Week for 200 children in a quite organized and careful way, and we recruited students and gave them accommodation. We advertised in *The Times* for our students – and then we'd give them a little honorarium, as well as accommodation, and it worked extremely well. But having got the money, it was wonderful being able to spend it not on keeping the building up but on doing something in the community. Obviously you can't keep going back to the livery companies for more money every year, so we came up with the idea of having a community carnival at the end of the week. One of the things they did with their artwork activities during the week was to make 'Jonah and the Whale', or something that could be a centrepiece for the carnival. Of course, South London is great for carnivals. Someone who worked for W H Smith used to get huge posters done for us and we found all sorts of people who would do things, and provide marquees, and someone who could bring a steam engine, and loads of bands; we even had a gigantic fairground organ which came all the way from Hampshire, which started my interest in fairground organs.

The carnival began with a huge procession all around the parish, and ended on Goose Green, adjacent to the church. On the Sunday at 9.30 a.m., the same time as the weekday activities had started, we had a carnival service, and of course they all turned up. So we had the bonus of the church being absolutely packed. I can remember on one occasion there was a circus clown who was due to come and take the sermon slot. Unfortunately, he got cold feet and didn't turn up, and that's the only other time I've had an interview like this. I ended up having to do the sermon, for which I was totally unprepared. But South London was great fun, and actually it was a bit like being brought up in the country because it was like a series of villages. I went around all the shops in Lordship Lane asking for prizes for the carnival and everybody coughed up. The carnival was a great community event; it raised enough money to fund the next year's children's week, which itself was a tangible piece of Christian service and witness.

Then you went to Cambridge and you met a very famous religious figure who became quite a formative influence on you.

Yes, it's strange, I went from South London to Great St Mary's, Cambridge. It was unusual for a curate post in those days as it was advertised with a competitive interview process. It wasn't one where somebody headhunted you. Stanley Booth-Clibborn, who was a descendant of General Booth, was the vicar; he was quite demanding on himself and his curates and very much into the Church and social issues, and I thought, 'I don't stand a chance with all these people being interviewed for the job.' I'm sure it was my reggae club which made him think, this chap's run a reggae club so perhaps he'll be all right. So I ended up at Great St Mary's, Cambridge, as a curate, and at one point the vicar had a sabbatical in Africa. By that time I was the senior curate – there were two of us – and so left in charge. We had a galaxy of amazing preachers come to Great St

Mary's in those days, mainly at 8.30 p.m. on Sunday nights – Robin Day preached, Cardinal Hume came, Michael Ramsey came – it was like this week after week. The vicar had been trying to get Mother Teresa. While he was on leave, it turned out she was to receive an honorary degree from the Duke of Edinburgh who was the Chancellor of the University. She agreed to come and preach at the University Church (Great St Mary's) where I was curate, after she'd received her honorary degree. As the vicar was in Africa, I got the joy of looking after her. I've still got the photograph; it's ironic, it's taken by the dustbins! So, there's me proudly receiving Mother Teresa at the church with the dustbins beside us, but it's appropriate somehow. The church was absolutely packed, with people sitting in the aisles and all across the floor of the chancel. Mother Teresa was quite a small person, so as I escorted her into church for the service and to preach, she had to pick her way through all the people who were there. It must have felt a bit like Calcutta! She preached for 40 minutes in English, which, when you think English was, whatever it was, her fifth language or something, it was a remarkable sermon. Most of it was about 'I'm not telling you to come and be kind to people in India, I'm telling you to come and be kind to people who sit next to you and who live down your street'. After her 40 minutes there was a collection and I said, 'Please be generous', and, of course, the poor churchwardens ended up with stacks of money falling out of their collecting bags. People even put their rings into the bag. All this despite the fact Mother Teresa had been very straight really, she hadn't tried to pull any emotional tricks. After the service somebody came up to me and said, 'I'm a businessman and I'd like to meet Mother Teresa, because I want to give her a cheque.' So I said to her, 'Mother, there's somebody here who'd like to give you a cheque', and she said to me, 'Well, tell them to put it in the bag like everybody else – I don't see people for money.' And I thought, 'Oh dear, how do I explain this?' But she was quite tough, with great integrity. When she left she said, 'If you come to Calcutta, do come and see me.' In those days Great St Mary's did a transcript of the sermon, so when it had been typed up by the secretary, I then sent it to her with a little thank-you note saying, 'It was a huge privilege, and here's the sermon.' She wrote back and said, 'I can't believe I went on for that long, God help the poor people who had to listen to me.' The letter was on a scrap of paper in biro – I've kept the letter. Apparently she often wrote them in the middle of the night. It ended up something like, 'God bless you in your vocation. Do you know why Jesus' head is bent upon the cross? Because he stoops to kiss us.' Then just, 'with love from Mother Teresa'.

As it happened, I ended up going to Calcutta the Christmas following,

completely by serendipity. The Cambridge Mission to Delhi was celebrating its centenary – which must have been in 1977 – and the college
chaplains were invited to apply to go. By that time I had been appointed
to be Chaplain at Jesus College (my three-year curacy had come to an
end), and somehow or other I ended up being chosen. The fact that I was
at the end of my curacy but with a chaplaincy still to go, I think they
thought, 'Well, we'll send him out because he's got a few years ahead of
him.' So I went out to Delhi for six weeks, and then spent two weeks in
Calcutta. I went to see Mother Teresa. I thought, having made contact
with her, 'She's got so much to do, she probably won't even remember
that she ever came to Cambridge.' But she said, 'Please come and see me
and I'll give you three-quarters of an hour.' So Lorna and I turned up at
the appointed time when we were in Calcutta and we went to see her.
She'd just come back from a cyclone in Andhra Pradesh – a horrendous
cyclone, where she'd been rolling up her sleeves and getting on with dis-
tributing aid – and that afternoon she had 90 novices she was admitting
to her community. I'm sure she's a saint just for this – she managed to
give us three-quarters of an hour of her time as if there was nobody else
in the world but us. I think to be able to do that, given the pressure she
was living under, was absolutely amazing. She listened and talked, and
at the end she just said, 'You're so lucky to have a vocation and you
must honour it, and God bless you in it. We've had our 45 minutes; we'll
say hello to Jesus and then I must move on.' We went to a chapel, had
a prayer, and then she blessed us and off we went. That three-quarters
of an hour had been totally ours, and the headmistress in her, for that
is what she had been, had the authority to conclude it and the gift of
being able to move on. So I'm sure that was a gift of some sanctity. We
then visited her Home for the Dying, which is in the Kali temple. It's a
working temple at the front, and we saw a family who brought a goat to
sacrifice to the goddess. Clearly they weren't a very rich family. The goat
was a gift, it was a genuine offering, and I think it looked as if the boy
was at puberty and that it was an offering at a moment of transition in
life. So we watched this goat being offered, and then we went round to
the back of the temple, and there were Mother Teresa's sisters in what
was like a cow shed with lots of little camp beds. In fact, although all the
people who came to the Home for the Dying were picked up from the
streets dying, a large percentage of them got better, amazingly. I thought
it would be pretty desperate and pretty awful going in. It was early in the
New Year when we were there. A lot of the sisters were just sitting by
these people in their beds, having fed them, holding hands and waving
sparklers. There was a great sense of joy, not misery, which transformed

everything. I've often thought in the light of that visit: what's Christian faith about? In the end it's allowing ourselves to offer our lives to God. Do you see your life as an offering, or do you see it as something for self-satisfaction? That temple was a real lesson; those people had come with their goat to sacrifice as a gift, and there was Mother Teresa showing that, in the end, the gift is what you do with your life and making it your offering. It was quite a signal.

You also showed a very practical bent at your next posting. I think, while you were there, the Bishop offered to give you a reference as a project manager?

It's funny how things work out. I was ordained in Southwark Cathedral by Bishop Mervyn Stockwood, who had previously been Vicar of Great St Mary's, Cambridge, and it was through him I ended up applying to Great St Mary's. He married Lorna and me at Great St Mary's; we met in Cambridge. I always thought I would probably go back and work in South London. When your children are young, there are some very good primary schools, so that would have been not unreasonable for the family. However, a Pharaoh arose that knew not Joseph. There was a new bishop and I wrote to say I'd like to return and he wrote back and said, 'No, the borders are closed, we don't take foreigners', and I protested 'I'm not a foreigner, I was ordained there.' Anyway, there was no going back to Southwark, and I ended up going to Northamptonshire as vicar of the market town with the racecourse at Towcester. It was strange, really, because I looked at a possible parish in Edmonton – the Bishop of Edmonton was Bill Westwood, and he was quite miffed with me after being offered the job, for turning it down because I didn't think it was right. He even came into my room at Jesus College in Cambridge; with a bang, bang on the door, he demanded, 'Why have you turned my job down?' I explained as diplomatically as possible that I had said 'Yes' to Towcester. Lo and behold, his next job was to be Bishop of Peterborough, so he turned up as my bishop anyway.

It's a strange story. I quite like projects, and was very happy organizing reggae clubs and a carnival, but ended up, arriving at this market town, faced with a different sort of project. There was a 'For Sale' notice outside the vicarage. Needless to say it was a lovely Queen Anne vicarage, but with a huge Victorian extension on the back, and I was told, 'You must understand that if you accept the job, the diocese can't possibly afford to keep the vicarage.' The problem was that even before I'd arrived one of the GPs had rung me up and said, 'It's horrendous, they're going to sell the vicarage, what are you going to do about it?' My response was,

'Can I get there first, please?' In fact, I soon discovered the way Towcester is laid out – there's an historic marketplace in the centre, and then loads of new housing estates that are satellites. In this historic centre you've got the town hall, the vicarage, the church, the old chantry house, and the post office. Heavens, if you're the parson for the community, it couldn't say it better with the post office on one side, the town hall the other, and bang on the market square. So I said to the initial bishop, who was Bill Westwood's predecessor, 'Look, I don't want to be a vicar who spends his time arguing about a vicarage, but they've got it wrong, it ought to stay here.' And he said, 'Well, as far as I'm concerned you can have a fight for it, so why don't you give it a go.' Then he retired and Bill Westwood arrived, so I wrote to Bishop Bill and said, 'Look, I'm stuck with this problem, and frankly if I haven't got the Bishop's support, I don't want to take it on.' Bishop Bill wrote me a letter a fortnight later and said, 'I was travelling through to Brackley, I stopped off at Towcester, I put a scarf around my neck and had a good look around and I take your point: go for it.' So we had quite a to-ing and fro-ing with the Church Commissioners about it. Now, as it happened, two old ladies lived in the adjacent chantry house, which was privately owned. One was 98, and she was one of the first lady doctors who had trained in Aberdeen, and she used to say to me, 'I'm looking after my elderly sister', who was 100. I can remember when it was the older sister's hundredth birthday, this nice GP had written to me and said, 'You better go and visit, because it's her hundredth birthday, and I think they want to leave the chantry house to the Church'. The 98-year-old was a bit of a spiritualist. She'd been a Congregationalist I think, and as I was chatting to her she said, 'I just feel that this house belongs spiritually with the Church and I'm going to leave it to the parish church'. And I thought, 'That's really lovely.' So, when she died it did indeed come to the parish. We consequently ended up with three projects running simultaneously; the tower had bits falling out of it, we were sitting in this dilapidated vicarage, and now we were left a chantry house falling to bits. So in the end, I said to the Bishop, 'If we throw the vicarage in, we'll raise the money and do the whole lot and the Church Commissioners won't have to pay for it.' So, great discussions ensued with the Church Commissioners. Eventually we got hold of the 'Green Guide', and interestingly the seventeenth-century vicarage was the same as the Church Commissioners' Green Guide standard except it had this huge, what the Prince of Wales might have called a 'Victorian carbuncle', on the back of it. Anyway, one of those eminent preachers at Great St Mary's had been Sir Ron Harris, who was then the boss of the Church Commissioners. I wrote and reminded him that he had said in his sermon that if people had a problem with the Church Commissioners they should get in touch with him. He responded by sending a committee down to the parish to assess the situation. However, the local Parsonages Board wouldn't let them report, so in the end the Church Commissioners rang me up and said, 'We'll give you a private report so you know what we think.' So one All Saints' Day I went up to London and they explained that the division scheme I'd put forward they were unhappy with, saying people sharing houses never get on, and all this, that and the other. However, they advised that if we could lose the back and the associated valley roof, it would be the right square footage and they'd support it. So I came back knowing the inside story. We went for planning permission to demolish the back and there was quite a furore. I'll always remember going to the Local History Society, who were one of the consultees in this process, and the planning request had gone in, and the chairman of the Local History Society said, 'Well, we certainly don't want to hear any more about this; we shan't be supporting part of the vicarage being demolished.' Somebody, who had done quite a lot of work for the society, very kindly interrupted, 'Well you've got the Vicar here. I think we should at least hear from him why he's supporting it.' So I said, 'Either you have a merchant banker in the vicarage as it is, or you lose the back of it and have a long-term solution for the Vicar's residence, which the Church Commissioners would support.' They had a vote and the society overwhelmingly voted to support the demolition plan, and the chairman and the treasurer banged their books on the table and walked out! I'm left thinking, 'What have I done?' Then the planning officer said he couldn't possibly support it, but there was a really enterprising chairman of the planning committee who came to the 8 o'clock service who said, 'We will find a solution.' However, then the Diocesan Parsonages Board suggested that 'If you give permission to demolish the back of it, we can still sell it with permission, because with the planning permission it may be worth even more.' However, the shrewd chairman of the planning committee came up with a plan: 'You are the freeholder as the Vicar, and we can give planning permission tied to a freeholder, not to the property. It makes sense, planning-wise, that the Vicar lives there, so it would make sense to tie it to you.' So he said, 'Come to the next planning meeting, sit in the public gallery. I'll propose that we override the planning officer, and that the permission is given to you only, so if you do move out, it'll lapse.' Amazingly, the Planning Committee voted to support it, so in fact it all went ahead, and then we had quite a big appeal to sort out the tower, to turn the chantry house into a parish centre and to modernize the vicarage, which we did without any financial help from the Church

Commissioners. Bishop Bill Westwood came for the grand service in December to open it, and Princess Margaret was coming, and it was all very exciting. We had the police putting the barriers out, sniffer dogs in the vicarage the night before Princess Margaret was coming, and we had 500 mugs celebrating Princess Margaret's visit. The phone went, and I answered it. The police were everywhere around the house, and it was a newspaper: 'Vicar, she's not coming, is she?' And I said, 'Pardon?' 'Yes, Princess Margaret, hasn't anyone told you?' So I thought, 'Oh dear', and I said, 'I have nothing else to say.' So I put the phone down and rang the Lord Lieutenant, and he said, 'Yes, I'm sorry, she's said she's not well and she's pulled out. I've been trying hard to find another Royal and I haven't succeeded. My last hope is Princess Alice.' She was the same age as the Queen Mother, and she lived, in those days, in Northamptonshire. And the good soul, aged 86, said, 'Yes, I'll turn out tomorrow.' So instead of Princess Margaret, we had Princess Alice, but she was absolutely brilliant. I'll always remember her going into the new chantry house/ parish centre, where the ladies were making tea in the kitchen, and into the kitchen went Princess Alice. They all pulled their hands out of the Fairy Liquid and curtseyed. She was marvellous, and we gave her a little present at the end, which was a piece of embroidery. She said, 'I shall ring Princess Margaret tonight to tell her what you've given me and make her jealous.'

That was good training for your next posting when you went to be, initially, Provost of St Edmundsbury Cathedral, where you had a really great project to pull off, which was touch and go.

It was spooky, really. Your bishop, if he's so minded, can send you to see the Archbishops' Appointments Secretary, in those days located at Westminster, and I'd been sent. I had this two-hour interview and then at the end he said, 'Well, you may or may not ever hear any more of this.' I can remember one of his questions was, 'Of all the jobs in the Church of England, what would you like to do?', and I said, 'Well, if you really want to know, I've always fancied being the Vicar of St Mary Redcliffe, Bristol.' He responded: 'Well, what about a cathedral?' I said, 'No, I'm not a cathedral man; I've never really thought of cathedrals', and left it at that. Then within six weeks or so, a letter came through the door from John Dennis, who was the Bishop of St Edmundsbury and Ipswich, saying, 'I'm inviting two or three people to come and see and be seen, to be Provost of St Edmundsbury. Would you like to be one of them?' Fancy me having said 'No' to the idea of a cathedral, and the first thing that happens is there's a letter through the letterbox about a cathedral.

But I thought I'll go and have a recce, and reflected that perhaps he had been quite clever – it's a parish church cathedral, and not unlike St Mary Redcliffe! So I put my hat in the ring and then ended up with the task. What I didn't know was that I was going to get a remarkable letter in my first week there, but what I did know was that the cathedral architect had been Stephen Dykes Bower – who was, in many ways, the last of the bearers of the tradition of the great Victorian architects. He had been the surveyor of the fabric at Westminster Abbey, and also had St Edmundsbury in his care, for which in the 1960s he had designed and built an inspired extension.

The Diocese of St Edmundsbury and Ipswich is basically the diocese of Suffolk. It was created in 1914, half of it coming from Norwich Diocese and half from Ely Diocese; originally the two areas represented East and West Suffolk, each with its own focus in Ipswich and Bury St Edmunds. Like much else we do backwards, Bury St Edmunds is identified ecclesiastically as St Edmundsbury, so the new diocese was named St Edmundsbury and Ipswich. It was decided by act of Parliament that the cathedral should be in Bury St Edmunds but the bishop's residence in Ipswich, so everybody felt that they had received something. There remained a further issue to settle: there were two substantial churches, both contenders for the dignity of the cathedral, sitting in a single churchyard in the centre of Bury St Edmunds – St Mary's and St James's. For various reasons they decided in the end St James's would be the cathedral, but having chosen St James's, it needed a lot of architectural work to turn it into a cathedral, and what with the First World War, the recession and the Second World War, no one got round to doing that work until the 1960s, and Dykes Bower was responsible for it. He managed to demolish the Gilbert Scott chancel – it wouldn't be allowed now – and all the stones were lost, so it was never rebuilt elsewhere. Instead of the Gilbert Scott small chancel, Dykes Bower designed a beautiful and more spacious quire, where there could be canons' stalls, and a crossing, which was supposed to have a tower above it, where a nave altar was located, so it's the only English cathedral, I think, designed to have a nave altar. Dykes Bower's design transformed a parish church into the architectural stature of a cathedral. However, the money ran out before they could build the tower, the north transept, and a further intended chapel and cloisters. Work stopped at the end of the 1960s. My predecessor at Bury (Ray Furnell, who became Dean of York) had built a cathedral centre, so when I arrived it had some really good modern facilities. The intended opening for a north transept had builder's felt and battening to secure it from the weather, so at first sight it could be mistaken for a building site. Dykes

Bower had just left spikes sticking out of the stump of a tower, so it did look terribly unfinished and rather ugly.

Dykes Bower had sent me a letter saying, 'Would you like to come and visit me?', when he knew I was appointed, and the only thing I thought I would do before I was installed was to go and visit him. He was then quite frail, and in his letter he had said, 'It takes me until about 3 o'clock in the afternoon to get up, so don't come before then.' I had my date all fixed, and sadly he died two weeks before I was due to go. He may have been going to tell me something that I discovered within the first week of taking up the job. A letter came from his solicitor saying, 'Stephen Dykes Bower has left £3 million in trust, which is to be spent on extensions to St Edmundsbury Cathedral, if the Dean co-operates with the intended vision, otherwise it is to go to Westminster Abbey.' It was quite unbelievable. Every time I met Michael Mayne, who was the Dean of Westminster, he'd say, 'Have you lost the money yet? Is it coming to us?' And I'd say, 'No, not if I can help it.' Dykes Bower was very canny; he set up trustees and an architectural adviser, and the money was drip-fed – we had to convince the trustees that we were spending it appropriately. Dykes Bower knew that even that generous sum would not complete a tower, so his instructions were that the north transept should be built and the chapel constructed, and any remaining money be spent on cloisters. Now, at the time, there was the Millennium Commission, an arm of the National Lottery, set up to celebrate the turn of the millennium with appropriate architectural symbols. It is very rare to have a gift of £3 million, and the existence of the Millennium Commission gave us the possibility of using it as a lever to achieve much more. We persuaded the trustees that if it included a tower, that would be fine, so long as the other things Dykes Bower specified were done as well. So we put in to the Millennium Commission the project 'to complete the cathedral' with a north transept, chapel, tower and some cloisters. It was a £12 million project, with the possibility of the Commission funding 50 per cent. In other words, should we be successful, the Cathedral would need to raise an additional £3 million in order to achieve the whole project.

The next problem was a design for the tower. There was one that Dykes Bower had done to a 'Low Countries' design, but it was turned down by the Millennium Commission. We then had a seminar to try to resource a design, but it didn't instantly come up with anything very marvellous. We went back in with another Dykes Bower design that was in the repertoire which had been hurriedly put together by Dykes Bower, and he had not greatly favoured it. The Millennium Commission turned that one down. An unknown outcome of the seminar was some homework being done by associates of Stephen Dykes Bower, which was announced through *The Times*. The architectural correspondent Marcus Binney ran an article entitled something like 'Soaring Solution for St Edmundsbury Cathedral', and a hitherto unseen design for a tower was illustrated – I just couldn't believe it. The first reaction was everybody being hurt at not being consulted, but then the beauty of the design began to speak. At the same time, there was a full-page article in *Private Eye*, which was sending up the Dome and saying that millennium projects lacked inspiration, and yet they turned down the opportunity of a cathedral in Bury St Edmunds. I think the Dykes Bower supporters probably had some friends at court, which meant *Private Eye* published this. It was the final weeks of the final round for applications. I cut both articles out and sent them to Tony Blair, and just said, 'This is the last chance for the St Edmundsbury project. There is the opportunity to do something really lasting for the millennium, and we can't actually get any support for it.' At the same time, we went to see Eric Sorensen, who was then the Chief Exec of the Millennium Commission, and his message was that as we had been turned down twice, it would be realistic to withdraw our application. I said, 'I don't see why I should withdraw. Why don't you shoot me and give me the application to take home?' He said, 'Well, I can't do that legally, if you don't withdraw then it's got to stay there.' My response was, 'Well, in that case I'll leave it, and you've got my phone number.' So I left it with him. I don't know quite what happened, whether it was sheer luck or whether the Prime Minister's office did intervene, because Tony Blair was quite pro doing some religious things with the millennium money, but I suddenly got a phone call from the Millennium Commission, with only three weeks to go, saying, 'Will you come and see us at once?' They showed considerable interest in the design from *The Times*, and said, 'If you want us seriously to consider this we'll have to have some proper plans; you'll have to articulate the justification, you'll have to have the quantity surveyor's report, and all the other necessary paperwork.' We pulled all of this together for the deadline, but not without strained professional relationships, and the day before they were due to announce the awards the architect withdrew the copyright on his design. I shall never forget processing out of Evensong one evening, in a dignified way and very calm, and the Head Verger said, 'The Millennium Commission is on the phone.' He thrust a mobile into my hand. I thought he was joking. It was Eric Sorensen, 'What the hell's going on? I have a letter from your architect withdrawing your design.' I said, 'Well, don't worry, he wants to see it done as much as the rest of us and we'll get the permission.' There was an abrupt reply: 'That's all I wanted to hear, thank you.' He put the phone down. The next morning a fax came through the cathedral office line from the Millennium Commission saying, 'Your £12 million project was awarded £6 million, on condition you can get the copyright on the design within three months. Please attend a press conference at 12 noon today at the Angel Hotel, Bury St Edmunds.' It took me six months to get the copyright settled, but the Millennium Commission held on. So it meant we had a £12 million project, £3 million from Dykes Bower, £6 million from Millennium Commission, and then we raised the other, as it turned out in the end, £3.5 million. It took most of my time there to complete it, and the letter from Tony Blair summoning me at the Queen's pleasure to Winchester arrived the weekend that Prince Charles, who was our Patron, was at St Edmundsbury Cathedral for the Celebration Service for the completion of the Millennium Tower and associated works. I was completely churned up. I was 59, and thinking that if I'm going to move I've got to get on with it, but it would be really nice to enjoy the achievement and not leave the moment it was completed. And how do you tell people when you've just raised all the money and everything together, that you're about to leave them all?

What swung your decision?

I think it was reflecting that if I'm going to do another job, I've got to get on with it. I'd done 11 years at Bury by that time, and thought perhaps somebody else should have a go.

And maybe Winchester will have another £20.5 million appeal to do?

Well, whereas I was interviewed for Bury St Edmunds, I didn't know my name was in for Winchester. My first inkling of what was going on was when the letter arrived from Tony Blair saying, 'The Queen has approved your nomination to Winchester, I hope you will accept. Please get in touch with my Appointment Secretary.' So I then had to ring the Appointment Secretary. You weren't allowed to come near the cathedral; you weren't allowed, in those days, to meet any of your future colleagues. What you had was the insight which the Crown Appointments Secretary had gleaned as to what he thought the challenges were. I did say to him, 'What about appeals?' 'No appeals,' he said. 'Nobody has mentioned that.' And then obviously you need to meet the bishop as a priority. Strangely enough, Bishop Michael Scott-Joynt had been, under the Runcie era, on the staff at Cuddesdon Theological College, and I'd seen him only once or twice since. He was the youngest member of staff when I was a student at Cuddesdon – and then, lo and behold, we met up again with me as his potential dean. I always remember Michael saying to me,

'We can't meet in Winchester at Wolvesey, because people will spot us and they'll guess what's going on. We can't meet at the House of Lords, it's too public. Let's be really incognito and go to 10 Downing Street.'

One of the things you do regularly is you take tours, particularly to the Middle East. What sparked all that?

Well, there have been two avenues in a way. As a student chaplain I used to take groups to Taizé, and used to quite enjoy that. Taizé is a religious community in France, in the beautiful Burgundy hills near Cluny. It was a very inspiring community with which to spend a week, and still is. In the 1970s, during the summer, there were 10,000 young people there each week. It was a great experience to take a group of students and be part of an international community and share the Brothers' religious life for a week in the simplicity of tents, with beautiful worship three times daily, shared basic meals, discussion, and meeting people. So taking pilgrimages was something that got into the bloodstream. Then, when I was Vicar of Towcester, someone said, 'Couldn't we have a pilgrimage to the Holy Land?', and I thought, 'Why not?' So we did some research, found a particular firm in Bristol, a family firm run by a Baptist family, who were very helpful and allowed you to choose your itinerary – you didn't have to have a set package. They would put it together for you. We had a parish pilgrimage, which was for ages 8–80. Quite a few young families came, and quite a few more senior people came. I think it was quite transformative for all of us who went on it. I hadn't realized how significant it would be. It was an eye-opener being in the Holy Land, in many different ways. Jerusalem is a city holy to three major world faiths, so the peace of Jerusalem remains key to world peace. There is the contemporary dilemma, which you cannot escape, and by worshipping with our Anglican brothers and sisters who are Arab congregations there are many heart-wrenching stories shared. A visit to Bethlehem is an encounter with deep tensions. Despite all this, it remains a place where faith is refreshed. You think that, 2,000 years on, the landscape will be different and there won't be much left that connects you to the biblical tradition, but in fact it couldn't be more opposite. Galilee is extraordinarily beautiful, and Tiberius remains the only major town – as it was in the time of our Lord – on the edge of the Sea of Galilee. Galilee is surprisingly unspoilt, and to have a Eucharist overlooking Galilee as the sun is setting is an amazing emotional experience. With my farming background, I had often read the New Testament and wondered, 'What's happened to God as Creator in all this?' When you visit, the penny drops – as one Franciscan put it, the geography of the Holy Land is the fifth Gospel.

You suddenly realize, with all the fishermen stories, the riot of spring flowers that 'excel Solomon in all his glory', the sheep and the goats being led out, the olive trees and the fig trees, the New Testament is loaded with the geography and the locality of Galilee. As one Jewish scholar has expressed it, Jesus is 'a child of the Galilee'. Once you have been to the Holy Land you can't read the New Testament again without the power of the geography coming back. And I find Jerusalem incredibly moving, despite all the signs of tension. I suppose the Old City, with its walls and narrow alleys, does have a lot of atmosphere to it. Then you've also got the original Jerusalem, the City of David, which Dame Kathleen Kenyon, who was a great English archaeologist, really discovered with her hand-bag single-handedly, and said, 'We're going to dig here.' And they found that it was the original City of David, and that's been hugely dug now. And there is the Church of the Holy Sepulchre, in all likelihood the place where Christ was crucified, and the location of the tomb and the place where the mystery of the resurrection was first witnessed. The Garden Tomb, which is an Anglican set-up, although without claim to authenticity, does give a sense of what the Holy Sepulchre site would originally have looked like before it was built over.

I am fascinated by the geography of the Holy Sepulchre site. It was an eighth-century BC limestone quarry, which was reopened by Herod the Great before becoming abandoned again. Once understood in this way, you see how it was that the crucifixion and the burial site could be so near to each other. There is an outcrop of rock which was never harvested by the quarry men because it was cracked and flawed, and so stuck out like a platform above the hollowed-out quarry; it would have provided a very suitable place for a visible public execution. Because you've got a quarry, you've got vertical cliffs in which there are a lot of first-century tombs carved into the limestone. An unused tomb nearby makes complete sense. So you've got the geography in one place of the crucifixion and burial. Once the quarry had been abandoned, after Herod the Great's time, debris would have accumulated in the bottom, which then produced the garden of St John's Gospel. So you have the biblical geography given a physical context. I'm convinced that geography also explains the significance that Psalm 118 acquired for the early Christians. It has got the verse about the stone which the builders rejected becoming the key cornerstone. It took on a new meaning in the light of the rejected Lord crucified on the rejected rock, but becoming the grounds of new hope in the resurrection. It may well point us to an annual liturgical marking of the death and resurrection of Christ at the site, from the first Christian Passover until the destruction of Jerusalem in AD 70. I am convinced that piece of geography gets as close to the resurrection as it is possible to be. The question to put to the resurrection of Christ is not 'Did it happen?' The New Testament wouldn't be here without it, and you almost touch it with the geography of the Holy Sepulchre. The question is, 'What was the significance of what happened?' And obviously if you're part of the Christian Church then what you bring with you is the interpretation of the resurrection as the initiative of God, as opposed to some freak or odd or other kind of token event. It is in the interpretation rather than the fact where faith takes over. So going to the Holy Land just bit me.

Over the years I've tried to expand the biblical context, so I have taken quite a lot of groups to Egypt, and there's lots about Egypt that connects with the Old Testament and its background. Another favourite destination is Jordan. If you join up Jordan and Sinai, then it is possible to include climbing up Mount Sinai on camels by night so that you're there at the top for the sunrise; it is an amazing experience. I did manage to take a group to Syria three years ago, before the present terrible civil war, and because Syria's tourism wasn't over-developed, people were incredibly welcoming. We went to visit the Patriarch of Antioch who lives in Damascus. Like the Bishop of Rome, the Patriarch of Antioch represents one of the great historic sees of Christendom. He arrived in his grand receiving chamber to meet our group saying, 'I'm 88 and I'm late.' One message we received was the good relations in Syria, then, between Christians and Muslims. He said, 'In the West you have dialogue, in Syria we get on and do things together.' It's so sad how all that's just broken up, so many lives destroyed and Christians frightened from the place where the faith was first established. Next week I'm taking a group to Greece in the footsteps of St Paul.

Questions from the audience

James, linking with what you've just been saying about the Holy Land, today there's a picture been posted on the Facebook website of a signed copy of the Bible. Who do you think would be the appropriate signator of the Bible, and why?

Well, Justin Welby, I suppose. There must be more behind this question of who signed it?

I imagine it was signed by the translator, some new translation, but whether it's appropriate the translator should sign the Bible, or perhaps someone else from biblical history should sign it, if that was possible, I just wondered what your opinion might be as to who the appropriate signator should be.

Well, even the twelfth-century Winchester Bible never got signed, did it? You think of these six artists who worked on it for a decade, they're anonymous. We don't know who they are and maybe being anonymous is quite important sometimes.

A few weeks ago, in the Sunday Telegraph, *there was a Matt cartoon on the front page of a middle-aged couple coming out of a service and the husband said, 'Lovely service, vicar, but I think you should leave God to the politicians.' In the light of David Cameron's recent comments, I wondered what your take on that was.*

I think that's interesting. I certainly would not want to leave politics to the politicians, so perhaps you shouldn't leave God to the Church either. I think it's very reasonable for the Church to have an influence on the way society develops. I was reflecting recently, as I was leading an assembly at St Swithun's School in Christian Aid Week, that often the Church is behind. For instance, we're catching up on the position of women – women have been doctors, women have been judges, women have been Queen in secular society – and the Church is perhaps about to catch up on women being bishops. But two areas where I think the Church has led, during my experience of ministry, is the hospice movement and world development issues. I reckon the hospice movement is partly due to the influence of Mother Teresa insisting on the dignity of people who are dying and that people aren't just economic units. If you really value people as children of God then their last hours, days, minutes, whatever it may be, are hugely significant. And then there was Dame Cicely Saunders who pioneered the hospice movement in the UK from her deeply Christian motivation. Now we take hospices for granted, and expect they'll be there, but they had to be pioneered, and I think the Christian conscience had a lot to do with that. The profile of world development owes a great deal to Christian compassion also. The Anglican communion gets a lot of bad press, but frankly keeping any family together is hard enough. When you've got a family across the world which is at hugely different places materially, economically and culturally, it is an enormous undertaking. For instance, the Anglican communion includes the UK, Uganda and North America, which all have vastly different perspectives and priorities. But one of the huge benefits of that global family is if one part hurts, another is aware of it. So if the price of coffee plummets in Tanzania or there's a civil war in South Sudan and huge swathes of the population are homeless, because we are a single communion, one body, one family, that information gets across. So I think there is a real Christian understanding that the answer to the question 'Who is my neighbour?' has to be global. The Church was quite early in picking that up, because of its international nature. Through Christian Aid Week, Tearfund, Cafod and various development agencies, the Christian conscience has had a huge impact in bringing that about. Now we've got UK Aid, and the commitment to 0.7 per cent of the Gross National Product ring-fenced for development. It seems to me that if that money is going to help people in Syria, if it's going to try and help women and girls who are victimized across the world, if it's going to try and sort things out in, say, a factory in Pakistan where maybe the garments there supply some of the shops in our high streets here, then UK Aid ought to be ring-fenced and is doing a very good job. It is perhaps the influence of the Christian conscience – maybe David Cameron is influenced by his Anglicanism. I did quote him on Easter Sunday in my sermon, saying that like most Anglicans he's not very regular about going to church, but it's rather helpful that it's there. So I hope politicians and faith do interact; it's vital that they do. And hopefully cathedrals can be part of that; surely that is what civic services, services for charities, legal services and Education Sunday are all about. They are all trying to celebrate the influence that faith can have on our nation.

I've never gone much for the Noah's Ark model of the Church, in which we're all in the ark and being saved from the rest going to perdition. I'm more into Jesus' idea of the presence of faith and the Church being the leaven in the lump. To return to the Creator bit again, that God's purpose is for the whole. When he calls people out for a special task, it must somehow be for the good of the whole. We are there to be leaven and salt so that in the end a whole world is offered to God.

I think that's a wonderful note on which to end this particular dialogue. In the previous dialogues you will remember that I've usually called on the Dean to thank the guest speaker, so I am very grateful to have this chance to say thank you to him. When I first tentatively suggested these dialogues to him he leapt on the idea, and he's written the most persuasive letters to the very distinguished panel of dialogue speakers we've had, which, clearly, they've all found irresistible. It is due to him that we have had such a distinguished group so far, and three more coming up in the Autumn. So I would like to say, very much, thank you, James, for all you've done for this, and hopefully it's aroused interest in the appeal, which was the whole point of the exercise.

9

Where all the great religions began

SIR MARK TULLY

It is a very great pleasure to introduce Sir Mark Tully. Most of you will have heard him from India, or here too with his other radio series, Something Understood. *I have been reading his books with great interest, and have listened to his broadcasts over the years with even greater interest. Mark, you were born in Calcutta, and you were there for the first several years before you came to our local school here at Twyford. Was that a cultural shock, or a weather shock, when you came to England after all the early years in India?*

I think it was more of a weather shock in a strange way, because our childhood in Calcutta was made as English as possible. The great fear of my parents was that we would in some way get 'Indianized'. So we were never allowed to speak or learn Indian languages; we had a European nanny whose main job was to stop us getting too close to the servants and learning Hindi from them, and that sort of thing. So when I came back here there were two big shocks. One was the weather, it was awful, it was about February or something like that and we came back to Winchester. The other shock was the fact that there were no servants – my mother doing the washing-up was a big shock.

Then you went to Marlborough. How was that?

Well, there are one or two Old Marlburians in the audience, so I had better be careful. I would say in my case not a success. That's all I would say.

As I have written in one of my books, the one thing I really enjoyed at Marlborough, and which I really took away from Marlborough, was the chapel and that has remained with me ever since. My love of the Anglican liturgy and Anglican worship, and indeed the Anglican Church, all comes from Marlborough College chapel. When I went back to Marlborough about five years ago to write a book called *India's Unending Journey*, which is stuff about my education, I was rather shocked to find that Marlborough, a school founded for the sons of the Anglican clergy, had one compulsory service a term, that was all. I went to that service and what so shocked me further was there was nothing Anglican about the service at all. It could have been Methodist or Baptist or any other, it had no liturgical shape at all. I thought that was a great mistake and was sad about it, and I wrote it in the book, and I haven't been back to Marlborough since.

Then you went to Cambridge to read theology. In fact, you intended to become a priest. What made you change your mind and take up broadcasting instead?

Well, my mind was changed for me to be honest, by the warden of the theological college who was a wonderful man, whom I was in contact with until he died, called Alan Webster. He went on to be Dean of St Paul's. There was a lovely occasion when I went to St Paul's and I was kneeling at the Communion rail and Alan was administering the Communion, and he saw me and he stopped and said, 'Hello, Mark, how are you? Come and see me afterwards for a chat', which I thought was lovely. But he said to me that he thought I wasn't really suited, and to be absolutely honest I didn't have the moral stability to be a priest, and the last thing I wanted to do was to let the Church down in any way. So between us we decided it would be much better if I did not go forward. But it was very amicable, and didn't in any way undermine my affection and love for the Anglican Church.

Then you joined the BBC and you went very quickly back to Delhi. Was that always your plan or was that by chance?

No, not at all, funnily enough. What happened was that first of all I went and worked for the Abbeyfield Society, which was a society for housing old people. I was in on the early days of that. I left that and I got a job in the personnel department of the BBC. I had to move from a lovely little cottage I was living in in Cheshire down to London, and I didn't like the move to London. I didn't like the personnel job because it was very boring indeed, and when the opportunity to go to Delhi was advertised

I put my name down for it and fortunately succeeded at the board. I thought I had wrecked it because during the board they said to me, 'You must speak very good Hindi, that will be very useful to you if you go out there.' Of course I had to say, 'I don't.' Then stupidly I said, 'But I can say Little Miss Moffat in Hindi.' And still I got the job. I think it was the hand of God, because after that India was open to me.

You do in fact speak very good Hindi now, though?

Well, not as good as it should be. One of the problems in India about Hindi, or any Indian language, you have to live at a certain level of society most of your time as a journalist. Everyone speaks to you in English, and it is really annoying when you carefully, in your best pronunciation, ask someone a question in Hindi and they come back and answer you in English.

You have written in your books quite a bit about Gandhi and Nehru, who were totally different both in character and in outlook, and also I think you said that Gandhi is now a prophet without honour in his own country. Is that true?

Yes, it is basically true. Gandhi is honoured in the letter, you might say, of national holidays and all the rest of it, but you certainly couldn't say he is honoured in the politics of the country. You couldn't really say he is honoured in economic planning or anything like that. You couldn't say, sadly, that he is honoured in the non-violence either.

How did he and Nehru really get on, or didn't they?

In one way they got on very well, because it was Gandhi who nom-inated Nehru, who chose Nehru to be his successor, but basically they were poles apart. Gandhi was a deeply religious man; Nehru claimed that he was agnostic, but strangely enough in his will he made a state-ment saying that he wanted to do something which was pretty Hindu, to have his ashes scattered on the Ganges. Nehru, in a sense, was much more practical than Gandhi, and Nehru did not at all share Gandhi's very fundamental belief that development should start in the villages, and be bottom up. Nehru wanted to have a powerful central government to control the direction in which the economy would develop.

Nehru wanted a secular state. Was that because he was afraid of tensions between the different religious communities?

Gandhi wanted a secular state very much. One of Gandhi's greatest dis-appointments was he wanted the Congress Party to be all-embracing, and that was why he was so strongly opposed to the Muslim League and to the demand for Pakistan. So they both wanted secularism, and both wanted it, I think, basically for two reasons. One for practical reasons, because for a country of such religious diversity if you didn't have secularism you could not say that one religion would be the dominant or the state religion or anything like that without causing an awful lot of trouble among the others. But the other reason was because they realized that this is the Indian tradition. If you think about it, India has been the historic home of all the world's great religions. Indian Christians believe that St Thomas came to India and preached in India and was martyred in Madras. Arab traders brought Islam to India at the time of the Prophet, and there were Jews in India. India has produced its own religions as well, and all these have lived side by side, basically on the principle that you let someone have their religion and you'll have your religion; you must not interfere in their religion, and they must not interfere in your religion. That long tradition of secularism was one which was one of the reasons why Nehru and Gandhi thought that India could be a secular country.

They went through a lot of communal violence at the time of Partition, and there have been further eruptions since, haven't there?

Yes. Funnily enough we have just been at the Cheltenham Festival today and had a session on Partition. You are absolutely right. One of the tragedies of Partition is it led to the transfer of population of probably 11 million people, and this was from areas particularly in Punjab. Before all the trouble over Partition broke out there was a famous Indian civil servant, British Indian civil servant, called Malcolm Darling, and he wrote of going through Punjab, and went on a tour to try and understand what the villagers in India were thinking about their future. He has a lovely description of some villages where people hardly knew whether they were Muslim or Hindu. So in that sort of socially cohesive, multi-religious culture you get all this dreadful violence breaking out over Partition. There are so many arguments over who was responsible for Partition, whether it was necessary or not, but I think we in Britain have to face the fact that we left India at a time when it was on the verge of chaos. We did not allow our soldiers to take part in the attempts to put down all the post-Partition violence, they were kept in their barracks. We probably did the whole job far too quickly. There are all sorts of reasons why over Pakistan, Nehru, Jinnah and Gandhi all made mistakes, but as Britain we also made grave errors at that time.

What about Indira Gandhi, Nehru's daughter? You are quite critical of her in your various books. She was regarded as the Great White Hope when she became Prime Minister. Was her response to the attack on the Golden Temple at Amritsar characteristic or was that something that shouldn't have happened?

Well, it was characteristic in a way, because one of the funny things about Indira Gandhi is that she, after winning the Bangladesh war, defeating the oldies in the Congress Party, to become sole leader of the Congress Party, winning an election handsomely, she was thought of as Queen of India. But within five years the country was in turmoil and she declared a state of emergency. If you look at her career, instead of being the decisive iron lady she was thought to be after the Bangladesh war, she was really something of a ditherer, and when things started to get almost out of control, she acted excessively. She acted excessively by breaking up the Congress Party, in my view. She acted excessively by declaring an emergency, and she was forced into taking some form of excessive action by dithering and dithering over the Punjab crisis as well.

But you said you went into the Golden Temple after that attack, and you've also said that you feel the presence of God in our great cathedrals here and in the great temples, including the Golden Temple of Amritsar. That of course was fatal for her?

Yes, well it was fatal to her and it is true, I've been to mosques, temples, churches, everything, and I would say that is one of the places where you really do feel the presence of God more than in many others. I mean it's silly to quantify it really, but it is the Golden Temple, so it was a great shock to anyone who loved that place that the army went in there and did what they did. It was really contrary to all Indira Gandhi stood for, in that it was contrary to her secularism and all the rest of it.

And was it inevitable that she would then be assassinated for that?

No, it wasn't inevitable. In fact it was an act of great courage which led to her assassination, because she was told that it made the Sikh communities so angry that she must not have a single Sikh in her security guards. She said, 'No, I am Prime Minister of all India, the Sikhs are part of India. I did that attack to stop people who wanted to separate Punjab from India and so I must have Sikhs in my bodyguard.' And, of course, it was two of those bodyguards who shot her.

I remember Peter Ustinov saying to me, he was waiting outside her house to interview her, he heard the shots, and then discovered what had happened, and the riots that he saw from his hotel room were the most terrifying he had ever seen.

Yes, there were the most dreadful riots, appalling riots broke out. They were basically not riots in one sense, in that a riot is very often between two different groups. This was just outright attacks on Sikhs, in Delhi; the police completely collapsed, the government collapsed, and the scandal of it all was that when eventually the government got itself organized and acted and called the army in, the whole thing stopped. So it was disgraceful, and it was something that has left something of a scar on the Sikh community, especially in this country. If you talk to Sikhs in this country they are as bitter over the riots as they are over the attack on the Golden Temple. Not all of them, but large numbers of them.

Then Rajiv Gandhi came to power. You've suggested that he was probably unfitted to take over the reins at that particular point.

He was inexperienced. He had never been a politician; he was educated at a very posh public school in India. Then he came to Cambridge, went to Imperial College, then became a pilot. In one of my books I write that you can hardly have a profession which is more removed from the population than someone sitting in an aeroplane 35,000 feet up. So until his younger brother died he was kept out of politics. When he was brought in he was very inexperienced, indeed he never really became a competent politician. He once said to me, 'You know, Mark, my trouble is I am not a very good politician.' But he was a man of great goodwill, and I believe if he had not been killed, and if he had become Prime Minister again things would have been very different. I remember my last interview with him, which was at 4 o'clock in the morning, when he was on a very slow journey from Jhansi to Kanpur, which should have taken about three hours but had taken all day because of the huge crowds who turned out to see him. I remember vividly him saying to me, 'You know, Mark, I want people like you to remember that I have learned my lessons and am going to be different this time.' So he knew that he had this weakness of not being a good politician.

You have argued that personality in Indian politics is even more important than, say, in this country or America.

Personality is very important, and we have just seen an example of that in the huge victory scored by Narendra Modi in the elections. A huge factor in that election has been Modi himself. He has had the personality and the communication skills, the ability to speak to convince masses of

Indians that he can bring change at last to India, revive the economy, end corruption, and all the rest of it. He is hugely responsible for, not solely, but hugely responsible for the amazing victory that the right-wing Hindu Bharatiya Janata Party (BJP) have won.

But you have held him responsible for the massacre in Gujarat when he was Governor?

I can't remember what I wrote. What I should have said was a lot of evidence pointed to his responsibility, but the fact is that there had been enquiries, there have been other enquiries as well, there was a special tribunal set up by the Supreme Court, and they found that Modi was not guilty of deliberately encouraging the riots or ordering the police to behave in the way that they did. It has to be said that, having seen the behaviour of the Delhi police in the Punjab riots and the Sikh riots in Delhi, it is possible to believe that the police would have on their own got out of control and behaved in the way that they did. So one can't be absolute about either things, but on the other hand one does have to say that Modi has been cleared by this special tribunal set up by the Supreme Court.

So are you optimistic about his government?

Well, I am not as optimistic as I would like to be, because I know that India is a very difficult country to govern. India has a very dysfunctional bureaucracy, and you cannot get things done in India unless you can get the bureaucracy to function. Modi has cracked the whip on the bureaucracy and told them you have got to get to work at 9 o'clock and all that. But still there is a lot of evidence that the bureaucracy goes to work, though what do they do at work? They can just push files around the place and try and avoid making decisions. A very small example. One of Modi's real crusades is to make India an investor-friendly destination, because the complications of investing in India are so great. The uncertainties of it are very great, and he wants to clear that up. One uncertainty is that when you come there and you do your tax deal you do it as the law stands at that time. Recently India has started introducing retroactive legislation, which means that suddenly, after you paid your tax in 1994 or 2004, whatever it is, you discover that you owe a whole lot more because this wretched other law has come into force. Now, Modi has categorically said taxation would have to be quite simple. I asked a senior member of the Tax Inland Revenue Service why this was not happening, and he had a very simple answer. He said the bureaucracy likes the status quo. So I think Modi has a big problem. As far as changing the bureaucracy, getting the bureaucracy to function, making India investment-friendly, he has all my support in wanting to do that, for what it's worth, which is not very much.

You have travelled around India a lot to the small villages as well as the big cities. How important is caste still in India?

Caste is changing. Caste is important, a lot of the politics particularly in North India is caste-based. You have caste parties, but it is changing undoubtedly, and there are several changes which are happening. Number one, of course, is urbanization, and urbanization is spreading way out of the big cities now. In an urbanized situation caste becomes less important. It is changing also because modern views are becoming more prevalent. It is changing in an interesting way in that those who are the underprivileged are now in some ways the privileged. Because they are the majority, either what we call other backward castes or former untouchables, or tribals. They are people who command tremendous clout now, because they vote by their castes, and they have got many more votes than the other castes have. So another way castes have changed is they are actually empowering the underprivileged or desperately underprivileged like the Dalits. Within the Dalit community you are getting a very prosperous section of that community, mainly because jobs and educational opportunities are reserved, a certain percentage of them have to go to the Dalits. And there is now an organization of Dalit capitalists, for instance. We had the thing that when I first went to India would have been absolutely unimaginable – we had not just the Dalit but a Dalit woman twice chief minister of India's most populous state. So that shows you the way it is changing, but still it becomes very important in people's lives, and the standard way to tell that is to look at the matrimonial advertisements even in a posh paper like the *Times of India*. Many of them will say, 'Brahmin boy wants Brahmin wife.' Quite often it will be a sub-caste as well: 'Very Sikh Akali Dal wants Sikh Akali Dal bride.' So it is still very much there, but it has changed quite dramatically.

How much is poverty related to caste?

Traditionally, yes of course, the Dalits were the poor people, and in a sense yes, now, because still those who don't get good education with the government are not getting educational opportunities, and that sort of thing. But I think poverty is much more due to maladministration, corruption, what I told you about the bureaucracy. India is still basically governed, administered rather than governed perhaps, in the same way as we the British administered it. When we were in charge, we had one main basic aim, which was to keep law and order. Whereas the Indian government is meant to be about developing, achieving some income parity, and bringing a great wave of new education, and all that sort of thing. Because of the government's inefficiency, corruption, slovenliness and all the rest of it, this doesn't happen as much as it could do.

How do you quantify the poverty in India? What percentage of the population would be considered poor?

There are so many different figures which are given for this, economists differ a great deal on it. So I never give a figure myself, but it is certainly into the hundreds of millions by many, and it's decreasing, there is no doubt about that. But the worrying thing is that the income disparity is still very wide. Poverty is decreasing, but it could decrease so much faster.

And now they are into space as well? That is a sharp contrast with that kind of poverty.

Yes. I had a long discussion on the BBC with someone whose name I will not mention about this, and he tried to tell me that it was disgraceful that India was wasting money on space. My answer was, and is, and would still be, that India – one of the things that Jawaharlal Nehru felt – as a colonial country had got scientific development at the rate that Britain wanted them to have basically. It had been allowed to industrialize at the rate Britain had wanted it to, and he got a degree in science from Cambridge, Trinity, and he was determined that India would never again be backward, and would be in the forefront of science. For my money, there are first of all many potential values of India's space science. There are values in the way that satellites can perform services, mapping territories, showing you what the state of harvests are, all sorts of things like that. There is also the prospect now where India will become a major launching station for satellites. So it is not entirely a commercial waste of time. India wants to increase its nuclear energy. So economically it is not nonsense. It is very insulting to say to India and Indians, 'Well, sorry boys, you are not ready to do this sort of thing', and that is effectively what people are saying when they talk about that. It is, I think, insulting.

There are also a lot of Indians who come to be educated in the West, either in this country or in America. You raise the prospect of what you call the 'baristocracy', people who studied law here who then go back to India and are part of the Marxist parties there.

Well, that was Calcutta. The West Bengal State was a Marxist state for a long time and it was dominated by people who the main economic adviser described to me as British returned baristocracy. They were – all of them. A chief minister who lasted for a long time was a member of one of the Chancery Lane Inns. So, yes, they were a big influence.

You have written quite a lot about religion, the Hindu majority, large Muslim minority, and Christians and other religions as well. You have said in one of your books that 'no religion has a monopoly of truth'.

Yes, this is something which I found very important and quite difficult for me to understand. When I went to India I was a good Anglican, in the sense of an observant Anglican, and I believed in the words of St John's Gospel, 'Jesus is the way, the truth and the light.' I went to the Cathedral for midnight mass at Christmas and the church was absolutely packed, and I was amazed to find there were Sikhs with turbans and Hindu ladies with red powder in their hair there, and all the rest of it. I came from Cambridge where my Roman Catholic friends would not come to an Anglican service; they wouldn't even come into an Anglican church, to be honest. I had friends in Trinity – they had that lovely chapel and they refused to go to it. So I was quite stunned by this when I saw it, and that is what started me to look into the religious traditions of India, and it is one of the truths in my view of all the religions which arose from India that truth is many-sided and there are many different ways to God. As I said, the India tradition is you believe in your way and you practise your way, but you don't stop someone else practising it. I remember the Bishop of Kingston came to India about three or four years ago, and I took him to meet a leading Muslim cleric and he said to him, 'I believe that for Christian theology religious pluralism is the great problem of the twenty-first century.' I personally solved it in a way which is probably theologically totally untenable, but I do not find any difficulty.

You describe going to one of the big Hindu festivals on the Ganges with hundreds of thousands of people there. What effect did that have on you?

I went again last year, it happens every 12 years. It is the biggest religious festival in the world; it is called the Kumbh Mela and millions of people come to it. It is very exciting. I spent about a week there both times. There are all sorts of different forms of Hinduism on display, there is even a group of Hindus who, when you go to them and say, 'What does bathing in the Ganges, which is the central ritual of the whole thing, mean?', they say, 'It is not different to having a bath under a tap.' So you have all this tremendous variety. You have the excitement of these huge crowds, and on the day of the big bathing it is quite frightening because the crowds are so huge. If you are doing recordings, and that sort of thing, you have to be right in with the crowds. Last year when we went, there was a bit of a stampede, and at one stage we really thought we were going to be pushed right back against the wooden barrier. It is a wonderful festival and I loved it, and it would be nice to think that I might be there in 12 years' time, but that might be a bit ambitious.

Have you ever felt endangered when you have been reporting?

Yes, mainly in riot situations. But, you know, I've not had any great acts of heroism to my credit. The most uncomfortable time I had was when it was almost obligatory that you had to go into Afghanistan with the Mujahideen, when the Soviets were there, and we were very roughly treated by the Mujahideen. They kept you walking all the time. If you are herding goats you make a noise like 'ssh sssh', and they would go behind us and make that noise. I said to the other guy who'd gone with me, 'They are treating us like goats.' When we came out I remember a lovely French chap from the AFP [Agence France-Presse], and he said, 'I know that we really are not meant to be on the side of the Soviets but after being with the Mujahideen for a week I think I am.'

The international problems in the China/India war almost destroyed Nehru, didn't they?

That was a tragedy and it was very badly handled by India, and Nehru had let the Defence Ministry get into a very bad state. It was in some ways a misunderstanding. It was a misconceived policy of India to have that forward policy, so if he wanted to move their troops and positions right up to the border that was misinterpreted by China, and it was a tragedy. One of the things about India I believe is that there is a great internal stability, because if you look at it you have the father of the nation assassinated, you had all the riots, and more bloodshed and transferred population of Partition, you had the China war, you had three Pakistan wars, you had the assassination of Indira Gandhi, and Rajiv Gandhi, you had the pulling down of the mosque in Ayodhya. You had all these events and somehow India was like a great big ship, it rocked and rolled but righted itself and went on. So I believe it has a great capacity to cope with these sorts of things, but obviously one wishes that they would not happen.

The other running sore which has been in the news again in the last few days is Kashmir. That seems to be insoluble. Pakistan and India don't ever seem to want to solve it or find any compromise.

No. I think there has been a lack of will on both sides really to find a compromise. In Pakistan undoubtedly the main problem is the army, because for the army, if you don't have Kashmir, you don't have hostility with India. At last Pakistanis just might start to ask why they are wasting such a huge percentage of their budget on the vast army. In India what has happened time and again is that politicians have just not had the guts to say we are going to go out to the people and tell them that it is in your interest and our interest and everyone's interest that we make some sacrifices and resolve this thing. There have been moments when this has been quite close to happening, but Pakistan has reneged on it, for instance when the Indian Prime Minister went by bus to Lahore, and soon after that Pakistan invaded a little bit of India in Kargil. Then there was the attack by the terrorists on the Taj Hotel and other hotels and buildings in Mumbai that set that back, and now we have had another setback again. So what happens is that they take a few steps forward, things look really good and then they pull back. But as I said, the army's the real problem in Pakistan, and in India the will to persuade the people of India that some compromise is in their interest is lacking.

How far is tradition important in the government of India? You've described the Nehru dynasty – his daughter became Prime Minister, and his grandson became Prime Minister. You said the Nehru dynasty is a bit like a Banyan tree, under which nothing else could flourish. How much of a problem is that?

Nepotism and dynasticism is a very prominent feature of Indian politics. In part it reflects the fact that dynasticism is a tradition in Indian life. Family is usually important and a traditionally brought-up Indian would say, 'Well, what's wrong?' It is part of the Indian tradition. It also fits in with something else which is that, we were talking about personalities before, and Indian parties seem to need one strong leader; they need to be built around a personality rather than around policies. It adds a bit of an aura to a person. Like in England you have the aura added to the royal family by the dynasticism there. So that is another reason why you get this dynasticism.

Is that going to continue?

For the moment it looks like it, yes. Of course, we have a Prime Minister now who is not dynastic. He started life, which he boasts very proudly of, working in a tea shop, and he has no family of his own, and he has risen to be Prime Minister of India. So it is not a universal phenomenon, but if you look around the states many of the leading politicians are in some way dynastic politicians.

Some of the more educated Indians want to copy Western traditions, and a lot of other Indians don't. You have also discussed the possibility of whether a marriage of East/West is possible.

Yes. I think in some ways it is possible, provided the Indian tradition is not swamped by it. But I think the really important thing in our relationship, the question we should really be asking is this. There are many Indians who want to live Western-style lives and live the sort of lives that all of you are able to live here. But if you think of the population of India, and by 2050 we may be up to well over 2.5 billion people, you think then of one or two things. I have an economist friend who has just written a book, and he has produced just three figures which are amazing to me. One is if that goes on and the average Indian consumes as much energy as the average Briton or American does now, then Indians will consume 75 per cent of the total amount of energy produced today. At the same time, India will emit more carbon dioxide than at present is calculated to be safe for the whole of the globe. Third, one of my pet hobby-horses, one-third of agricultural land will be lost to the wretched motor car. So you see if India develops in that way, how are we all going to cope with it? But you cannot sit in England and say, 'We're all right here, thank you very much, but you can't develop like us.' That is what much of the climate dialogue sounds like to Indian people. So really the marriage should be about you in Britain, you in America, thinking about how you need to change your lifestyle, so that we can build up a parity, whereby the lifestyles of the Indians and the British are so environmentally free and energy-economic, that everyone enjoys roughly the same standard and style of life. I believe very firmly that we would all live much better lives if we were more energy conscious – I am a devoted railway man. I have to tell you therefore the car is my bitter enemy for that reason, but again I thought today, driving into Winchester, it took about half an hour probably from when we first entered Winchester to get here. I just thought what an inefficient method of transport this is. So we have all got to think about how we are going to change the way we live so that we can accommodate the energy needs of those who need to use much more energy than they do at the moment.

You're not very keen on the importation of Western-style supermarkets and McDonald's and all those sorts of places in India?

I am not. I am losing the battle. I like shopping in small shops, and I like to go down to the little market at the end of the road, or there is another one across the road where everyone says good morning to you, and you have a little chat as you buy your bread or whatever it is, and it is all like shopping in this country used to be. But there is a big problem, which supermarkets say they are the only people who can deliver, which is that getting the food to the small shops has proved very expensive and very wasteful in India and there are no adequate supply chains. I would always argue, 'Why can't we create supply chains for small shops?' but the supermarketeers and many others say that is just idealism.

You have also written that you couldn't now leave India. Why is that?

I may have said that, but I would put it differently now. I'm often asked in India if I would ever leave it, and I say that it is in the hands of God; of course, I will leave it one day, and at the moment I have no plans. One of the things I have imbibed from India, perhaps over-imbibed, is a belief that so much of our life is guided, because when I look at the way I went to India, the way I stayed in India, and the opportunities that came up at just the right moment to continue in India, I can see that it was laid out for me, in a way. So when I say it is in the hands of God I do mean that, but I can't say that something won't happen which will lead me to think I have to leave India. But I have no plans to, and I do know that if I ever left India there would be a big hole in my life, that is certainly true.

What is the most important thing you have learnt since living in India?

Probably the most important thing I have learnt is to believe that there are many different ways to God. I found it hugely reassuring, because it made me think that if people in so many different cultures, so many different parts of the world, so many different times of history are in some fundamental way all doing the same thing, feeling the same way and searching for the same thing, then surely that is very strong evidence for the existence of God. I would be the last person to deny that frequently one is desperately in search of evidence for the existence of God. I think that is the most important thing I have learnt.

How different is the relationship between religion and politics in India and, say, here?

Much more important in politics, unfortunately, in a way because politicians do use religion to attract voters. The Congress Party has made a practice of trying to attract Muslim voters, by doing special favours or making out things for them. One part of the BJP, which is now in power, has very much gone out to try and persuade people to vote as Hindus, and the Hindu bit of it is in my view very negative, because you are basically saying you are voting for Hindus because in some way your religion is under threat, which it is not at all in India. So we do have that, but still basically one can say India is a secular country, and there is a secularism about politics as well, and even the hardcore bits of the BJP say they respect all religions, and say that they are secularists, but they are against what they call pseudo-secularism, and by that they mean the Congress Party's attempt to woo the Muslim vote.

One last question before I throw this open. You have reported from Delhi for quite a long while and you have, always as far as one can tell, told the truth as you've seen it. It has occasionally got you into trouble. You were once threatened with lashes, weren't you?

Yes. What happened was that when the emergency was declared, when Indira Gandhi withdrew virtually all civil rights, postponed the election and took the dictatorial powers, of course there was great panic at that time, and the rumour went around saying that the BBC has reported that the major Dalit leader of the Congress Party has resigned in protest against this. The Information Minister was called up by one of the flunkeys – Indira Gandhi had some pretty doubtful flunkeys – and this one had got hold of the information list and said to the Minister, 'You must get hold of Mark Tully, give him a good beating, put him in prison, because he has reported this.' Fortunately, the Information Minister went to All-India-Radio monitoring and found there was no such report at all, and he went to see the Minister and said (a) Mark Tully has not said this and (b) it is your job to put people in prison, not mine. The Information Minister told me all of this and I have written about it in a book called *Raj to Rajiv*.

I think that is a good moment to throw this open.

Questions from the audience

You said at one point that poverty could decrease so much faster. In what way?

Basically if the government was more efficient, if the government was not so corrupt, then the services that the government offered would improve.

You can take it from the bottom level with the government's rural unemployment guarantee scheme where sometimes as little as 50 per cent goes into the pockets of the people who should get the money from the work. You can take it from Rajiv Gandhi's own statement where he famously said, 'If as Prime Minister I want to give 100 rupees to some rural development scheme or some village, I know that only 15 rupees will actually reach there.' So there is a huge amount of wastage just in that. And then you take it up to the Education Services; if the Education Services were efficient and properly run we would have many more educated Indians able to do the sort of jobs which it is necessary to have a good level of education for. And then again another example, the obstructive, bureaucratic attitude to foreign investment, the way that bureaucrats, described well by a friend of mine as the Abominable Indian No-Man, saying no to foreign investors, making India an unattractive investment destination, if we got more and more foreign investment then there would be more and more jobs, and that would of course also decrease poverty. Those are three examples of how the corruption and inefficiency of the government prevents, or slows down, the decreases in poverty.

Would you like to make some comment, Mark, about the situation last year when we had the student in Delhi who was gang-raped and subsequently murdered by the group there? I am asking from the perspective of Indian women. Whether that terrible event has changed the situation in relation to women, and fear of domestic violence, or fear of violence in itself? A national or international issue as such.

That was an appalling incident. Let's face it, there are other incidents of rape in India. Traditional Indian culture, as in many ways ours was, has that basically the man was the boss. The danger of the coverage of these sort of stories is that you get an exaggerated view of what is happening. You leave out completely a very powerful women's movement that there is in India. There's a wonderful NGO called SEVA, which is entirely dedicated to the upliftment of poor women. There are so many Indians and activists who are campaigning for this, but you don't change cultural attitudes overnight. It wasn't the culture of India to rape, but some people think of it as a follow-on of an excess of violence in your patrilineal culture. The other interesting thing about this, a relevant and sad thing, was said to me by a leading Indian sociologist. He said, 'The other thing which is never reported is what about the people who committed the rape? Why did they do it?' And that draws you to consider the impact of the really appalling living conditions that some people have in Indian cities and the hopelessness of their lives. These were young men who really were living in dreadful, extreme poverty – that's not quite the right word – I would say more in squalor and in hopeless lives really. So you do also have to consider that factor.

With your experience of India I am not sure how far you would talk about Pakistan. Would you ever see an accommodation between Pakistan and India and this difficult hoohah at the frontiers?

I can't see one at the moment. Sadly, we had a classic example of this only very recently when everyone was very pleased, Modi invited the Pakistan Prime Minister to come to India for his swearing-in. There was a lot of speculation in India – will the Pakistan Prime Minister dare to come? Will the army be angry with him? He came and there were not substantive talks but an agreement to restart civil service-level talks, and then just before those talks were due to start, India pulled out of them. And so once again you had this, what I was talking about, this stop–start thing. There isn't the political will in India yet, or in Pakistan as far as I can see, to overcome this problem. But one of the interesting things is that the BJP, which is in power, is traditionally the party that shouts loudest if there is to be any accommodation with Pakistan. When the BJP were in power in the late 1990s and the early part of this century a major step forward was taken by the Prime Minister, by that bus journey to Lahore. It was a good thing the BJP was in power for Indo–Pakistan relations, because then if they did take a decision to do something about it, they couldn't oppose it in the way they would do if they were out of power. So nothing is impossible, but there is no real sign on the horizon. But one thing is important to remember, that big efforts go on all the time on what is called 'track two diplomacy', and there are lots of Indians and lots of Pakistanis who really wish all this nonsense would stop. One of the big drivers which could be for it to stop is economy, because one of the tragedies of South Asia post-independence is the lack of regional economic co-operation. Businessmen in Pakistan and businessmen in India know what a resolution for stopping all these problems would mean to them in economic and business terms.

Could you tell us how you see the relationship between India and China evolving in the next two decades, seeing as they are two of the world's most populous countries and both probably expanding their economies?

It is a very complicated situation. We have just had the Chinese leader come to India, and talks were held. Just before the talks were held there was what India claims was an incursion across the line of control. As you know, there is a major border dispute between India and China.

But the Indian policy at the moment is to try and pursue good relations with China, and good trade relations with China, and put the border issue on the back-burner. Talks continue and continue and continue on the border issue and don't seem to make much progress, although the Chinese leader did say this time that he really wanted to solve that. But I think that what is going to go on for some time yet is that the border issue will be discussed at official level, and that sort of thing. Discussions will go on, there will be periodical little disputes over whether the Chinese have come across the line of control or not, because the line of control is not properly demarcated, and the economic relationship will expand. What India wants out of that relationship is to have far more trade in manufactured goods, in services like IT, because at the moment India is providing raw materials and China is providing manufactured goods in India. So there's a very serious imbalance. So I think and hope that the economic relationship will develop, will become more balanced. I don't see why it shouldn't do. As for the border talks, it would be wonderful if it could be resolved, but it will not lead to a big brake on the development of the other relationship.

You said you would like to be optimistic about Modi's prospects, and if he succeeds I guess the prospects for the BJP are very good. How do you see the prospects of the Congress Party after their electoral defeat?

You are right to ask that question, because the Congress Party is in a miserable position now. It doesn't even have enough seats in Parliament to be the opposition, the official opposition party, because you have to have 10 per cent of the seats. The Gandhi family is, for the moment anyhow, discredited because Rahul Gandhi, the young son of Rajiv and Sonia, not so young now, led the election campaign with disastrous results. The weakness of the Congress Party is that it is all built around the Gandhi family, and if you ask any Congressman, 'Why don't you grow a new leadership? Why do you go on depending on the Gandhi family?' they say, 'Because if you take the Gandhi family out it would be like taking the cornerstone out of the arch, the arch would collapse.' So at the moment the dilemma in the Congress Party is that the Gandhi family seems to have lost its vote-pulling; Rahul Gandhi is showing no signs of being a vote-catcher, and no signs of being an effective leader of the party while in opposition. Yet if we do away with them we are going to split up. So they are in a complete quandary at the moment. There is the prospect, a possibility that some Congressmen feel, that Rahul Gandhi's sister Priyanka would be much more charismatic, and much more able to win votes, and that sort of thing. So that is a possibility, but there are doubts about her health, and also she has a husband with a rather unsavoury reputation. I would just add one word of caution, with a little story about the hazards of being a broadcaster. When Rajiv Gandhi was defeated a lot of people said that it was the end of the Gandhi dynasty. I was interviewed on the *PM* programme, and the interviewer kept on trying to persuade me to say that the Congress Party, the Gandhi family, is definitely finished. I said I had seen the Gandhi family and its ups and its downs – I had seen Indira Gandhi after her defeat, a humiliating defeat in 1977 – and I would not be premature in writing off the Gandhi family. And as the guy said, 'Well OK, Mark', and then he didn't switch off the microphone; I could still hear the programme. So he then said to the audience, 'Well, Mark Tully says that the Gandhi family is not finished' and – I can't remember the name of the reporter – 'but our reporter Joe Bloggs says it is finished.' I'm still cautious about saying they are finished. The one thing you have to realize, there are several states in which the Congress and BJP are the only two major parties, so there is a big vacuum, and politics move in India, they are not static, and so you can't write off Congress, and you can't write off the Gandhi family. But both of them have really serious problems that they have to face, and neither of them as yet show any signs of doing so.

The microphone is coming to the Dean for one last word. Can I just say that Sir Mark will be signing copies of his books outside immediately after we leave this room and you will have had some impressions over the last hour of just what you are likely to be reading.

There is something, John, I always say about that, and that is that one of the things which I believe is not culturally safe, is alien to Indian culture, is consumerism, and I think one of the great things we should do with our economies is to try and find economies that do not regard consumerism as the driving energy of the economy. I have written about that in one of my books, but having said that, that means I have absolutely no right to try and persuade you to buy my books!

The Dean

Sir Mark, it is my privilege to pass a vote of thanks for your being with us tonight and all that you have shared. I can remember once someone saying to me when I was reading theology, 'What on earth do you do with a degree in theology?' Well, there are all sorts of avenues for a degree in theology and you are a fine example of how to use it successfully. India is something of a miracle. As a subcontinent with a huge diversity of population, it somehow hangs together as a democracy. I loved your suggestion that one could think of it as a rolling boat that somehow does right itself despite community convulsions from time to time. To have you with us for an evening with your prodigious knowledge which runs so deeply, and your love of India, but also your ability to communicate that to us here in Winchester, is just a great privilege. You are a great interpreter, and to understand another culture and civilization and another human adventure takes someone with a huge breadth of knowledge who can span our two cultures, and you've done that for us tonight.

10

Liking difficult places

JOHN SIMPSON

It gives me very great pleasure to welcome John Simpson tonight. Some of you were hoping to hear him in February, but as you may remember that very day the BBC sent him to Kiev. I am particularly grateful to him because in fact he is off to Kabul tomorrow. But he still insisted on coming to us tonight, which we all deeply appreciate.

I couldn't do it twice could I?

In fact we are very lucky he is here at all because, John, you came under enemy fire on the very day of your birth?

Well I did, yes, or even indeed slightly before. My father was back from the army on leave, and my mother was mountainously pregnant with me. They were lying in bed side by side at four or five in the morning, and a V1 rocket destroyed the house next door, and the ceiling came in, making my mother all the more like an alp I suppose, and my father danced up and down in rage, completely naked, shouting appalling things apparently. I didn't, of course, hear this – well, if I did, I didn't remember. Shouting insults and things about Goering and Hitler, and he seemed to bring Himmler into it too. He put on his clothes and got my mother out of bed. They were lucky to have survived, as you can imagine, and he took her round to King's Cross station in London, and put his hand in his pocket and brought out a bunch of coins and notes, and stuck them down on the counter of the ticket office and said rather grandly, 'Take her to wherever this will go.' It took them quite a lot of time to work out where this would go, and which class and everything. Eventually it turned out it would take her to Blackpool, so she went to Blackpool, which took two and a half days because of the heavy bombing. It was a train full of soldiers who treated her like royalty apparently, and were wonderful to her. Then, when she got to Blackpool, she had just enough money to get a taxi to take her to the rather more upmarket place called Cleveleys, where I was born. I left at the age of two days or five days or something, and I have never been back. But everywhere I go I always duly write in the book, or when applying for a passport, I put Cleveleys. So in places like Iran, Cleveleys is a presence which others perhaps would know about.

When you were aged only seven and your parents separated, you were given the choice of which parent you wanted to live with, which was quite a decision for a seven-year-old, wasn't it?

Yes it was. I am sitting here looking at my eight-year-old son – I know it doesn't seem terribly likely at my age. But by some miracle of whatever we had a son when I was 61, and he's sitting in front here. It does come to me quite a lot, this moment. I spent a lot of my life thinking that was a pretty dreadful thing to do, giving that decision to a kid to make at that age. I now realize entirely what happened, in a way I don't think my parents could explain to me. My father and I had been out. We had been to the Festival of Britain, and we came back to my mother, my long-suffering mother – my father was a really difficult person; with the best will in the world he was not easy to live with or to be with. My mother was all dressed up, in a hat, I remember, with a little feather in it, and a beautiful green coat, and she had her case and my case beside her. She was sitting on the stairs as we came in, and she said she was leaving, and that she was taking me with her. I now understand why my father did it; he really just did it, as I would now if such a dreadful thing happened, which I don't think it will. 'Well, don't you think the boy should decide what happens to him?' It seems such an awful thing to say to your seven-year-old son – decide who is going to look after you for the rest of your life. But it really wasn't like that. I, being a very serious-minded kid, thought that I had to make this judgement of Solomon between them, and so I thought, 'My mother is a war widow, she has two children by her first marriage. She's got those two, and my poor old father doesn't have any kids, so I had better stay with him.' A strange look, well I like to think that a strange look, passed across his face, which was one, of course, of horror at the thought, so that was that. I have told this story once or twice and people do get very judgemental, and are inclined to shake their heads about the cruelty of parents that could make a little boy have to choose. But I actually think it was just one of those spur-of-the-moment things that my father said just to gain a bit of time. Perhaps even to dissuade my mother from doing it or from going. Although I think he was quite glad that she had gone.

Your father was a Christian Scientist, and so were you at that stage.

I was brought up as a Christian Scientist and I still have great affection for it as a religion. It is weird and it's difficult to follow, but it is a very open kind of thing, and it is up to you. My father loved it (a) because it was American, and he loved American things, and (b) because he hated all kinds of authority figures, so he loathed doctors. The idea that you can cut doctors out of the whole equation by healing yourself through mental means, that was mother's milk to him, he adored that notion. I was brought up with it. It gave me a very good ethical and moral grounding that I am very grateful for, though I don't suppose I have lived up to those things at all. I stopped being one at some stage and now I am an Anglican, and I turn up pretty regularly. I live in Ireland at the moment, so Rafe and I go to Church of Ireland; sometimes we go to St Patrick's Cathedral which is rather nice. But my wife is a very firm atheist. She doesn't try and stop us going but she makes the lunch on those days.

The other thing that surprised me in your memoir is that you had a year off school, when you were quite young, and you read so voraciously that you were ahead of the other children when you actually went to school.

Yes, that is true. My dear father, who really was an oddball, no question about it, he was determined to send me to a fee-paying school. I don't think he was right, to be honest, because the fee-paying school he chose was a pretty useless one. But nevertheless he felt that it was a step up on the ladder. Our family had been quite a wealthy family, kind of middle class, they ran a big building company. It went belly-up in the Second World War. It started to go downhill in the First World War, and then really was finished off by the Second World War. He had been brought up to something better than he was now used to, so he had always wanted to 'get us back', dear old boy, to where we had been socially. Which he did manage to do, but that meant that he did not want me to get into the school system at all, he didn't want me to appear. Well, thank God we didn't have a computer then. He didn't want me to exist officially. So from the age of five, when I should have gone to school, he kept me at home. I had been at home before, but I wasn't allowed to go out of the house in the hours of daylight, I was only allowed to creep out at night-time. I read the contents of the bookcases all through. At the age of five and six, I didn't understand any of it really, and I only looked at the pictures mostly. But it was one of the ways that I kept myself going. So he would go off in the mornings to work and I would be there, hiding at home, trying not to make a noise. I loved it actually. Because to be a journalist is always to be slightly at odds with authority of all kinds; now at the grand old age of 70, I still feel that, I get a real kick out of doing things that I am not supposed to – going into countries that don't want me and dressing up as something. That for me is absolutely heavenly, and I adore it. Even on the occasions I have been caught I feel that I am doing the right thing as opposed to the wrong thing.

Did you always want to be a BBC reporter?

No, I didn't know what I wanted to be, I liked journalism. At Cambridge I was a journalist, in fact I edited *Granta* magazine, which was the big Cambridge University, slightly upmarket one. Not a newspaper, but a literary magazine. Then very soon after I left, no doubt partly because I was a useless manager, it was taken over by an American writer who first of all published it as a national literary magazine in Britain, and then went back to America with it and it is now quite a famous thing. I always liked to say, 'Oh yes, I was editor of *Granta*', and just leave it at that. Actually, it was a sort of crappy, over-exaggerated, fanciful undergraduate magazine when I was the editor. But it gave me a taste for the whole business, and then I was fortunate enough to land a job at the BBC at the age of 22, and became a temporary half-pay sub-editor, and that's something I still feel about my work with the BBC which is still temporary and, God knows, it is half-pay.

On your first day as a reporter you were assaulted by the Prime Minister?

Yes, slightly embarrassing, I was. We were all very innocent at that stage. This was 1970; Harold Wilson was the Prime Minister. He was just about to call a general election. We only knew this because there were articles in the paper that suggested it, completely unsourced. In those days the lobby was a pretty disgraceful outfit which did more or less what it was told – perhaps I'm being too unkind, but it did do a lot of that. So the political editor of the *Daily X* would say, I think, 'I imagine that the Prime Minister about now is thinking of holding an election.' Whereas, the Prime Minister's Press Secretary had said to him, 'You know he's going to call an election, quite soon.' I was deeply innocent of all this. I was 24 and knew nothing about this, and my boss had been the head of the BBC

World Service. So he knew nothing about the intricacies and the appalling nature of British political reporting either. So he said to me, 'I keep reading all this stuff in the papers about an election coming up. I tell you what, Harold Wilson is going off to his constituency from Euston station in London. Just go and ask him.' So I thought, 'Well, this is my first day, that's not bad, I am going to be speaking to the Prime Minister and it's a story of national importance. God, I really have arrived.' So I went down to Platform 7 at Euston station, characteristically rather late, and found the whole platform absolutely plastered with television camera crews, because in those days a British election was a matter of national and international importance. There were American camera crews there and Australian ones, the odd French one, as well as the British ones, and loads and loads and loads of photographers. And me with my tape-recorder standing in front of them because I'd only just arrived, and people saying, 'Get out of the way, sonny, can't see round your head.' So I was sort of dodging. Then Harold Wilson arrives, comes walking down the platform, and I looked round, and I thought nobody's doing anything, they are all smiling in a sort of ingratiating way, but they are not actually going to ask him anything. So I thought, well, somebody's got to, so I stepped out and said to him, 'Good morning, Prime Minister, the newspapers at the moment are full of speculation that there is going to be an election soon, and I just wondered, do you have anything to say about it?' Actually I didn't say any of that because I said 'Excuse me Prime ...' when the whole world kind of exploded, because Harold Wilson, though not always regarded as much of a politician, did have as it turned out a very good left hook. He punched me really hard in the stomach and tried to wrestle the microphone out of my hand while saying things like, 'You know this is an outrage. Your Director General knows that I never do these things. This is appalling. I shall put in a complaint to your Director General the moment I get to Huyton.' Then he got on the train. I was standing there gasping, and all the journalists laughing. Somebody said to me, 'You don't ask the Prime Minister a question, old boy.' I looked at my watch, and it was ten to eleven, it wasn't even lunchtime. I'd been physically assaulted by the Prime Minister and was clearly going to lose my job on my first day out. Actually, Harold Wilson obviously changed his mind – perhaps he never intended to. There is a slightly sad side-effect to that, which is that within six or seven years he was showing the symptoms of Alzheimer's, and probably even at that stage knew that it wasn't a good thing to just talk off the cuff to journalists, and never, never did it. But what an introduction to a career which was full of violence and aggression, and that was just from the BBC, and the Conservative and the Labour Parties.

Talking of violence and aggression, what was your experience of Saddam Hussein?

I don't know how far I can trust you and everyone else here. I actually rather liked Saddam Hussein. Obviously he had certain moral limitations – shall we put it that way – he can be said to be responsible for the deaths of probably a million and a half people. We are not talking about a kind of liberal democrat politician here. On the other hand, I saw him hanged and that was a horrible, horrible experience, and it's affected my thinking about him ever since. I thought that was disgusting, and I admired him for the way he behaved at the end. I saw him during his trial, I was there during the trial, and I didn't get a chance to get a word with him, but I exchanged a lot of glances during it. I can't remember how long it lasted, but quite a long time. Of course, he held Iraq together; he didn't hold it together in a particularly attractive way, and dreadful things were done under his name and as a result of him. But he wasn't a lunatic; his sons were disgusting characters, horrible, horrible characters. Colonel Gadaffi was mad but also a horrible character, who did the most horrible things. Saddam wasn't like that. Can I tell you a story? A friend of mine, an American journalist, went to see Saddam quite early on in his time as President, and he got an interview with him for the *New York Times*. He's sitting down there, and he's thinking, with this bloke I could end up dead as a result of this interview, but at the same time I can't go back to the *New York Times* without asking him about the nature of his power and his extraordinary unpleasant way of wielding it. So he said to him, 'There are people in your country who say that you are quite cruel and brutal', and there was a bit of a pause, and Saddam got up and grabbed him by the lapel. Didn't say a word, dragged him out of the room and down the stairs into the courtyard where all the cars were kept, jumped into his Range Rover; all the guards weren't expecting any of this, so they were appalled at first, then throwing themselves into their vehicles to try and keep up with him. He speeds off down into the centre of Baghdad at 60/70 miles an hour. Everybody, policemen, locals, everybody knew his car, everybody throwing themselves aside, so as not to have anything to do with him, and not to get in his way. Suddenly, as he is driving along, Saddam sees an old man by the side of the road. He screeches to a halt, he jumps out of his car with his swagger stick (he was a great Anglophile, and the army was already based on the British model – he encouraged that – so he had a swagger stick with him), and he was wearing uniform. The first words he said to the journalist were, 'Come with me.' So the journalist hopped, really nervously, out of the car. He got his swagger stick and stuck it under the chin of this poor old man, and he said, 'This journalist from America thinks that I am a tyrant and that everybody hates me. Do you hate me?' The old man said, 'Oh no, Saddam, we really, really, really love you, Saddam, I really love you.' Saddam laughed and laughed and jumped back in the car, and he said, 'You see, that's how you treat people.' Well, I know it is an ugly story but it shows a certain sense of humour, doesn't it? I didn't dislike him as much as I disliked lots and lots and lots of people. I just felt that he did all these things because he knew that, as has been proved really, you can't keep Iraq together unless you are pretty brutal about it. But I agree, ethically it is a difficult argument to make, and so I think I should shut up now.

But do you still have his statue?

I do, yes. I didn't know you knew about that. I went to one of his smaller palaces, after he was overthrown. It is the little palace that he had when he used to review the troops when they went through – you remember those swords that were up on either end of the parade ground, whose arms were modelled on his arms, made by a British company of course. I went in there, and there was an Iraqi officer who was selling stuff, I don't know how he was there and what he was doing. There was this rather charming little statue of Saddam, who used to hold his hand out in an irritating way when he was in public. And so there he was, there was his statue. We've got it at home now. We put a funny sort of hat on it. But I had to take it through the airport in Kuwait, which of course Saddam had captured and treated very brutally. I am quite an innocent, as you see, and I got my colleagues to make a wooden box to fit this thing, which looked disturbingly like a coffin. I thought, well, that will cover it up, nobody will look. Anyway, I had to go through; it was fine going down, the RAF flew us down to Kuwait as they used to do, it was too dangerous to drive at that stage. So we got out of the helicopter in Kuwait, and I was carrying the coffin with me – it was very light, the statue was made of resin or something, very light indeed. I had to check in to catch my flight back to London, and it was at that point that I realized these x-ray machines are actually rather good. Because there he was. There was a scream of anger from the chap who was looking at the screen, and I wandered round, as if I was interested to see what it was, pretending it wasn't me that was the owner of this thing. And there it was, you could see everything, you could see the cap badge on his beret, you could see his moustache lying hair by hair, and his hand stuck out like that. A lot of these characters gathered round me, Kuwaiti army people. I'm sure I shouldn't say this, but I am not at all fond of Kuwait, and I have had a rather nasty set of experiences from Kuwaitis. So I thought, they are going to shoot me, they are going to shoot me, they were so wild, they were screaming and shouting. But in the end a more senior and sensible one came out and said, 'It's just a statue.' He was quite insulting to me, but at least I got the statue out. By this stage, the coffin had fallen apart, so I just had Saddam, and queuing up was a slight problem, because people kept coming up and wanting to tell me what they thought about people who would have statues of Saddam. I got on the plane and the BA crew were absolutely delightful. They gave him a seat, and they strapped him in, and gave him a meal too, which I thought was really good.

You have specialized in reporting from the other side in conflicts. You reported from Baghdad during the Kuwait invasion, and you reported from Belgrade during the war against Kosovo. Was that tricky?

It was, yes it was very tricky. It was tricky in two ways. It was tricky because we weren't the most popular people, as you can imagine; in fact, we had real problems in the streets – I am talking about Belgrade here – from people who wanted to grab us as representatives of the country, one of the countries that was bombing them. So maybe you can understand it, I personally don't understand that attitude. But then I have to say that the British public's attitude wasn't always very good either. I had huge amounts of hate-mail from people who said it was disgusting that I should go to Belgrade and see the effects of British and allied bombing. Almost every one of them ended up as though this was a killer argument, 'After all you wouldn't have been in Berlin during the Second World War.' Well that is true: (a) I wasn't born properly, but (b) it wasn't possible, of course, because we were at war. This wasn't a war in Belgrade in 1999; it wasn't even a war properly I would say in Iraq in 1991 or indeed in 2003; it was so one-sided that I don't think it counted as a real war. But anyway, apart from anything else, I think if the British, American, French, Canadian taxpayers are paying for this, they might as well know where their money is going to, and what the effects of these things were. I realized after a while people didn't want to know about the effects of the bombing of Belgrade or anywhere else; they didn't want to know that bombs go astray, bombs do always go astray, and we are always told about smart bombs and how they can see the colour of your eyes from space or whatever it is. Which is true – the technology of these things is absolutely remarkable, but there are always, always, every time these things are let off, there are mistakes and they always go astray. So often they kill real people, people like us. I don't have an axe to grind at all; I thought it was perfectly right that we should put pressure on Slobodan Milošević to force him to back down in Kosovo, I thought it perfectly right. But we should know about these things, we shouldn't hide the knowledge from ourselves, or hide ourselves from the knowledge. If the BBC or any other organization had been able to have a correspondent in Berlin during the Second World War, we would have jumped at the chance because you need to know what is going on. OK, fine that Goebbels' propaganda ministry would have cut back everything they said and controlled it terribly, but who didn't know that? Everyone knew that. In fact, in Belgrade, and in Iraq in 1991 and 2003, we were remarkably free of controls, it was always possible to get round them. I remember that once we did have to present our stuff to the censors in Iraq in 1991, and we used to report that. We'd say that a report was put together under the controls that exist, under the propaganda controls. But it was always possible to get round these guys by using expressions they didn't know. I remember, for instance, saying that there was a big demo that was turned out under the barrel of a gun by Saddam's people to support him in the last few days before the bombing started. I remember writing in the script, 'These people are going through the motions', which was entirely true, I don't suppose anybody was voluntarily there. The censor, who was a particularly unpleasant character, said to me 'What is this "motions"?' So I said, 'Oh you know, they are going through the motions, they are chanting "Saddam", they are waving their fists.' He knew there was something dodgy about it, but he didn't do anything to stop it, so it was always possible to tell people what was really, really going on. I just think, I'm not in the business of telling people less than they know, I want to tell them more if possible. Even if it is only a tiny percentage more, I still think it is worth it. But, as I say, I kept the mail for quite a long time, because I thought it shed a particular light on British public opinion. It was extraordinary how people didn't want to be told bad things, they only wanted to be told positive things – we are hitting all the targets, civilians are perfectly safe. Alas, it's never true in my experience.

And it wasn't true in your own experience where you were hit by what is euphemistically called 'friendly fire'?

Yes, terribly friendly. This was in 2003 during the invasion of Iraq. Again, it just annoys me that we were given the impression that this was the battle of El Alamein, Waterloo and everything, all over. The Iraqi army was entirely filled with people that didn't want to fight. There was scarcely anybody that did want to fight, and funnily enough the people that went down to the front line were the ones that most wanted to get

away from Saddam. People volunteered to go down, that was true, absolutely true, when Saddam said all my front-line soldiers have volunteered,
it was absolutely true – they wanted to get away from Saddam. They
never thought, either in 1999 or in 2003, that there would be fighting,
they thought that it would stop. So I was always rather sympathetic to
the poor old soldiers. In both the wars, the Americans had vehicles, they
kept it quite quiet but they had vehicles as big as this room, earth-moving
vehicles, and heavily armoured. They just drove towards the Iraqi lines
and buried these soldiers alive. I didn't like that very much either. Anyway,
on the day that this started, we headed off across no man's land and we
found ourselves on top of a hill with Saddam's tanks in the valley firing. I
don't know whether they were really firing at us, they seemed to be firing
over our heads really. We'd joined up with a group of American Special
Forces, soldiers, people I really like. There must have been about 60 or 70
of us, and there were 20 vehicles, perhaps even more, most of them those
armoured Humvees and American, definitely clearly American, vehicles,
some one or two armoured personnel carriers and stuff like that, plus
our broken-down old car that we were trying to rent. Every one of these
vehicles had a patch of orange material of some kind. We'd just bought
ours in a bazaar and it didn't really match the others that much, but on
the roofs of the cars you tied this thing over the whole of the roof of the
car, to show that you were on the Western coalition side, praying that
the Americans wouldn't bomb you. Good luck! The Captain radioed up
to a plane that was flying round and round and round for ages; it must
have been there for ten minutes flying round above us, looking down at
us. The Captain radioed up and said, 'We are in such and such a position,
and Iraqi tanks are down there and they are in ...', whatever the other
position was. Map reference positions, you know? After another three
or four minutes of flying over us at only about 1,000 feet, with this glare
of orange material on every single vehicle, and I'd never seen such a big
stars and stripes before, it was absolutely enormous, about the size of
this stage. Anyway the American pilot put a 1,000lb bomb right down
in the middle of us all, killed 18 people, who were burned alive, not a
very nice business. It killed my translator, whom I was very fond of, and
damaged most of the rest of us. I have a large piece of shrapnel in my
backside, and I am pretty much completely deaf in this ear. I was lucky,
one of our group who came with us got injured, quite badly injured in
the neck, and left quite quickly. He managed to get a lift to hospital in
the nearby town, and we didn't know. The security man and I thought
he was one of the burnt people, so we had to go round, finding all the
bodies and trying to work out who they were from the stuff on them,

and their faces, and whether this chap we were responsible for was there. Not a nice thing, and it is not a memory I like to dwell on, but I did a *Panorama* programme about it afterwards and I rather thought it was a bit too me, me, me. I didn't really like the whole idea of doing it. But anyway we did it, and I suppose it was a clear-cut case where the Americans wouldn't admit any kind of responsibility. In the end, after we had pestered them for months, the Pentagon said I could come on my own to see the Admiral who had been in charge of the ship from which this plane had gone – it was a ship-borne US navy plane, an F15, I think – and I could get a briefing from him. That was all they were prepared to do, and it was nice. I got a cameraman to stand outside in the car park of the Pentagon – there is a big car park, as you might imagine – and I said to him, 'Stand here. I don't know how long I am going to be, but I am going to go in there and I am obviously going to come out in a really, really bad mood, and I want you to be running the moment I walk up because I want you to get that first reaction, that first anger.' Anyway, I went in there, and the Admiral was a really charming bloke, exactly my age and, rather like me, had a bit of a tummy on him, and I was anticipating some sort of shaven-haired character whose eyebrows bristled at the mention of America, and all that kind of stuff. Not a bit of it, he was really laid-back and funny and charming, and he said, 'I am really so sorry about what happened to you, but you know we don't accept responsibility on these occasions, even though it was really clear-cut, and even though 18 people were killed; it was the worst loss of life in a friendly-fire incident during the war. I am sorry, what can I say? I am sorry.' I said, 'Did you give the guys a bad time?' He said, 'Not really.' Somehow or other that was better than him saying, 'Yes, I told them ...' He said, 'No, not really.' They had to go off again and fly the next day; he said, 'I thought their morale would be shot through if I went on at them.' Anyway, he gave me a couple of tots of whisky, rather good whisky, and I came out, and the cameraman said, 'Yes, yes, I'm ready, I'm ready', and I said, 'Oh shut up, let's go and have a hamburger somewhere.'

You have often been the first in the front line. You were first into Kabul during the invasion, I think, but you made a rather rash statement.

Yes, I did, how stupid of me. I never seem to learn – clearly I haven't learnt this evening, because if you are representing an outfit like the BBC, you have really got to be so careful. Almost all the newspapers, for one reason or another, have got it in for the BBC, and they want to do the BBC down. It is true that the BBC, seven of us, were the first people into Kabul when it fell in 2001. We had good contacts with the pro-Western forces that had captured it, who decided not to go into Kabul themselves but to stay outside. So, there was Kabul still full of Taliban, and we managed to persuade them to let us drive in – it is a long walk. In journalistic terms, we cleaned up, but unfortunately I made a joke, which I have often regretted. I haven't regretted making jokes in general, but I regretted this one. There was a lovely lady some people may, I am sure, will remember, called Sue Macgregor, who used to present the *Today* programme. We were four and a half hours or something in front of London, and so it was lunchtime by the time I got on the *Today* programme. By that stage the Taliban had really either fled or been sorted out by people in Kabul itself, not again by this northern alliance grouping, so there were bodies all over the place. Sue Macgregor said to me, 'There's one thing I can't understand. You say that the Taliban have finished in Kabul, that they've surrendered, run for it or whatever, and yet the northern alliance haven't entered the city. So who liberated it?' And I said, 'Well, I suppose the BBC did', laughing, terrible. There is this awful man, he's probably in the audience, I hope so, Piers Morgan, you know him. Somehow or other, I don't know quite why, I got up his nose, big time, quite early on in the thing. I also did something rather dopey. It wasn't my idea, but we got into Afghanistan before the invasion dressed as women, because you can get away with anything if you are dressed as a woman. (I told my wife that she still did.) Nobody looked at you or anything. So we were able to get in, even though they said they would shoot anybody they found, or cut their heads off. We managed to spend a couple of days roaming around in Afghanistan. It got a bit of attention. Somehow or other, I am not quite sure why, Piers Morgan really took against this, and the next time I knew or heard anything, it was somebody sent me – people are always so nice about sending you these things. It was a full-page spread – it might even have been the front page – that said, 'What a burka', and then it went on for some days after this about it; I don't know why. I thought it was a rather tasteless trick myself. So Piers Morgan then picked up this thing and said that I had claimed I'd singlehandedly liberated Kabul. In fact, it was the BBC team that was in there first, and I suppose that got up the noses of lots of other journalists. Not that the *Daily Mirror* had any representatives in Iraq. I think they just stayed back in London and wrote things, as the *Sun* did. But the *Sun* didn't have anybody there either, and I don't think the *Daily Mail* did. They just used to sit there in London and write this kind of headline about these things. But I don't care, these things happen. I was at a thing like this in Northern Ireland in August. You would think it was quite a quiet month and the kind of place where nobody would pay any attention, but somebody in the audience said to me something about the way the BBC was managed. I said, 'Absolutely catastrophic' as a joke, and everybody laughed. Then about half an hour later somebody said, 'Do they have a lot of women managers in the BBC?' And I said, 'Look, for God's sake, most of my bosses seem to be women, and they are tough, I can tell you', or something like that. Anyway, it was all put together and because it was August there wasn't any other news about, so, 'Simpson says tough women are catastrophic governing the BBC'. I did have one or two letters to write, actually. If you work for the BBC, that is what the newspapers do to you, and so one of the women said, 'Well, I was rather chuffed to think that I was a tough woman at the BBC.' Something like that. The other three said, 'Believe me, they've said worse things about us and I understand.' But still, a friend of mine sent me a thing from the newspapers about how wonderful it was to have women in management. As though I didn't know.

You said, in fact, that if you hear during this sort of thing going on about the morality of it, their craft, you reach for the off switch.

I do a bit. I've always remembered something that somebody said to me decades ago now, a friend of mine in the BBC, a journalist. He said to me, 'Have you ever noticed, the only people who use the word "journalistically" as a term of praise are other journalists? Everybody else uses the word "journalistically" as a term of abuse.' I have always thought that was absolutely true.

One last question before I throw this open. You have also said that you don't see your role just as the observer and sometimes you need to get involved, as you did in Tiananmen Square.

Did I say that? I'm rather trying to keep that bit quiet, but I probably let it slip. I do see my job purely as being an observer, in terms of telling people what is going on. I promise you I don't – you are free not to believe me – but I believe that I don't have an agenda; I am sure I do, of course. I have an agenda in that I don't think that killing people or torturing people, or indeed cutting their heads off with small knives, is a good thing, but by and large I do not believe that I have a political agenda, that I think one type of political party is better than another type – I think they are all useless. I really do try my utmost, as indeed does everybody that I know of among my colleagues, to be absolutely dead straight about what I have seen. I am sure that I have not been as straight as I ought to be, but it is always because I have misunderstood the situation or wasn't aware of some particular fact about it, which happens of course, very often when you are in the heat of something that's going on; you can't possibly look back at it from a distance and see what is going on. But to the best of my ability I try to be honest, I do, I promise you that is true. I don't think at the same time that you are *just* an observer. You know the old title of that film 'I am a camera'. I don't think I am a camera, I don't think I am a machine that registers what is going on and then puts out a script. I am a human being with duties, I would say, as well as everything else. So once or twice, only I think twice, I felt it necessary to intervene, to stop people killing other people; I wouldn't want to have it on my conscience. So I was in Tiananmen Square on the night of the massacre, and I was right beside an armoured personnel carrier from the Chinese army, which had driven through the Square for reasons that were very questionable indeed. I think the Chinese army wanted sacrificial victims to be killed by the students, and then they could say, 'Look, the people you think are so wonderful', and indeed there was quite a large element of real rough characters in the Square that night, people that wanted to kill soldiers and to bring down the communist state. So there were students who were entirely peaceful, and there were these other characters. This armoured personnel carrier had the misfortune to be stopped and brought to a halt by the actions of people that wanted to kill somebody. So the crowd set fire to this thing, and after a while the crew decided they couldn't stay in it any longer, so they jumped out. The first one that jumped out was smashed and killed by the crowd. The second one, I didn't know this was going to happen, the second soldier that got out was attacked. I don't think he was killed but he was very badly injured. As a third one came out, I thought I can't take this any more, this is nothing to do with being a reporter, being honest and straight and open about reporting this. I don't want to see another person being murdered in front of me. So I'm afraid I rather got involved. I managed to persuade the cameraman not to show me doing this, but there was a certain amount of bad language in English over the soundtrack as I was shouting at them. I think everybody was so amazed that this rather large European was wading in that they stopped, and then the students came and saved the others. I am not ashamed of it. I wouldn't normally raise it, but I think you are not a machine, you are a human being, and one of the basic principles of all of us is that we do not want to see human beings killed. I did the same in Iraq. I always seem to take the side of the bad guys, in a way. There was an American soldier who was going to shoot an old man standing on a roof, and he was screaming, 'Sniper, sniper', and I whacked him with a stick. It was a great feeling. I had this large piece of shrapnel in my backside, and it was extremely painful, and I was hobbling around with a stick. It was in a place called Tikrit, Saddam's home town, and the Americans had just taken it over. I mean they'd just captured it, about half an hour before. So they were all terribly jittery, understandably, and this guy raised his rifle to blow away some poor completely innocent old boy. Even I could see – I was three times the age of the soldier – I could see perfectly clearly what was going to happen. I whacked this soldier over the back of the neck with my walking stick. I felt great, and he stopped, and, because they were a civilized army then, the officer agreed with me. That was the only thing that did rather upset me; the officer had a funny look on his face, I couldn't work out what it was, a sort of half a smile. Then I realized I had seen that look on the face of the parents of terribly ill-behaved kids that were completely out of control – I can't do ... what can I do? But at least after I whacked this chap it was the Captain that persuaded both the soldier and the others not to do anything to the man that had jabbed him with a stick. I felt better for that, I don't deny it.

Questions from the audience

What should we think of the Persians? It is now quite a few years since the arrival of the Ayatollah Khomeini – are they now good guys or bad guys?

They've matured, and changed very, very much indeed. I haven't been back there since 2009 when there was, if you recall, a presidential election, which was stolen by the incumbent Mahmoud Ahmadinejad, who had deep-set eyes and didn't wear ties, and things like that, a bit of a nutter. Do you remember he went to the United Nations General Assembly and said he saw a green light shining in his eyes? And he said some very careless things. As a sayer of careless things myself I felt rather sympathetic to him, but at least I don't imagine that I have seen the light of Islam shining in my eyes at such moments. But he stole the election. There were these huge demonstrations which reminded me so much of being in Iran during the 1978–79 revolution, and I thought for a moment it was going to succeed, but it didn't because they shot people down. So bad things still happen, very nasty bad people have got more power than they ought to in Iran, but it's a different country. They have not been able to change the nature of the country. In 2009, and I am sure it hasn't changed, having a meal in a restaurant was a real problem because you didn't have much time to eat, people kept on coming over to you and saying how wonderful it was to see somebody from the West. Where was I from? 'Britain.' 'Oh, I've got cousins in Manchester.' And as you got up at the end or called for the bill at the end, 'Oh no, somebody's already paid for it.' This is a particular thing in Tehran, but it was also true in the two or three provincial cities we went to. People have worked out ways of living with a loony government, an extremist, loony government. To be honest, the government is now headed by a really serious moderate figure, whom we would find very easy to do a deal with if it weren't for the religious hierarchy behind him, who hold the real power still, or most of it. But they have had to accommodate the feelings in society, the atmosphere of society, as much as society has had to accommodate them. So they live on a kind of ... well, women wear scarves in the streets, because there is always a chance that some head-banger will come and cause trouble, but it is the flimsiest of scarves and it is right down by the level of the ears, and they wear figure-hugging clothes, as they do in any other country in the Middle East or the general area. Again sometimes there are clampdowns on that, though as far as I know there hasn't been one for some time. I think it is gradually falling apart, added to which I think what was behind your question was the fact that of course we find ourselves on something of a similar side as contrasted with Islamic State, and all these other real heavy-duty Sunni Islam head-bangers. Iran being the major Shiite power is terrified of people like Islamic State, so we might not want them to get involved, they might have problems getting involved, but we both want the same thing in Syria and in Iraq.

This goes back to your desire to tell it like it is. Back in July I was watching one of your reports from Gaza, and you were probably the only reporter to be brutally honest about what the Israelis were doing there. About the same time was when the aeroplane was shot down, the Malaysian aeroplane. They were quick to jump on the Western governments there and condemn Putin and Russia, but when it comes to Israel why do you feel they are quiet and just let them slaughter with impunity?

It is really, really difficult. I don't go there very much. I am not very welcomed by the government there, to be honest. I've got a lot of Israeli friends, but they are not numbered among the political elite. I wasn't like Jon Snow, who went there and said, 'This is disgraceful, what is happening in Gaza.' I didn't do that because I don't think that is my function; I don't think I am paid to dig out the adjectives and show what I think. But I can tell you, it is not the first time it has happened to me – in fact, it's about the sixth time. It is very, very painful to see a first-world army and airforce using the highest quality of weaponry against ordinary people. I mean, that doesn't feel good. At the same time, I do understand that life was made intolerable by Hamas, and that public opinion in Israel wanted something done about it. It is the most difficult subject that I know to report on. I like difficult places, I like places where you can come unstuck in an instant. In an evening you can lose your job by going live and talking live about these things. I enjoy that. What I don't enjoy is the horrible complexity of reporting on Israel and the Palestinians. In the past, I was on the Israeli side, but I have wanted to report on the Palestinian side because it's clearer. I found myself when I was there the other month saying that on the one hand Israel is killing what turned out to be hundreds of Palestinians, and on the other hand there are five, or whatever it was, civilians on the Israeli side, as though there was some kind of balance and that I am uncomfortable. But I did it because I think that was what was required, and it was certainly true that the Israeli, particularly the Israeli airforce, where I have got quite a lot of contacts, were telling me just privately how much effort they went to to try and avoid civilian casualties. It faded, alas, as the thing went on. But they developed this new system, which they called 'knocking on the roof', of telling the people who lived in the building that it would soon be a target in the next few hours or a day or so. They would drop little lead balls on the roof, and people would realize that they had got to get out. I am told, although I wasn't there, that Hamas are often trying to get people to stop leaving the houses. Just because one set of tactics is distasteful doesn't mean to say that the other side is all fine and pure and white. That is one of the biggest problems that any journalist faces anywhere: to try and show why these things are happening, not just what is happening. But I was glad when I left, I had had enough; I find it very difficult. I don't think it is my job to preach about what is happening, but I do think you have to be absolutely honest, and I got into a certain amount of trouble for doing that.

Do you agree that there is a tendency today for journalists, reporters, politicians and other personalities to apologize when people take offence to what they say publicly, even though offence probably should not be taken? Sometimes those apologies are said to be in case they offend other people. Why should they even say that if they stand by what they have said in the first place? Judy Finnigan recently, for example, spoke candidly and with some wisdom and experience about the question of whether the footballer who had been convicted and jailed for rape should be allowed to revert back to his job. The result was this awful trolling, and things like this. Why should people not be able to speak freely in the democratic society that you support and have done for many years without having to apologize?

I am afraid I think it comes down to economics. Judy Finnigan's audience was in danger perhaps, I don't know, but her bosses must have thought their audience was in danger of falling away or even collapsing, and it is more important to them to keep the audience than it is to allow somebody to say what they honestly think. I would love to say that the BBC doesn't care about these things, and that it just simply wants its employees to say what they believe to be the case regardless of public opinion, but it ain't so. This allows me to head off on to something which is nothing about what you are asking about, but why change the habits of a lifetime? I believe that the BBC is now in its last stages, that the present Secretary of State for the Arts will do a really savage number on the BBC when it comes to negotiating the renewed licence fee, and that the cuts that we have been seeing in the last four or five years will be as nothing to the cuts that we are going to see. And I think that the BBC has one last ten-year charter left to it and, because the government will ensure the licence fee is cut back savagely, those ten years will be the last effective years of the BBC as I have known it all my life. I am sure something called the BBC will exist, but in order to continue it will have, for instance, to take advertising. It will have to find other ways of financing itself, and will probably be like a slightly better version of NPR and these other outfits in the United States that get by by passing the begging bowl around to everybody. I think that is what is going to happen. It's nothing like what you asked me about, is it? I just thought I'd better sling that in. I mean, what do I care? I am 70, I shall be 80 by that time, 84 or something; you can put up with it yourselves as far as I'm concerned. I shall be out of it, hopefully somewhere warm, taking no notice any longer, if indeed I am capable of taking notice of anything. But I do think that is what is happening. Every day you read *The Times*, the *Daily Telegraph*, the *Daily Mail*, not to mention some of the other trash that passes itself off as newspapers, and you see story after story after story about the BBC's waste of money, and so forth. Some of them are true, some of them are not true. It is not a co-ordinated campaign in any way; I can't imagine there is anything that links the *Sun* newspaper and the *Daily Telegraph*. I don't know, I think I can actually, but there is a desire to see an end to the BBC. The people of this country wouldn't agree with it, but there is a definite desire to see an end to public-service broadcasting as funded by a licence fee, and the government, desperate as it will be either before or after a Conservative government, desperate to keep as much support as it can in the public, will want to encourage that. So I think perhaps it doesn't matter, perhaps we'll just be able to get our news information from the Murdoch organization. You can imagine I don't feel hugely enthusiastic about that. Anyway, thank you, I am sorry to have rambled on so much, and I apologize for not answering your question. I didn't really want to, but I know exactly what you mean, and I think you are probably right. Having been through this experience recently in County Tyrone at a literary festival, where I thought this place is so isolated nobody will ever know anything I say here, I am safe. And there was an ancient character who about 40 years ago worked for the *Irish Times* who was busy writing it all down in slow, and I must say inaccurate, shorthand, but he still managed to find the phone numbers of the *Sun*, the *Express*, all the rest of them, and so I was quite famous for a day or so after that, and infamous as far as my bosses were concerned. So no doubt if there is anybody here from the *Irish Times*, or any other newspaper who has been writing it down – I notice the Dean has been writing some stuff down – I suspect you will be on to the *Sun* tomorrow morning.

(John Miller) There is a representative of the Hampshire Chronicle, *I know, here.*

Just point him out and I will beat him to death.

The Dean

John, thank you very much – we have had a delightful evening. I was thinking if you had a biblical chum it would probably be the prophet Elijah who was always taking off in his chariot of fire. His disciples were always saying, 'Can we go and see where he has landed now?' We are really grateful that your chariot of fire landed in Winchester tonight. With all the claims on your time and attention, thank you so much for finding time to be with us in Winchester. I think it has just been a sheer delight for us to be in your company. It is marvellous that you do risk it. It is really nice that you are so honest and open and humorous with us. The thing that has struck me tonight, and I don't know how far this will be true for everybody, is that you have had to cope with some quite gruesome situations – Kosovo, Baghdad, Tiananmen Square – yet you have managed to hold on to your humanity in a quite amazing way. Clearly one of the ways you hold on to your humanity is your tremendous sense of humour. I sometimes think about judges (judges' lodgings are in the Cathedral Close), who sometimes turn up after Evensong, after they've had a tough day. Somehow they survive it, and it is that ability that you have got, to come out with your humanity intact, and share something which has been really hopeful for us. One can be realistic about the world, but come out too with a sense of goodness, loving kindness and just a wonderful sense of humanity. So for sharing that with us, thank you very much indeed on behalf of us all.

11

Things to say to psychotic dictators

ARCHBISHOP ROWAN WILLIAMS

(Professor Joy Carter, Vice-Chancellor, Winchester University) My Lord, Mr Dean, Distinguished Guests, Ladies and Gentlemen. Good Evening, and welcome to you all. It is my pleasure to welcome you here tonight on behalf of the Cathedral, and on behalf of the University.

Tonight we welcome Lord Williams of Oystermouth, a wonderful title for a wonderful person. He is of course the former Archbishop of Canterbury. He stepped down in 2012 after ten years of distinguished office. He is a renowned academic and theologian, not to mention poet and linguist. Lord Williams is now Master of Magdalene College, Cambridge, which doesn't stop him from being a regular visitor to Winchester University, and we are always delighted to see him. It is a real honour to welcome him here tonight.

Finally, asking the questions is one John Miller who is probably known to almost everybody in this room.

Thank you very much Vice-Chancellor. Lord Williams, can I begin at the beginning? You were born to Presbyterian parents. As a schoolboy you decided to join the Anglican Church and your parents followed you. How did all that happen?

Not quite as dramatic as it sounds really. I didn't actively preach Anglicanism over the breakfast table to my parents. But we'd moved house and there wasn't locally a Presbyterian chapel that was as lively as the one we had been part of, where we'd been before, and one Sunday morning I just slunk away very early to the parish church to see what happened there. And I liked it, and I came back and said so. So we started going, and it was a mixture of a very engaged and colourful worship, it was a fairly Anglo-Catholic parish but not extreme. Wonderful preaching and teaching from one of the best priests I have ever known in my life, who had such creativity, such theological depth and such personal holiness, that he set standards for all of us that really stuck. I remember many years later, at his funeral, having a conversation with somebody who had been in the choir with me as a schoolgirl, and she said, 'I just hope that our children have somebody who does for them what Eddy did for us when we were teenagers.' I thought that was a wonderful tribute. So yes, that's how it happened.

As a boy you had a nasty attack of meningitis?

I did, yes, which left me with a non-functioning left ear, and several years of susceptibility to all sorts of illnesses, and lots and lots of attacks of bronchitis and that sort of thing. So I was a very weedy child, and that gave me the opportunity of spending lots of time in bed reading books. With the results you see.

But also as a boy you had a party trick of being able to put your leg over your neck. Can you still do it now?

Well, I am not proposing to.

You'd acted at school, but at Cambridge you played God? Was that a portent of things to come?

Yes, I had done quite a bit of acting in school, not very much at Cambridge, but some friends of mine and I put on a medieval mystery play, in my second year. It was a twelfth-century French play called *The Play of Adam*, and the *figura dei*, a representation of God, is a character in that. So in those days, with a false beard and a large gold crown, and various other things, I did what I could. I have never had romantic leads, I am afraid, in plays I have been in. I am still trying to work out why.

Dogberry you played twice?

Dogberry, yes; not many people know that. That really was casting against type.

You had very much an academic career. In fact, I think you were only a part-time parish priest, you were never a full-time parish priest. People thought you would stay at Oxford or Cambridge as you moved between the two for ever. Did you think that?

No, I didn't really. The parish period had been very important to me, and I did feel I hadn't been ordained just to write books. So the question was, and it was getting quite an interesting question by my late thirties, 'What's possible that will allow that pastoral priest living to flourish a bit more?' A bit out of the blue came this invitation to go back to Wales as a bishop.

Before we get to that, while you were still in academia you were arrested on a CND demonstration.

Yes, that's right. It was on Ash Wednesday, and the little Christian CND group in Cambridge decided that we would go and say some prayers at the RAF base at Alconbury. We were fairly determined to make it a bit difficult for them to arrest us, because we didn't want to do anything openly criminal, so we carefully put blankets over the barbed wires, so that we didn't cut it, and climbed over, and scattered some ashes and said some prayers, and were rounded up at rifle-point. That was an interesting experience, but they couldn't work out what to charge us with afterwards, so I don't actually have a criminal record, I hasten to add.

But you had to miss Evensong.

I had to miss Evensong. Yes. I don't think the college director of music ever quite forgave me for that.

You had a couple of very formative visits abroad, the first one to India, which opened your eyes, I think, very significantly?

Yes. My wife grew up in India. She spent the first eight years of her life in India, having been born to a missionary family. When the opportunity arose very shortly after we were married to go to India for a few weeks we both leapt at it. She wanted to revisit the site of her childhood, and I was very eager to discover India. I had always been fascinated by it. I'd been fascinated by some aspects of Hinduism and also the Christian history of India, which especially in the South is such an important element. So we went and spent some time in Delhi, and we took the train down to Bangalore. If you want to see India, travelling second-class on an Indian train is quite a good way of doing it. You meet the entire world and it takes 48 hours. Then we had a bit of time in Kerala, in the college where Jane had grown up, her father had been principal, and in all sorts of ways that was a very, deeply moving, deeply engaging time.

Were you taken aback by the poverty?

I was taken aback by the poverty, and then taken aback by how easily I got used to it; that was one of the things that shocked me most in a sense. I realized that after ten days I was walking past beggars in the street and thinking, 'Oh, there's another beggar', and then realizing – what have I just thought? But it was becoming routine, and on the train journey, I don't know if this still happens, but 35 years ago it did, at every station a great crowd of children would swarm on to the train, and they'd sweep under the seats, and they'd pretend to do a bit of cleaning, and then they would ask for money. Again I realized I was feeling impatient. I caught myself thinking, 'And this is how it gets like this, you get used to it, you stop noticing, you stop sensing the human reality.' It is so easy.

And your visit to South Africa had a similar effect on you?

A wonderful and very stretching time. It was the mid-80s, so a very difficult period, when the Bantustan system was still in place, apartheid was still in place, there were pass raids, it seemed to be getting worse at that point. My wife and I were there for rather more than two months, I think it must have been nine or ten weeks. We were signed up to do refresher courses for clergy around South Africa in different centres, and to give a couple of lectures and some sermons in Johannesburg. It involved us in meeting a whole lot of people whose witness was extra-ordinarily courageous, and vivid and wonderful. We met Desmond Tutu for the first time on that trip, and he remained a fast friend. But I think the people I remember most in some ways are not the big names – to say ordinary people sounds patronizing, I don't mean that – but people who had no particular professional commitment to activism or protest, but who just could not put up in silence with the injustices, and put them-selves very much at risk. I remember one housewife in Pietermaritzburg, whom we got to know a bit. A few months later we heard that she had been arrested and interrogated, and she sent us an account of that. It is people like that, the routine heroism of people who were just doggedly witnessing to the fact that this wouldn't do in the eyes of God. The other memory I have, which is quite a painful one, is of one particular priest I talked to a bit. An African priest, whose life had quite clearly been wrecked by his experience of interrogation and torture in prison. He was alcoholic, and clearly in a very bad way, and I felt how many lives like that, individual lives are just ruined because of this system? So huge inspiration from people, a huge sense of the personal cost, and mostly just wonderful people to meet and get to know.

When you were offered to be Bishop of Monmouth was it the appeal of going back to Wales that attracted you?

Yes, yes it was. I had long wanted to go back in some way. I'd started working again on my Welsh, trying to get it back up to a reasonable level, and then of course I found myself in a diocese where very few people spoke Welsh. It was a very affirming, homecoming sort of feeling. The years we had in Monmouth, I think, were the happiest of our lives.

Your wife was initially reportedly less enthusiastic.

Well yes, she tells the story of the first visit we made to Newport which was the See city. I don't know if anybody from Newport is here or this is going straight back into the *South Wales Argus*, but it has to be said that Newport is not superficially one of the more picturesque or charming towns in Wales. The Bishop's house is in a very challenged bit of the town, or the city as it now is. Coming from Oxford and having a house in the precincts of Christchurch, a sixteenth-century house with a beautiful view of Christchurch meadow, Newport felt a bit different. What made it for us was predictably the people, and the immense warmth of a town which we'd really got to love.

Was it a natural progression then to become Archbishop of Wales?

Well, in Wales the Archbishop is elected on a sort of Buggins-turn principle. There are six bishops in Wales, there isn't a separate Archbishop's diocese. So we just take it in turns. By 1999 I was the senior serving Bishop in Wales rather surprisingly, so I thought it was predictable, but again a wonderfully happy time.

It was while you were Archbishop of Wales that you were in New York on 9/11. That was a near-death experience, wasn't it?

I suppose it was, yes. Well I say that, it was an experience where, for all any of us knew, our lives were at risk. We were two blocks away from the twin towers, and nobody really knew what was going on, and how severe the risk was. In the event, now we know in retrospect, we were probably not at risk directly. But that morning was so completely chaotic that we took it for granted that anything might happen.

The dust was rather overwhelming, wasn't it?

The dust yes, like a snowstorm, when we got out into the street. I remember one of the workmen in the building where we were handed out some little masks on elastic cords, because they had been having some construction work there, and he happened to have a little stock of these masks, and we were happy to have those as we went out. I kept mine for quite a long time in my chapel, just as a little reminder. Yes, the dust and also the sound of the towers coming down, which I can't describe.

And you all prayed together at one point?

We did. We were trying to get away from the collapsing towers, the second tower had just come down, we were escorting some children from the crèche in the building. As you can imagine, you have about 20 under-fives in that situation, and all of us bumbling our way down the street. There was a portacabin, because they were doing some construction work. We dived into that, and one of the workers there, who didn't know us from Adam, just put his arms round our shoulders and said, 'I guess it's time that we said a few prayers.' This little group of bishops, abbots, and all the rest of it, quite rightly submitted to the authority. I mean it seriously, the authority of a believing person who said what we need to do is pray.

There was a lady in your group who said, 'If we are going to die there is nobody I'd rather die with more than you, Archbishop'?

Not to me personally at all, but to all of us. She simply said, 'If I had to choose the company I'd die with, it would be these people, this group.' That again is something I keep thinking about.

You wrote a little book afterwards, called Written in the Dust.' *There is a quote in there I notice where you said, 'In the global village it shows how quickly fire can jump from roof to roof.'*

Yes, that's right. That sense that violence, distress, insecurity, if you are from a certain place, a certain class, a certain country, you can kid yourself that it is a long way off, and suddenly with this appalling brutality and violence it's there on your doorstep. And what you think would be a place most remote from threat and insecurity and butchery, there it is.

Does that experience still stay with you very much?

It does. I can't quite believe in retrospect that I was there, if that makes any sense. I went back a couple of years later to the site, and just paced out where we had walked and run that morning, and one of the most moving things on that visit was to go into the little church of St Paul's, which is on the edge of Ground Zero – through the year or so that followed 9/11 that little church had a really extraordinary ministry. People from the local parish were staffing it 24 hours a day, providing shelter and refreshment for people working on the site, and so there were fire-men and police who would come in. The thing I remember is that, just before 9/11 this rather exquisite little eighteenth-century church had been redecorated, it had all been whitewashed inside. And these newly white-washed pews were stained and scratched throughout, because people had been lying down on the pews to sleep for an hour or two, and their shoes had scarred the paintwork. The church authorities had decided, 'We leave it like that, we don't whitewash it over, because this is what this church has been and meant', and it is one of those experiences which I describe somewhere as a glimpse of the Church being itself. You know, I have seen the church, and it works.

The following year you became Archbishop of Canterbury. You joked before you went that you felt like St Augustine going to evangelize the savage English.

Yes, I learnt early on never to make jokes in public because, saving your presence, a lot of journalists have professionally no sense of humour. Anything that looks like irony is very dangerous. So I learnt that the hard way.

In fact, though, some people might say you did meet some savage English at the Synod?

I couldn't possibly comment. [Laughter]

You were always in favour of the ordination of women, and you came to change your mind about women bishops. That was a really difficult issue for you as Archbishop of Canterbury, wasn't it?

I don't know that I changed my mind about women bishops, I wasn't quite sure about what rate it was coming. I think what I said when I was first appointed and asked about this was, 'I would like to see us thinking well in advance about how we are going to provide for a dissident minor-ity, rather than making things up on the hoof.' I had a slight feeling that when women were ordained as priests the provision made for the minor-ity was put together a bit rapidly, and I wanted to give us a bit longer to think about it. Easier said than done, as I discovered.

Very early on in your time as Archbishop, Gene Robinson was made Bishop of New Hampshire. That caused quite a problem with your followers, didn't it?

Yes it did. I had of course written, when I was still a professor, about my views on the question generally of homosexuality, and whether the

Church ought to rethink its ethical position, and put forward a case for doing that rethinking, but what I had hoped was that the Church together would make up its mind. I wasn't very happy about piecemeal picking off of localities where it was all right and localities where it wasn't. That may be an unrealistic hope, but I just wished very much that we could have kept in step in thinking about that. I felt, rightly or wrongly, that the ordination of Gene Robinson in some ways polarized even further an already rather polarized situation, which is why I wasn't at all happy about it. But all of that was of course among the most painful bits of the last ten years, and the way it played out here in the nomination of Jeffrey John as a Bishop and the withdrawal of that. Yes, I look back and think that was just awful for everybody involved. Not least Jeffrey.

You persuaded Jeffrey John to withdraw, because you thought this would divide the Anglican communion?

Yes, and because at that time quite a lot of my colleagues said they could not take part in the ordination of Jeffrey. And I felt that is not a good start for anybody's ministry as a bishop, or indeed, I suppose I have to be honest, for mine as an archbishop. I just didn't want to begin with a wedge driven right into the middle of the collegiality of the bishops. Rightly or wrongly, that was one of the things that shaped my reaction there.

The fiercest opposition came from Africa, didn't it?

Some of it, but also Latin America to some extent.

Archbishop Akinola from Nigeria was particularly virulent, wasn't he?

Oh, he had a lot to say on the subject, yes. I felt that as a sadness, because I had had quite a bit to do directly and indirectly with churches in Africa. Not just South Africa. I had made a visit to Uganda as Archbishop of Wales, which I had immensely enjoyed and profited from, so it wasn't a matter of distant figures sounding off, these were people I knew, had worked with, had prayed with, and loved, and that all made it harder too.

You also went to see President Mugabe.

I did yes. My word, yes. I have occasionally said that one of the files I have left to my successor is 'Things to say to psychotic dictators'. That was the end of quite a long story really because our church in Zimbabwe, many of you will know this better than I, our church in Zimbabwe had been very deeply divided, because of Mugabe, and the then Bishop of Harare in the middle of the 2000s was somebody very close to Mugabe, who had been accused of all sorts of things – intimidation of his own clergy, death threats against his clergy, that sort of thing, and uncritical support of Mugabe's regime. I had quite a lot of pressure to denounce this Bishop or depose him. I couldn't depose him. I did meet him eventually, and tried to persuade him that he had to distance himself from a regime which was increasingly nakedly immoral. He said that, yes, he would sign a statement about the freedom of the Church to be critical of the government, and then went back to Harare and tore it up. So I thought, OK that's it. I didn't try to be diplomatic after that, and eventually happily the Church of the Province of Central Africa deposed and excommunicated him. He then seized a lot of church property, and created a schism in the Church there. It was all really horrible, but state security apparatus was of course backing this man, although he had only a tiny percentage of the Anglicans in the country. My going there was one way of saying, 'There is only one Bishop of Harare I recognize and it's not him.' The bishops there said, 'Will you go to the President and just tell him not to?' So I said 'Yes' and I went with this large dossier of human rights abuses and atrocities against the churches and others, and delivered it to him physically. We had an hour and a half with him, and it was all very hard work, but the real heavy lifting was done by the wonderful Archbishop of Cape Town who was with us, and also the Archbishop of Central Africa. These were people who couldn't be written off as colonial stooges, and I still remember the Archbishop of Cape Town, Thabo Magoba, a great man, saying directly to Mugabe, 'You call yourself a Christian? So what's this about?'

You were also concerned about the position of Christians in the Middle East.

Very much so.

And you went to see President Bashar al-Assad.

I did, yes.

How was that?

That was in the days when Syria looked like a reasonable model of co-existence between Christians and Muslims, and when it looked as though Bashar was going to be a reforming president. The messages we carried away from that meeting were really very positive. Of course that just underlines the tragedy of what happened since, I think. President Assad has been completely taken over by some of his father's most hawkish advisers, and internal divisions, and buried divisions between different groups in Syria of course come to light with horrific effect. But I also recall one of my best friends in the region, a very senior Orthodox cleric, said to me about Syria, 'If it all dissolves, the problem will not be just Muslim against Christian, it will be Muslim against Muslim', and before it got to the present state he was predicting already the savage Sunni–Shia hostility that's evolved – he was a very prescient man.

You have also been to Jerusalem. How different is that experience, how special is that experience?

There is a saying in the Talmud that Jerusalem is for the testing of hearts, and I think that is absolutely right. I can recall the first time I went to Jerusalem, thinking literally, 'So this place actually exists, it is real, the one we hear about, the one we sing about, it's a real place.' 'Now our feet are standing within thy gates, O Jerusalem', as the psalmist says, and suddenly realizing what that meant. So I have always had a passionate love for the city, in ways that I find quite difficult to explain, and of course it is partly because of what happened there. Also, because of that, I guess like a lot of other people, I feel very acutely the intensity of suffering, suspicion, division, pain, hatred, fear that surrounds it. Every time I have gone it's felt worse in some ways. So yes, the testing of hearts – you discover what matters to you in Jerusalem.

Did you feel under pressure to say anything about the Israeli/Palestinian stand-off?

All the time. Of course any comment you make is played into the zero-sum politics of the region. I have in my time been accused of being in the pay of the Israeli government, and being in the pay of the Palestinian authority. Because if you qualify your support of either side you are immediately seen as a traitor by a lot of people. And that is very hard if you have real friends on both sides, and if you don't want to say that one side is blameless and one side is unspeakably evil. I think the policies of the government of Israel need challenging in the deepest way. I also think that Hamas in Gaza is a terrible regime, and that the Palestinians have been betrayed by their own leadership in some ways. Trying to say that all together is not making friends anywhere.

The whole Muslim thing is such a minefield. You got into terrible trouble when you talked about bringing sharia law to this country.

I vaguely remember that, yes – another caution about thinking aloud in public too much. I was invited simply to give a lecture on Islam and British law, which obliged me to think a little bit about what the relation ought to be between a community law if you like, religiously sanctioned, and the law of the land. It is clear to me that you cannot have a no-go area for the law of the land. Everyone as a citizen has absolutely inalienable civic rights. So it is not a matter of fencing off any area. The question I was asking was, 'Is it thinkable that certain issues are, as it were, franchised to sharia courts?' This is perhaps about inheritance or about finance or whatever. I am still not quite sure what the exact answer to that is, but that was the question I thought worth asking. But, yes, of course it was then all about public beheadings in Trafalgar Square, wasn't it?

The Sun *newspaper rather ran with it, didn't it?*

Yes, a vivid memory that. It is a complicated issue, I think. I was try-ing in the lecture to say as clearly as I could that there really are issues about, for example, the rights and dignities of women not being up for negotiation; you can't alienate once again the rights of women. You can't enshrine in British law the inferiority of women. Some forms of sharia practice, I won't say sharia law, have that risk around them, to put it mildly. So you have to think how you balance that if you are franchising anything to sharia courts. But one of the more interesting comments I had on the evening I gave the lecture – there were in fact a number of very good sharp questions from the lawyers I was talking to – was a comment from a Muslim lawyer who said, 'If you have sharia courts operating unrecognized, unmonitored as it were, privately in ghettos as it were, that is a great deal worse than asking how you bring that a bit more into the light, or train people better, or work out what the balance and so forth is.'

You also expressed regret at the manner of the killing of Osama Bin Laden.

Yes. I couldn't exactly feel sorry that he was dead, to be honest, and yet what I think I said was, 'Any Christian is bound to feel that the killing of an unarmed man in cold blood is not a good thing.' I don't know what else was possible. I know military people there as elsewhere make appall-ingly difficult decisions under pressure and at short notice, but I don't want us to pretend that a killing in cold blood is a good thing in itself.

You had a happier relationship with Pope Benedict. You went to the Vatican and also welcomed the Pope here.

That's right, yes. It is a bit of a paradox, isn't it, that over the last ten or fifteen years, at the personal level, relations between the hierarchies and the leadership have been very warm, whereas at the institutional level it hasn't seemed to be thawing very much? I came to respect and like Pope Benedict and his great encyclicals; the three big encyclicals that he wrote are wonderful compositions. Not my questions obviously, but he found – I think I said so at the time – he found a register, a way of speaking about deep theological and ethical issues, which was clear and rooted in very rich theological reflection and biblical interpretation. I envied the clarity and directness, and the richness altogether of his style.

It is reported that when you were very young you toyed with the idea of becoming a Roman Catholic monk.

I did. I felt the attraction of a life of contemplation, I suppose. If the most important thing you can do in life is to love and adore God, then you try to make some opportunities to learn how to do it. And if we are going to spend eternity, please God, loving and adoring and nothing much else, then we'd better get used to it. So that had its attractions, and I was hugely helped by several communities, especially Roman Catholic communities, which is why I thought about it as a possibility. I think two of the things that made me think again were, first of all, the experience of teaching in an Anglican theological college, and the level of respect I felt for my students. I thought, here are people, very prayerful, intelligent, serious people, getting ready for ministry in the Church of England, and the Church of England needs to be taken seriously because here are serious prayerful people involved in it. It sounds a bit odd put like that perhaps, but that did weigh with me, and I've never been quite convinced that you can simply say the Church of England doesn't work and the Roman Catholic Church does, or one is wrong and one is right. It was a rather more personal thing, but that did work for me a bit. Then by providence, or whatever, I found myself being nudged in the direction of teaching, of research things that were offered, things that seemed right to go forward with. And so I suppose sometime around when I was about 27, I said finally, 'Yes, I will offer myself for ordination in the Church of England', and settled with that, but kept those relationships with the monasteries.

One of your responsibilities as Archbishop was dealing with the government about issues like same-sex marriage, and the government legislation didn't particularly help you, did it?

I think we were all a bit taken aback at how fast that went. Remember, we'd been given cast-iron assurances that the civil partnerships legislation was not the first step to same-sex marriage, and then we found that within 24 months that was very much on the agenda. I still feel that it was an over-rapid process for a very big social change, but that is water under the bridge.

But the whole business about same-sex marriage in church is still an ongoing problem, isn't it?

I think back to the earlier question. I think unless and until the Church has more of a coherent theological perspective on same-sex relationships, licensing same-sex marriages in churches will be premature. And we are not there yet, as others in this hall will I'm sure confirm.

You also debated with Richard Dawkins. Was that a useful experience?

Yes it was. I have done it twice now – well, I suppose three times – I did a television thing with him once. For all the ferocity of his public pronouncements he can be a really engaging person to argue with, because he's not nearly as monochrome in his views as people might imagine. And he did, in the Oxford discussion that we had, eventually say that he wasn't sure God didn't exist. OK, that's a foot in the door somewhere. What I always find frustrating, sometimes with Richard, sometimes with others, is the feeling that Christianity, the theology they're attacking, bears so little relationship to what I believe, and what a lot of people believe. All this stuff about belief in God being like belief in the tooth fairy – that's the point at which I really feel they're not thinking. There is not a great body of reflective theology about tooth fairies; there are no great works of art inspired by tooth fairies, there's no tooth fairy equivalent of Winchester Cathedral, or the St Matthew Passion, and I do feel you've got to weigh all those on a list.

There is debate about whether we now live in a post-Christian society. Do you believe that we do?

Well, it's a phrase I've used, and been slapped on the wrist for using. But what I meant by post-Christian was quite clearly we are no longer in a Christendom society, where the default setting for most people is Christian belief. That's just a fact. On the other hand, the background, the hinterland of our history and our culture is Christian and you can't deny it. The furniture of our culture is still Christian. What the Church is challenged to do in that context is to try and make the most of the fact that that background is not invisible, and not without effective presence in people's lives. In so many communities people still do believe; it seems in all probability that the Church is there on their behalf, and that's not trivial. So that's where I'd say post-Christian doesn't mean non-Christian, let alone anti-Christian. There's a huge gulf of ignorance, but the furniture remains there.

You weren't happy with the Prince of Wales saying he'd be happy to take the oath as 'Defender of Faith', rather than 'the Faith'.

Not entirely, because the title of Defender of the Faith doesn't just mean somebody who's publicly nice about religion. It does mean in its context something that's tied up with the constitutional relationship with the Christian Church, the Church of England. So I don't want to muddle our categories here, just as I don't particularly want to see an inter-faith coronation. I think there are many ways of celebrating a new reign, when it comes, which I hope will be long delayed, with inter-faith representations, but the Coronation Service is a service of Holy Communion, in the course of which somebody is made a monarch, just as ordination is a service of Holy Communion, in the course of which somebody is made a deacon or a priest, that's what the coronation is. So long as you have the constitutional relationship with the Church, that's the way it is, so I just want to be clear on where we are with that. If at some point somebody wanted to unscramble the whole thing, well I won't say good luck to them, because I don't really mean that, but it's going to mean a lot more work than some people think. But that's what would be needed, not just a little bit of massaging of the language.

In her introduction, Joy mentioned that you were a poet. What drives you to write poetry?

One of two things, I suppose. I believe very strongly that poetry is an aural thing, it's about what you hear, and that poetry is about doing musical things with language. If the palaeontologists and neuroscientists are right, we were singing before we were speaking, as human beings evolutionarily, and probably therefore we were producing poetry before we were producing prose. There's the amazing discovery that you can make strange unexpected noises, and resonances and echoes, in the noises you make. You see children discovering that, don't you? Poetry has something to do with that, so one of the motives is hearing something, hearing connections. You think, yes, that's the shape, the rhythm, the music of a phrase I need to get down, and connected with that is seeing the connection between things, experiences, elements in your environment, which you want to express in the connected words of a poem. I don't think it's ever a good idea to start writing poetry with an idea, or a message. Some of the worst poetry is written because there are messages and ideas, and you're just trying to translate them into verse.

The best poetry is poetry that really does listen and work with the sound and flow of language.

Given all the enormous pressures on your time as Archbishop, did you find time to write poetry in that ten years?

Yes, I published two books in that time. It helped quite a bit to have lots of travelling to do.

And you never took your mobile phone?

No. I was usually travelling with staff who could be contacted in emergency. But I really didn't like the idea of being quite so directly accessible. I needed a bit of protected time, and used it on plane journeys especially, to draft some poems, and catch up with other things.

You were quoted in the last few weeks of your time as Archbishop that you were looking forward to having your life back.

Yes, I think that was mostly about the sense that if you're living in public, as a public person, you do feel you're everybody's property all the time, and you're always talking to everybody. I was hoping to get a bit more space that wasn't dictated by all that – with limited success so far, he said, looking out at the audience.

Douglas Hurd, who was in the very first of these dialogues, was quoted when you got into terrible trouble over the sharia law, saying that you weren't a politician, that it might have helped if you'd had an adviser; on the other hand you should draw comfort from the fact that Jesus himself would not have had a good ride from our tabloid press.

I'm sure he wouldn't. Definitely somebody who didn't measure his words, who wasn't seen in the right company, and had all sorts of unsavoury and controversial ideas.

Now that you have more time, you've said that you vowed never to write an autobiography; have you reconsidered that?

No. I've said this in front of witnesses, and I'll say it again.

So meanwhile we have to make do with the biography by Rupert Short, which I must say I did find very useful, and thoughtful.

Rupert is a former student of mine, so I think he is quite kind.

Questions from the audience

Would you care to comment on the Bill now before the House of Lords concerning assisted dying? I wonder whether you agree with your successor in the view that he took on that issue in an article in The Times *three or four months ago when it was being debated in the House of Lords, in which he used the parable of the good Samaritan to argue against changing the present law concerning that matter. Would you comment on that please?*

Yes. I think broadly speaking I would agree with my successor about that. I have never been persuaded that a change in the law is the right way to go forward. There are two or three things which weigh heavily with me here. The first is, as soon as you try to define in law the kinds of condition that might justify an appeal or a licence for assisted dying, you are in danger of creating categories of illness or disability or whatever which the law tells you are capable of being terminated. In a context where people may come under pressure, where you can't guarantee that there won't be some pressure to save money to expedite things, I think that is a bit risky, to put it mildly. My second concern is that in the discussion overall it is very often represented as a straightforward stand-off between people who believe that the sick should be kept alive at all costs and in all circumstances, and people who want to be merciful and compassionate and end their suffering. I once tried to define what I meant by euthanasia in terms of initiating a new process whose primary purpose was to accelerate death. In other words, I think the routine medical practices whereby you can scale down or wind down some kinds of care, knowing that it will shorten life, are a morally acceptable part of how we approach death and dying. To introduce a new process, by beginning this in order to accelerate death, that is where my moral hackles begin to rise, and I am not sure that we have got this entirely clear. I sometimes meet the objection, 'Well, you want to keep people alive at all costs, whatever the circumstances.' I say, 'Well, it's not quite like that.' I don't think it is particularly Christian just to want to keep people alive, but the limits of medical intervention, the point at which you scale down or whatever, those seem to me perfectly capable of being accommodated within a fairly traditional Christian ethic. So those are a couple of my concerns, and on the first one I have noted in the House of Lords debates that two or three of the quite severely disabled peers who sit in the Lords have made quite strong speeches against a legal definition of conditions that might justify this. Because they say, given that sort of condition, I live with it. It is very difficult to generalize on this. We have been faced again and again with really heartbreakingly difficult individual cases. I'm just not sure; well, hard cases make bad law, they say. So uncomfortably, with a very strong sense of unfinished business in the discussion, I don't want to see the law changed.

Joy has introduced you as a patron of cathedral universities, and I was wondering: the University of Winchester, with its Anglican foundation, is a university I have experienced to be very inspiring, welcoming and nurturing towards its students. I was wondering whether you could comment on how you think institutions with, for example, an Anglican foundation should or could approach the inclusion and celebration of a multi-faith community, where the question that sometimes arises is about an act of effort needed to make sure that in celebrations such as graduation, other faiths are visible and included and can contribute, or is the living of what you may call Christian values enough in itself to ensure that these parties are heard and included?

Thank you, that is a very interesting question indeed. It seems to me that to celebrate a Christian or an Anglican identity is just that. It is to say, 'This is where we come from, this is the ground in the centre.' That does not have to be exclusive; it simply means somebody is holding the ring for a religious perspective. And that somebody happens to be Anglican in this context. Precisely because of that, as I hope in the establishment of the Church nationally, part of the responsibility of the Anglican presence is to make room for others. I think in primary and secondary schools, in universities, in other contexts, that is one of the historic legacies the Church of England inherits, the responsibility to make room. It is not in that sense an exclusive privilege. We have the power to define the boundaries; it's more we have the responsibility to see that whatever religious perspective comes up clearly, creatively, honestly with commitment in this community is honoured and recognized. That is what it is to belong to that tradition and to work within it.

Lord Williams, you said earlier in relation to the sharia law question, if I understood you correctly, that everyone has an inalienable right to the law of the land, and nothing should be fenced off by reason of religion. I wonder what you would say to those in the Church who would fence off certain aspects of the body's grace for those in licensed ministry today?

Difficult question. Or rather, two difficult questions. Let me try and disentangle. It seems to me absolutely axiomatic that the law of the land, its privileges and liberties, do belong to everyone, whatever their sexual orientation, their gender, whatever. That question of civic right and dignity to everybody should not be in dispute, whether in this country or any other. The question of what disciplines the Church requires of its ordained ministers is a more complicated one. It is not just about civil liberties or civil rights, and has to be discussed in terms of where the Church's own thinking is. That is why it is not so self-evident that there are rights involved here. I know where I feel more comfortable here, but I know that the Church overall struggles bitterly over this. But one of the things which I found quite important to try and say in the debates over the last decade or so, to some churches in other cultural contexts is, 'Can we not move a little bit further towards the recognition that the civic right and the human dignity are the same? We will work on the theological and ethical stuff, but can we at least go that far?' Sometimes the answer is 'No, we can't', and that is very hard. I may say now as chair of the trustees of Christian Aid that the same question occurs sometimes in the work of Christian Aid, where we want to say some quite strong things about the persecution or discrimination against people of homosexual orientation practice in some countries, and that is our philosophy. To say that without wholly alienating people we want to work with in other ways on quite important priorities – that is a pig of an issue.

As the former Archbishop would know, there is quite a distinct difference between law and sin. Would he have any comment on whether the Church should stand in the way of signing through laws that could potentially open the doors for sin?

I don't think that the Church can have or should have a veto on legislation. Because if it is true that legislation can't make people holy, if discipleship and holiness and virtue depend on our freedom, I am very wary of suggesting that the Church should be trying to apply the standards of the Kingdom of God to the coercive patterns of the law. That is where I stand on that. There have been, there are, other views. In the sixteenth century, people like the great Puritan Cartwright were saying the Law of Moses should be the law of the land. If that means that we have to make adultery a capital offence, well let's do it, said Cartwright. Some others I think pointed out realistically this could be a rather complicated exercise. It seems to me that the relation between crime and sin has always, right from the beginnings of Church–State interaction, been a complex one, and I don't think it would help if we took it for granted that all sins should be crimes. To say that isn't to say they are any less sins.

As a Welsh Anglican, I want to refer back to the question about the coronation, the question from a postgraduate student about the graduation ceremony in an Anglican cathedral accommodating a multi-faith society and civic culture. As an Anglican I have always felt slightly embarrassed by what I call a 'little Englander', about the Church of England. I always considered myself an Anglican, ever since my time with you at Mirfield. The question is how far is an Anglican/English establishment a bit of a perplexing anomaly given the fragmentation, or the threat of fragmentation, of a British identity? A kind of atavistic reversion to English, a sense of English identity. Aren't these questions going to be raised at the next coronation? And how far do you reflect on them yourself in relation to an Anglican future, where England has to find, for example, that the Queen is often referred to as the Queen of England, but when she was crowned she wasn't just 'of England', it was also as Head of the Commonwealth? Can you reflect on that complexity of identity and its political attraction?

Thank you. I think with the Establishment and all that it means, I am very much inclined to say I wouldn't start from here. The anomalous character of it is clear enough. That means that the challenge as I see it is to decide between two alternatives. One is to try and unscramble and reconceive the nature of our public space in this country; the other is to ask what we can make of that legacy or that tradition that is positive towards the changing character of our country. Because I take our history and our cultural legacy quite seriously, I am not very convinced that it would be easy or indeed possible just to say we will start from somewhere else – we have already started. So my instinct is to go for the second option. How do we make it work positively, not negatively? That hasn't always been how the Church of England has worked, frankly. And it does us good from time to time to remember that up until the third decade of the nineteenth century, this was still in important respects a confessional society, with exclusive laws that imposed disabilities on non-Anglicans. We have been there, we have done this exclusive stuff. It is not as if we have always been benign and lovely. Even if we are now. Very gradually I think the sheer weight of the kind of experience you've described, the kind of experience of being at the front end of multiplicity and diversity in a local community, has pushed us, or many of us as Anglicans in this country, to think of how the Establishment, and all that that means, should work positively. On balance I don't think we've made too bad a job of it. That is not to say that in an ideal world that is the sort of structure we would want to create. But if you can't just start from a blank slate, the question is how do you make the most of where you are? I quite agree it is going to be an issue when the next reign begins, I suspect we haven't thought hard enough about it just yet.

A few months ago I wrote a letter to The Times *which was published, suggesting that the tradition, the historical role of the Archbishop of Canterbury, be divided among two people, one who would be the head of the English church in England, and one the moderator of the worldwide Anglican communion, because those two roles seem so often in conflict. Do you agree?*

My first instinct is to say, 'Just the two?' There are quite a few other roles involved. It is a really serious issue, which I felt was coming more and more into focus during my time. Indeed, once or twice I raised a similar question, whether, whatever the historic role of the Archbishop of Canterbury in respect to other Anglican provinces, there shouldn't be a more deliberately intentional and presidential role for the communion, which wasn't tied to that, so I think it is worth reflecting on. The odd fact is, though, that Canterbury for quite a lot of Anglican provinces around the world still retains some serious spiritual meaning. And I wouldn't want to lose that. At the last Lambeth Conference, the decision to begin with a retreat in Canterbury Cathedral for the bishops – a couple of days of quiet and reflection in the Cathedral – was a very deliberate attempt to let the tradition and the prayer of that place speak, in ways people were very open to. I wouldn't want to dismantle that, but there really is a question about whether in 20 or 30 years' time it will feel honest or realistic that the president of a worldwide Christian fellowship should always automatically be the senior metropolitan of the Church of England. So work in progress I think.

The Dean

Lord Williams, former Archbishop, we have been enormously privileged to have you with us. I feel a bit as though Christmas has come already, partly because, in our pre-Advent group in the Cathedral, we have been using your book Being Christian. *This evening has been absolutely brilliant – to be allowed in a sense to be with you as you share yourself, and be given that sense of the way you look out on the world, whether it was the Twin Towers, or Wales, or whether it was your poetic soul – you let us see a new world by sharing your insights with us, and the way you see it.*

It is John's final interview in the series and I think we shouldn't let this go without saying to John Miller a huge appreciation. You have been a superlative interviewer; you are amazing at doing your research; you have a hugely retentive mind; you master your brief and, as I said to Bishop Rowan, you will be shrewd with your questioning but there will be no tricks. So thank you.